LAN Switching and Wireless
CCNA Exploration Labs and Study Guide

Allan Johnson

Cisco Press

800 East 96th Street

Indianapolis, Indiana 46240 USA

LAN Switching and Wireless
CCNA Exploration Labs and Study Guide

Allan Johnson

Copyright© 2008 Cisco Systems, Inc.

Published by:
Cisco Press
800 East 96th Street
Indianapolis, IN 46240 USA

Printed in the United States of America

Fourth Printing, January 2010

Library of Congress Cataloging-in-Publication Data:

Johnson, Allan, 1962-
  LAN switching and wireless : CCNA exploration labs and study guide /
Allan Johnson.
     p. cm.
  ISBN-13: 978-1-58713-202-5 (pbk.)
  ISBN-10: 1-58713-202-8 (pbk.)
 1. Wireless LANs—Examinations—Study guides.
2. Packet switching—Examinations—Study guides.
3. Telecommunications engineers—Certification—Examinations—Study guides.
4. Routing (Computer network management)—Examinations—Study guides.
5. Telecommunication—Switching systems Examinations—Study guides. I.
Title.
  TK5105.78.J64 2008
  004.6'8—dc22
2008014858

ISBN-13: 978-1-58713-202-5

ISBN-10: 1-58713-202-8

Publisher
Paul Boger

Associate Publisher
Dave Dusthimer

Cisco Representative
Anthony Wolfenden

Cisco Press Program Manager
Jeff Brady

Executive Editor
Mary Beth Ray

Production Manager
Patrick Kanouse

Development Editor
Andrew Cupp

Senior Project Editor
Tonya Simpson

Copy Editor
Bill McManus

Technical Editors
Bruce R. Gottwig
Khalid Rubayi
Tara Skibar
Linda C. Watson

Editorial Assistant
Vanessa Evans

Book and Cover Designer
Louisa Adair

Composition
Mark Shirar

Proofreader
Leslie Joseph

Warning and Disclaimer

This book is designed to provide information about LAN switching and wireless as part of the Cisco Networking Academy CCNA Exploration curriculum. Every effort has been made to make this book as complete and as accurate as possible, but no warranty or fitness is implied.

The information is provided on an "as is" basis. The authors, Cisco Press, and Cisco Systems, Inc. shall have neither liability nor responsibility to any person or entity with respect to any loss or damages arising from the information contained in this book or from the use of the discs or programs that may accompany it.

The opinions expressed in this book belong to the author and are not necessarily those of Cisco Systems, Inc.

Trademark Acknowledgments

All terms mentioned in this book that are known to be trademarks or service marks have been appropriately capitalized. Cisco Press or Cisco Systems, Inc. cannot attest to the accuracy of this information. Use of a term in this book should not be regarded as affecting the validity of any trademark or service mark.

Corporate and Government Sales

The publisher offers excellent discounts on this book when ordered in quantity for bulk purchases or special sales, which may include electronic versions and/or custom covers and content particular to your business, training goals, marketing focus, and branding interests. For more information, please contact: **U.S. Corporate and Government Sales** 1-800-382-3419
corpsales@pearsontechgroup.com

For sales outside the United States please contact: **International Sales**
international@pearsoned.com

Feedback Information

At Cisco Press, our goal is to create in-depth technical books of the highest quality and value. Each book is crafted with care and precision, undergoing rigorous development that involves the unique expertise of members from the professional technical community.

Readers' feedback is a natural continuation of this process. If you have any comments regarding how we could improve the quality of this book, or otherwise alter it to better suit your needs, you can contact us through e-mail at feedback@ciscopress.com. Please make sure to include the book title and ISBN in your message.

We greatly appreciate your assistance.

Americas Headquarters
Cisco Systems, Inc.
170 West Tasman Drive
San Jose, CA 95134-1706
USA
www.cisco.com
Tel: 408 526-4000
800 553-NETS (6387)
Fax: 408 527-0883

Asia Pacific Headquarters
Cisco Systems, Inc.
168 Robinson Road
#28-01 Capital Tower
Singapore 068912
www.cisco.com
Tel: +65 6317 7777
Fax: +65 6317 7799

Europe Headquarters
Cisco Systems International BV
Haarlerbergpark
Haarlerbergweg 13-19
1101 CH Amsterdam
The Netherlands
www-europe.cisco.com
Tel: +31 0 800 020 0791
Fax: +31 0 20 357 1100

Cisco has more than 200 offices worldwide. Addresses, phone numbers, and fax numbers are listed on the Cisco Website at **www.cisco.com/go/offices.**

About the Author

Allan Johnson entered the academic world in 1999 after 10 years as a business owner/operator to dedicate his efforts to his passion for teaching. He holds both an MBA and an M.Ed. in occupational training and development. He is an information technology instructor at Del Mar College in Corpus Christi, Texas. In 2003, Allan began to commit much of his time and energy to the CCNA Instructional Support Team providing services to Networking Academy instructors worldwide and creating training materials. He now works full time for the Academy in Learning Systems Development.

About the Technical Reviewers

Bruce R. Gottwig has spent most of his professional career teaching both at the K–12 and post-secondary levels. He earned an M.Ed. in Educational Technology and is currently working toward an Ed.D. in Educational Leadership. He is currently the curriculum lead and instructor for the Computer Information Technology Network support degree and certification program at Montana State University–Great Falls. Since 1998 he has also been an instructor and program director for the Montana State University–Great Falls Local, Regional Cisco Networking Academy and Cisco Academy Training Center for Sponsored Curriculum. He also teaches for Lesley University in its M.Ed. program in Educational Technology. Throughout his years in educational technology, Bruce has earned his CCNA, CCNP, CompTIA A+, Network+, Server+, and World Organization of Webmasters CPW certifications and continues to learn and pass his learning to others.

Khalid Rubayi teaches courses for the Electronics and Computer Technology Department at Victor Valley Community College in Victorville, California. He teaches all networking courses offered by the Cisco Networking Academy, including CCNA, CCNP, Security, and Wireless. He has a BS and MS in Electrical Engineering from Northrop University. He holds CCNA, CCNP, and CCAI certifications.

Tara Skibar, CCNP, was first introduced to networking in 1994 when she enlisted in the Air Force. After serving for four years as a network technician, she became an instructor. Tara has worked with major telecom companies in the United States and Europe. She has worked for the Cisco Networking Academy since 2003 as a subject matter expert for the CCNP assessment development team and for the CCNP certification exams. Most recently, Tara was the assessment lead for the newly modified CCNA curriculum and traveled with a group of development folks to Manila, Philippines, for the small market trial. Tara has a BS in Information Technology and is working toward a master's in Information Systems.

Linda C. Watson has been involved with the Cisco Networking Academy for ten years. She began as a student in version 1.1, and in the last eight years has been an instructor and director of the Academy program at Chandler-Gilbert Community College in Chandler, Arizona. After completing her own career change, she especially enjoys helping students transition from novices in the networking field to certified IT professionals. Linda has an MBA from Arizona State University and holds CCNA, CCAI, A+, and MCSE certifications.

Dedication

For my wife, Becky. Without the sacrifices you made during the project, this work would not have come to fruition. Thank you for providing me the comfort and resting place only you can give.

Acknowledgments

The reader will certainly benefit from the many hours devoted to this effort by the technical editors. A team of no less than four people served admirably as my second pair of eyes, finding and correcting technical inaccuracies and grammatical errors. Thank you Bruce Gottwig, Khalid Rubayi, Tara Skibar, and Linda Watson for doing an outstanding job.

Mary Beth Ray, executive editor, you amaze me with your ability to juggle multiple projects at once, steering each from beginning to end. I can always count on you to make the tough decisions.

This is my second project with Andrew Cupp as development editor. His dedication to perfection pays dividends in countless, unseen ways. Thank you again, Drew, for providing me with much-needed guidance and support. This book could not be a reality without your persistence.

Last, I cannot forget to thank all my students—past and present—who have helped me over the years to create engaging and exciting activities and labs. There is no better way to test the effectiveness of an activity or lab than to give it to a team of dedicated students. They excel at finding the obscurest of errors! I could have never done this without all your support.

Contents at a Glance

Contents

Icons Used in This Book

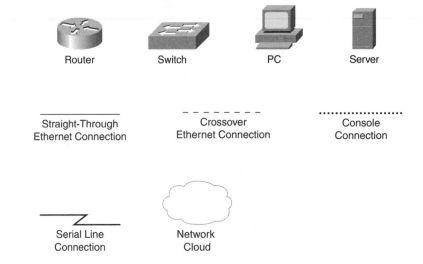

Router   Switch   PC   Server

Straight-Through   Crossover   Console
Ethernet Connection   Ethernet Connection   Connection

Serial Line   Network
Connection   Cloud

Command Syntax Conventions

The conventions used to present command syntax in this book are the same conventions used in the IOS Command Reference. The Command Reference describes these conventions as follows:

- **Boldface** indicates commands and keywords that are entered literally as shown. In actual configuration examples and output (not general command syntax), boldface indicates commands that are manually input by the user (such as a **show** command).

- *Italics* indicate arguments for which you supply actual values.

- Vertical bars (|) separate alternative, mutually exclusive elements.

- Square brackets [ ] indicate optional elements.

- Braces { } indicate a required choice.

- Braces within brackets [{ }] indicate a required choice within an optional element.

Introduction

The Cisco Networking Academy is a comprehensive e-learning program that provides students with Internet technology skills. A Networking Academy delivers web-based content, online assessment, student performance tracking, and hands-on labs to prepare students for industry-standard certifications. The CCNA curriculum includes four courses oriented around the topics on the Cisco Certified Network Associate (CCNA) certification.

LAN Switching and Wireless, CCNA Exploration Labs and Study Guide is a supplement to your classroom and laboratory experience with the Cisco Networking Academy. In order to be successful on the exam and achieve your CCNA certification, you should do everything in your power to arm yourself with a variety of tools and training materials to support your learning efforts. This Labs and Study Guide is just such a collection of tools. Used to its fullest extent, it will help you gain the knowledge and practice the skills associated with the content area of the CCNA Exploration LAN Switching and Wireless course. Specifically, this book will help you work on these main areas:

- LAN design principles and concepts
- Ethernet operation with switches
- Basic switch configuration and security
- VLAN concepts and configuration
- VTP concepts and configuration
- STP, RSTP, and rapid PVST+ concepts and configuration
- Inter-VLAN routing concepts and configuration
- LAN wireless concepts and security issues
- LAN wireless configuration using Linksys WRT300N routers
- Troubleshooting LAN switching and wireless configurations

Labs and Study Guides similar to this one are also available for the other three courses: *Network Fundamentals, CCNA Exploration Labs and Study Guide*, *Routing Protocols and Concepts, CCNA Exploration Labs and Study Guide*, and *Accessing the WAN, CCNA Exploration Labs and Study Guide*.

Audience for This Book

This book's main audience is anyone taking the *CCNA Exploration LAN Switching and Wireless course* of the Cisco Networking Academy curriculum. Many Academies use this book as a required tool in the course, while other Academies recommend the Labs and Study Guides as an additional source of study and practice materials.

The secondary audiences for this book include people taking CCNA-related classes from professional training organizations. This book can also be used for college- and university-level networking courses, as well as anyone wanting to gain a detailed understanding of basic switching and wireless technologies.

Goals and Methods

The most important goal of this book is to help you pass the CCNA exam (640-802). Passing this foundation exam means that you not only have the required knowledge of the technologies covered by the exam, but that you can plan, design, implement, operate, and troubleshoot these technologies. In other words, these exams are rigorously application based. You can view the exam topics any time at http://www.cisco.com/go/certifications. The topics are divided into eight categories:

- Describe how a network works

- Configure, verify, and troubleshoot a switch with VLANs and inter-switch communications

- Implement an IP addressing scheme and IP services to meet network requirements in a medium-sized enterprise branch office network

- Configure, verify, and troubleshoot basic router operation and routing on Cisco devices

- Explain and select the appropriate administrative tasks required for a WLAN

- Identify security threats to a network and describe general methods to mitigate those threats

- Implement, verify, and troubleshoot NAT and ACLs in a medium-sized enterprise branch office network

- Implement and verify WAN links

The LAN Switching and Wireless course focuses on the second, fifth, and sixth bullets.

The Study Guide portion of each chapter offers exercises that help you learn the LAN switching and wireless concepts as well as the configurations crucial to your success as a CCNA exam candidate. Each chapter is slightly different and includes some or all of the following types of exercises:

- Vocabulary matching and completion

- Skill-building activities and scenarios

- Configuration scenarios

- Concept questions

- Internet research

Packet Tracer
□ Activity

In the configuration chapters, you'll find many Packet Tracer Activities that work with the Cisco Packet Tracer tool. Packet Tracer allows you to create networks, visualize how packets flow in the network, and use basic testing tools to determine whether the network would work. When you see this icon, you can use Packet Tracer with the listed file to perform a task suggested in this book. The activity files are available in this book's CD-ROM; Packet Tracer software, however, is available through the Academy Connection website. Ask your instructor for access to Packet Tracer.

The Labs and Activities portion of each chapter includes a Command Reference table, all the online Curriculum Labs, and a Packet Tracer Skills Integration Challenge Activity. The Curriculum Labs are divided into three categories:

- **Basic:** The Basic Labs are procedural in nature and assume you have no experience configuring the technologies that are the topic of the lab.

- **Challenge:** The Challenge Labs are implementation in nature and assume you have a firm enough grasp on the technologies to "go it alone." These labs often only give you a general requirement that you must implement fully without the details of each small step. In other words, you must use the knowledge and skills you gained in the chapter text, activities, and Basic Lab to successfully complete the Challenge Labs. Avoid the temptation to work through the Challenge Lab by flipping back through the Basic Lab when you are not sure of a command. Do not try to short-circuit your CCNA training. You need a deep understanding CCNA knowledge and skills to ultimately be successful on the CCNA exam.

■ **Troubleshooting:** The Troubleshooting Labs will ask you to fix a broken network. These labs include corrupted scripts you purposefully load onto the routers. Then you use troubleshooting techniques to isolate problems and implement a solution. By the end of the lab, you should have a functional network with full end-to-end connectivity.

Most of the hands-on labs include Packet Tracer Companion Activities where you can use Packet Tracer to complete a simulation of the lab.

Each chapter also includes a culminating activity called the Packet Tracer Skills Integration Challenge. These activities require you to pull together several skills learned from the chapter—and from previous chapters and courses—to successfully complete one comprehensive exercise.

A Word About Packet Tracer

Packet Tracer is a self-paced, visual, interactive teaching and learning tool developed by Cisco. Lab activities are an important part of networking education. However, lab equipment can be a scarce resource. Packet Tracer provides a visual simulation of equipment and network processes to offset the challenge of limited equipment. Students can spend as much time as they like completing standard lab exercises through Packet Tracer, and have the option to work from home. Although Packet Tracer is not a substitute for real equipment, it allows students to practice using a command-line interface. This "e-doing" capability is a fundamental component of learning how to configure routers and switches from the command line.

Packet Tracer v4.x is available only to Cisco Networking Academies through the Academy Connection website.

How This Book Is Organized

Because the content of *LAN Switching and Wireless, CCNA Exploration Companion Guide* and the online curriculum is sequential, you should work through this Labs and Study Guide in order beginning with Chapter 1.

The book covers the major topic headings in the same sequence as the online curriculum for the *CCNA Exploration LAN Switching and Wireless course*. This book has seven chapters, with the same numbers and names as the online course chapters.

If necessary, a chapter uses a single topology for the exercises in the Study Guide portion. The single topology per chapter allows for better continuity and easier understanding of switching commands, operations, and outputs. However, the topology is different from the one used in the online curriculum and the *Companion Guide*. A different topology affords you the opportunity to practice your knowledge and skills without just simply recording the information you find in the text.

■ **Chapter 1, "LAN Design":** The exercises in the Study Guide portion focus on LAN design concepts, including vocabulary and the three-layer hierarchical model. The Labs and Activities portion includes a Basic Lab, a Challenge Lab, a Troubleshooting Lab, and a Packet Tracer Skills Integration Challenge activity.

■ **Chapter 2, "Basic Switch Concepts and Configuration":** The exercises in the Study Guide portion help you understand basic Ethernet and switching concepts, including building the MAC address table and collision and broadcast domains. Then, the Packet Tracer exercises cover, in detail, how to configure a switch, including basic switch management and configuring switch security. The Labs and Activities portion includes two Basic Labs, a Challenge Lab, and a Packet Tracer Skills Integration Challenge activity.

- **Chapter 3, "VLANs":** The exercises in the Study Guide portion focus on the concepts of VLANs, including benefits of VLANs and types of VLANs. The exercises then cover VLAN trunking concepts before moving into a section devoted to a VLAN and trunk configuration Packet Tracer exercise. The Labs and Activities portion includes a Basic Lab, a Challenge Lab, a Troubleshooting Lab, and a Packet Tracer Skills Integration Challenge activity.

- **Chapter 4, "VTP":** The exercises in the Study Guide portion are devoted to VTP concepts and configuration, including vocabulary, VTP modes, an Internet research exercise, and a VTP Packet Tracer exercise. The Labs and Activities portion includes a Basic Lab, a Challenge Lab, a Troubleshooting Lab, and a Packet Tracer Skills Integration Challenge activity.

- **Chapter 5, "STP":** The exercises in the Study Guide portion focus on the concept of redundant LAN topologies, using STP and its variants to stop loops, and the commands to manipulate root bridge elections. The Labs and Activities portion of the chapter includes a Basic Lab, a Challenge Lab, a Troubleshooting Lab, and a Packet Tracer Skills Integration Challenge activity.

- **Chapter 6, "Inter-VLAN Routing":** This short chapter focuses on how to configure inter-VLAN routing, including two Packet Tracer exercises. The Labs and Activities portion includes a Basic Lab, a Challenge Lab, a Troubleshooting Lab, and a Packet Tracer Skills Integration Challenge activity.

- **Chapter 7, "Basic Wireless Concepts and Configuration":** The exercises in the Study Guide portion begin with wireless LAN concepts, including standards, operation, and security. The exercises then cover wireless configuration for LAN access using a Linksys WRT300N, including a Packet Tracer exercise. The Labs and Activities portion of the chapter includes a Basic Lab, a Challenge Lab, a Troubleshooting Lab, and a Packet Tracer Skills Integration Challenge activity.

About the CD-ROM

The CD-ROM included with this book has all the Packet Tracer Activity, Packet Tracer Companion, and Packet Tracer Challenge files that are referenced throughout the book, indicated by the Packet Tracer Activity, Packet Tracer Companion, and Packet Tracer Challenge icons.

Updates to these files can be obtained from the website for this book at http://www.ciscopress.com/title/1587132028. The files will be updated to cover any subsequent releases of Packet Tracer.

About the Cisco Press Website for This Book

Cisco Press may provide additional content that can be accessed by registering your individual book at the Ciscopress.com website. Becoming a member and registering is free, and you then gain access to exclusive deals on other resources from Cisco Press.

To register this book, go to www.ciscopress.com/bookstore/register.asp and log into your account or create a free account if you do not have one already. Then enter the ISBN located on the back cover of this book.

After you register the book, it will appear on your Account page under Registered Products and you can access any online material from there.

CHAPTER 1

LAN Design

A properly designed LAN is a fundamental requirement for doing business. You must understand what a well-designed LAN is and be able to select appropriate devices to support the network specifications of a small or medium-sized business.

The Study Guide portion of this chapter uses a combination of matching, fill-in-the-blank, and open-ended question exercises to test your knowledge of LAN design.

The Labs and Activities portion of this chapter includes all the online curriculum labs and Packet Tracer activities to help you review information and skills you learned in the first course, Exploration Network Fundamentals.

As you work through this chapter, use Chapter 1 in *LAN Switching and Wireless, CCNA Exploration Companion Guide* or use the corresponding Chapter 1 in the Exploration LAN Switching and Wireless online curriculum for assistance.

Study Guide

Switched LAN Architecture

Compared to other network designs, a hierarchical network is easier to manage and expand, and problems are solved more quickly. Each layer provides specific functions that define its role within the overall network. By separating the various functions that exist on a network, not only is the network more manageable, but the network design becomes modular, which facilitates scalability and performance.

Vocabulary Exercise: Matching

Match the definition on the left with a term on the right. All definitions and terms are used exactly one time.

Definitions

a. Classifying and prioritizing traffic based on type of data.

b. Allow you to segment the traffic on a switch into separate subnetworks.

c. Controls which end devices are allowed to communicate on the network.

d. Distribution layer and core layer are combined into one layer.

e. High-speed backbone of the internetwork capable of forwarding large amounts of data quickly.

f. Determine the design requirements for a network.

g. Access layer switches can be configured with this option to provide control over which devices are allowed to connect to the network.

h. Cisco proprietary link aggregation technology.

i. Properly designed hierarchical networks can achieve near wire speed between all devices.

j. Consistency between the switches at each layer allows for rapid recovery and simplified troubleshooting.

k. Dramatically increases availability.

l. Controls the flow of network traffic using policies and delineates broadcast domains by performing routing functions between virtual LANs (VLANs).

m. The process of combining voice and video communications on a data network.

n. The modularity of the hierarchical design facilitates ease of network expansion.

Terms

___ access layer

___ business goals

___ collapsed core

___ convergence

___ core layer

___ distribution layer

___ EtherChannel

___ manageability

___ performance

___ port security

___ Quality of Service (QoS)

___ redundancy

___ scalability

___ VLANs

Vocabulary Exercise: Completion

Complete the paragraphs that follow by filling in the appropriate words and phrases.

The Hierarchical Network Model

The typical hierarchical design model is broken up into three layers: _____, _____, and _____. Draw an example of a three-layer hierarchical network design in the blank space provided in Figure 1-1.

Figure 1-1   Three-Layer Hierarchical Network Example

The main purpose of the _____ layer is to provide a means of connecting devices to the network and controlling which devices are allowed to communicate on the network.

The _____ layer aggregates the data received from the _____ layer switches before it is transmitted to the _____ layer for routing to its final destination. The _____ layer controls the flow of network traffic using policies and delineates _____ domains by performing routing functions between _____ defined at the _____ layer.

The _____ layer is critical for interconnectivity between _____ layer devices. It can also connect to Internet resources.

There are many benefits associated with hierarchical network designs:

- _____: The modularity of the design allows you to replicate design elements as the network grows. Because each instance of the module is consistent, expansion is easy to plan and implement.

- _____: Access layer switches are connected to two different distribution layer switches. Distribution layer switches are connected to two or more core layer switches to ensure path availability if a core switch fails.

- _____: Data is sent through aggregated switch port links from the access layer to the distribution layer at near wire speed in most cases.

- _____: You have the flexibility to use more advanced policies at the distribution layer. You may apply access control policies that define which communication protocols are deployed on your network and where they are permitted to go.

- _____: Each layer of the hierarchical design performs specific functions that are consistent throughout that layer. Consistency between the switches at each layer allows for rapid recovery and simplified troubleshooting.

- _____: Because hierarchical networks are modular in nature and scale very easily, they are easy to maintain.

Principles of Hierarchical Network Design

When designing a hierarchical network topology, consider the network _____, which is the number of devices that a packet has to cross before it reaches its destination. Keeping the network _____ low ensures low and predictable _____ between devices.

Each layer in the hierarchical network model is a possible candidate for _____, which allows multiple switch port links to be combined so as to achieve higher throughput between switches.

_____ can be provided in a number of ways, including by doubling up the network connections between devices or doubling the devices themselves.

Design requirements, such as the level of performance or redundancy necessary, are determined by the _____ of the organization.

What Is a Converged Network?

Convergence is the process of combining _____ and _____ communications on a data network. Converged networks have existed for a while now, but were only feasible in large enterprise organizations because of the high network costs. Converged networks also required extensive management in relation to Quality of Service (QoS), because voice and video data traffic needed to be _____ and _____ on the network. Few individuals had the expertise in voice, video, and data networks to make convergence feasible and functional. In addition, _____ equipment hinders the process of moving toward a converged network.

What are two benefits to implementing a converged network as opposed to implementing three separate networks?

_____

_____

Converged networks give you options that had not existed previously. There is no need for an expensive handset phone or videoconferencing equipment. You can accomplish the same function using special _____ integrated with a personal computer. With the addition of inexpensive webcams, _____ can be added to a softphone.

Three-Layer Hierarchical Model Exercise

For each of the following figures, indicate whether the scenario is an **access** layer function, **distribution** layer function, or **core** layer function.

Figure 1-2   Scenario 1

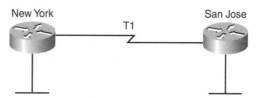

In Figure 1-2, the _____ layer is responsible for connecting New York and San Jose across a T1 link.

Figure 1-3   Scenario 2

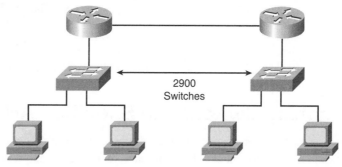

In Figure 1-3, the _____ layer is using 2900 series switches to connect end users to the network.

Figure 1-4   Scenario 3

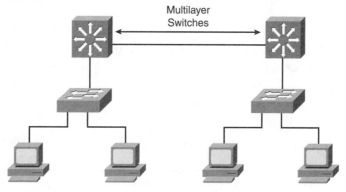

In Figure 1-4, the _____ layer is using multilayer switches for inter-VLAN routing.

Figure 1-5   Scenario 4

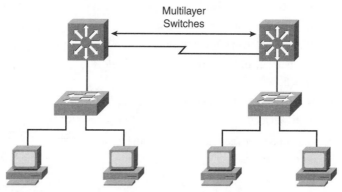

In Figure 1-5, the _____ layer is using multilayer switches between remote sites across a WAN link for fast switching and no packet manipulation.

Figure 1-6   Scenario 5

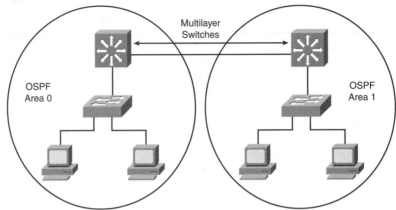

In Figure 1-6, the _____ layer is using multilayer switches to summarize OSPF routes.

Matching Switches to Specific LAN Functions

Selecting switches for each of the layers of the hierarchical design requires knowing details about traffic flows, the user community demands, data storage needs, and server availability.

Vocabulary Exercise: Matching

Match the definition on the left with a term on the right. All definitions and terms are used exactly one time.

Definitions

a. A graphical representation of a network infrastructure.

b. Cannot add hardware features or options beyond those that originally came with the switch.

c. Allow installation of different line cards.

d. A process of measuring the bandwidth usage on a network and analyzing the data for the purpose of performance tuning, capacity planning, and making hardware improvement decisions.

e. Reduces bottlenecks of traffic by allowing up to eight switch ports to be bound together for data communications.

f. The number of ports available on a single switch.

g. Uses the network cable to deliver electricity to devices.

h. Generated between data storage devices on the network.

i. Interconnected using a special backplane cable.

j. Typically traverses multiple switches to reach its destination.

k. Defines the capabilities of a switch by classifying how much data the switch can process per second.

l. Also known as Layer 3 switches.

m. A process of identifying various groups and their impact on network performance.

Terms

_____ client-server traffic

_____ fixed configuration switches

_____ forwarding rates

_____ link aggregation

_____ modular switches

_____ multilayer switches

_____ port density

_____ Power over Ethernet (PoE)

_____ server-server traffic

_____ stackable switches

_____ topology diagram

_____ traffic flow analysis

_____ user community analysis

Layer Features of the Hierarchical Model Exercise

Check the appropriate column in Table 1-1 to identify which feature belongs to each layer. Some features may belong to more than one layer.

Table 1-1   Features at Each Layer of the Hierarchical Model

Feature	Access	Distribution	Core
Bandwidth aggregation			
Fast Ethernet/Gigabit Ethernet			
Gigabit Ethernet/10-Gigabit Ethernet			
High forwarding rate			
Very high forwarding rate			
Layer 3 support			
Port security			
Power over Ethernet (PoE)			
Quality of Service (QoS)			
Redundant components			
Security policies/access control lists			
VLANs			

Labs and Activities

Command Reference

The labs for this first chapter review the configuration skills you acquired in previous courses. In Table 1-2, record the command, *including the correct prompt*, that fits the description. Fill in any blanks with the appropriate missing information.

Table 1-2   Commands for Basic Router Configuration

Command	Description
	Switches from user EXEC mode to privileged EXEC mode
	Switches back from privileged EXEC mode to user EXEC mode
	Moves into global configuration mode
	Names the router CISCO
	Sets the enable password to **class** and encrypts it
	Configures a message-of-the-day banner that uses # as the delimiting character and displays the following when users attempt to log in: Authorized Access Only
	Enters console line configuration mode
	Sets the console password to **cisco**
	Enables password checking when users log in
	Enters line configuration mode for five Telnet lines
	Enters interface configuration mode for Fa0/0
	Sets an interface address as 192.168.1.1/24
	Configures an interface with the text Link to ISP, which is used to describe the purpose of the link
	Activates an interface
	Saves the current configuration to NVRAM
	Displays the current configuration in RAM
	Displays the configuration saved in NVRAM
	Tests end-to-end connectivity with a remote destination at 192.168.1.1

Command	Description
	Begins a remote management session on a device at 192.168.1.1

Lab 1-1: Review of Concepts from Exploration 1 (1.3.1)

Learning Objectives

Upon completion of this lab, you will be able to

- Create a logical topology given network requirements
- Create subnets to meet host requirements
- Configure the physical topology
- Configure the logical topology
- Verify network connectivity
- Configure and verify passwords

Scenario

In this lab, you will design and configure a small routed network and verify connectivity across multiple network devices. This requires creating and assigning two subnetwork blocks, connecting hosts and network devices, and configuring host computers and one Cisco router for basic network connectivity. Switch1 has a default configuration and does not require additional configuration. You will use common commands to test and document the network. The zero subnet is used.

Figure 1-7 shows the topology diagram for this lab.

Figure 1-7   Topology Diagram for Lab 1-1

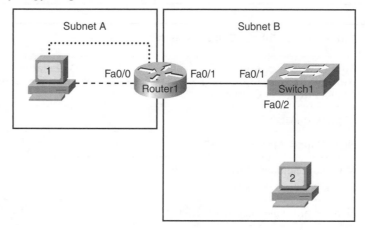

Task 1: Design a Logical LAN Topology

Step 1.   Design an IP addressing scheme.

Given the IP address block of 192.168.7.0/24, design an IP addressing scheme that satisfies the following requirements:

- Subnet A has 110 hosts.
- Subnet B has 54 hosts.
- Subnet zero is used.
- Create the smallest possible subnets that satisfy the requirements for hosts.
- Complete the calculations for Subnet A in Table 1-3.
- Complete the calculations for Subnet B in Table 1-4.
- No subnet calculators may be used.

Table 1-3   Subnet Calculations for Subnet A

Subnet Specification	Calculation
Number of bits in the subnet	
IP mask (binary)	
New IP mask (decimal)	
Maximum number of usable subnets (including the 0 subnet)	
Number of usable hosts per subnet	
IP subnetwork address	
First IP host address	
Last IP host address	

Table 1-4   Subnet Calculations for Subnet B

Subnet Specification	Calculation
Number of bits in the subnet	
IP mask (binary)	
New IP mask (decimal)	
Maximum number of usable subnets (including the 0 subnet)	
Number of usable hosts per subnet	
IP network address	
First IP host address	
Last IP host address	

Step 2. Record the IP address information for each device:

- Assign the first usable IP address in the subnet to the hosts and record the information in Table 1-5.

- Assign the last usable IP address to the router interface and record the information in Table 1-5.

Table 1-5   IP Address Assignments

Device	IP Address	Subnet Mask	Default Gateway
Host1			
Router1-Fa0/0			
Host2			
Router1-Fa0/1			

Before proceeding, verify your IP addresses with the instructor.

Task 2: Configure the Physical Topology

Step 1. Cable the network.

Refer to Figure 1-7 and Table 1-6 to determine the necessary cables needed to connect the devices.

Table 1-6   Choosing the Correct Cable

Link	Cable Type
Host1 to Router1 Fa0/0	Crossover
Switch1 to Router1 Fa0/1	Straight-through
Switch1 to Host2	Straight-through
Host1 and Router1 console	Rollover

Step 2. Physically connect lab devices.

Cable the network devices as shown in Figure 1-7 and power all devices.

Step 3. Inspect the network connections.

Verify the connections visually. Link lights on the router, switch, and hosts should be green. You will not have a link light for the console connection, but it should be firmly attached at both ends.

Task 3: Configure the Logical Topology

Step 1.   Configure the host computers.

Configure the static IP address, subnet mask, and gateway for each host computer.

Note: The following directions are for Windows XP. To configure hosts using other operating systems, refer to the operating system manual.

To configure the host, choose **Start > Control Panel > Network Connections > Local Area Connection** and then click the **Properties** button. In the Local Area Connection Properties dialog box, click **Internet Protocol (TCP/IP)** and click the **Properties** button, as shown in Figure 1-8.

Figure 1-8   Setting Properties for Internet Protocol (TCP/IP)

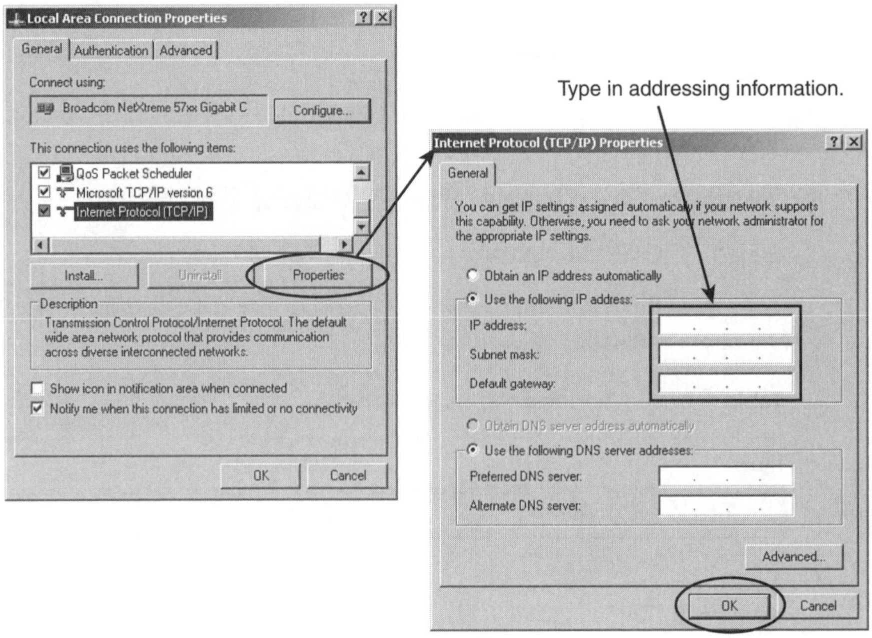

In the TCP/IP Properties dialog box for each host, enter the IP address, subnet mask, and the default gateway you recorded previously in Table 1-5.

After configuring each host computer, open a command window on the host by choosing **Start > Run**. When prompted to type the name of a program, enter **cmd** in the text box. From the command window, display and verify the host network settings with the **ipconfig** command. The settings should match what you recorded previously in Table 1-5.

Step 2.   Configure Router1.

From Host1, establish a console session with Router1. Directions for creating a console connection using Tera Term or HyperTerminal are in the appendixes at the end of this lab.

From the router console, enter the following commands:

```
Router>enable
Router#config terminal
Enter configuration commands, one per line. End with CNTL/Z.
Router(config)#hostname Router1
```

```
Router1(config)#enable secret class
Router1(config)#line console 0
Router1(config-line)#password cisco
Router1(config-line)#login
Router1(config-line)#line vty 0 4
Router1(config-line)#password cisco
Router1(config-line)#login
Router1(config-line)#interface fa0/0
Router1(config-if)#ip address 192.168.7.126  255.255.255.128
Router1(config-if)#no shutdown
Router1(config-if)#description connection to host1
Router1(config-if)#interface fa0/1
Router1(config-if)#description connection to switch1
Router1(config-if)#ip address 192.168.7.190 255.255.255.192
Router1(config-if)#no shutdown
Router1(config-if)#end
Router1#
```

Task 4: Verify Network Connectivity

Use the **ping** command to verify network connectivity.

Note: If pings to the host computers fail, temporarily disable the computer firewall and retest. To disable a Windows firewall, choose **Start > Control Panel > Windows Firewall**, click the **Off** radio button, and then click **OK**.

Use Table 1-7 to verify connectivity with each network device. Take corrective action to establish connectivity if a test fails.

Table 1-7   Connectivity Verification

From	To	IP Address	Ping Results
Host1	NIC IP address	192.168.7.1	
Host1	Router1, Fa0/0	192.168.7.126	
Host1	Router1, Fa0/1	192.168.7.190	
Host1	Host2	192.168.7.129	
Host2	NIC IP address	192.168.7.129	
Host2	Router1, Fa0/1	192.168.7.190	
Host2	Router1, Fa0/0	192.168.7.126	
Host2	Host1	192.168.7.1	

In addition to the **ping** command, what other Windows command is useful in displaying network delay and breaks in the path to the destination?

_____

Task 5: Verify Passwords

Step 1. Telnet to Router1 from Host2 to verify the Telnet password.

You should be able to telnet to either FastEthernet interface of the router.

In a command window on Host 2, type

`C:\>telnet 192.168.7.190`

When you are prompted for the Telnet password, type **cisco** and press **Enter**.

Was the telnet successful? _____

Step 2. Verify that the enable secret password has been set.

From the Telnet session, enter privileged EXEC mode and verify it is password protected:

`Router1>enable`

Were you prompted for the enable secret password? _____

Step 3. Verify that the console is password protected.

Terminate and then re-establish the console connection from Host1 to the router to verify that the console is password protected.

Depending on the Telnet client that you are using, the session can usually be terminated with **Ctrl**-]. When the session is re-established, you should be prompted for the console password before being allowed access to the command-line interface.

Task 6: Reflection

How are Telnet access and console access different? When might it make sense to set different passwords on these two access ports?

_____

_____

_____

_____

Why does the switch between Host2 and the router not require configuration with an IP address to forward packets?

_____

_____

_____

Task 7: Clean Up

Unless directed otherwise by your instructor, erase the configurations and reload the switches. Disconnect and store the cabling. For PC hosts that are normally connected to other networks (such as the school LAN or to the Internet), reconnect the appropriate cabling and restore the TCP/IP settings.

Packet Tracer
☐ Companion

Review of Concepts from Exploration 1 (1.3.1)

You can now open the file LSG03-Lab131.pka on the CD-ROM that accompanies this book to repeat this hands-on lab using Packet Tracer. Remember, however, that Packet Tracer is not a substitute for a hands-on lab experience with real equipment.

Appendix 1A: Installing and Configuring Tera Term for Use in Windows XP

Tera Term is a free terminal-emulation program for Windows. It can be used in the lab environment in place of Windows HyperTerminal. Tera Term can be obtained at the following URL:

http://hp.vector.co.jp/authors/VA002416/teraterm.html

Download the ttermp23.zip file for Windows95/NT, unzip it, and install Tera Term. This version is compatible with XP and Vista.

Step 1.   Open Tera Term.

Step 2.   Assign the serial port.

To use Tera Term to connect to the router console, click the **Serial** radio button, as shown in Figure 1-9.

Step 3.   Set the serial port parameter.

Choose the appropriate parameter from the **Port** drop-down list. Normally, your connection is through COM1. If you are unsure what port to use, ask your instructor for assistance. When you are finished, click **OK**.

Figure 1-9   Tera Term: New Connection Dialog Box

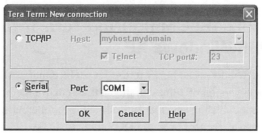

Step 4.   Configure settings.

Tera Term has some settings that can be changed to make it more convenient to use. Choose **Setup > Terminal** to open the Terminal Setup dialog box, and then check the **Term Size = Win Size** check box, as shown in Figure 1-10. This setting allows command output to remain visible when the Tera Term window is resized. Click **OK** to close the Terminal Setup dialog box.

Figure 1-10   Tera Term: Terminal Setup Dialog Box

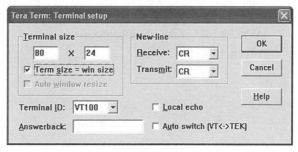

Step 5.   Change the scroll buffer number.

Choose **Setup > Window** and, in the Window Setup dialog box, change the **Scroll Buffer** number to a number higher than 100, as shown in Figure 1-11. This setting allows you to scroll up and view previous commands and outputs. If there are only 100 lines available in the buffer, only the last 100 lines of output are visible. For example, set the scroll buffer to 1000 lines.

Figure 1-11   Tera Term: Window Setup Dialog Box

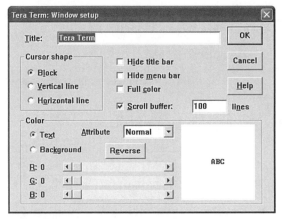

Appendix 1B: Configuring Tera Term as the Default Telnet Client in Windows XP

By default, Windows can be set to use HyperTerminal as the Telnet client. Windows can also be set to use the DOS version of Telnet. In the NetLab environment, you can change the Telnet client to Local Telnet Client, which means that NetLab will open the current Windows default Telnet client. This can be set to HyperTerminal or to the DOS-like version of Telnet embedded in the Windows operating system.

Complete the following steps to change your default Telnet client to Tera Term (or any other Telnet client):

Step 1.   Open the Folder Options dialog box.

Double-click **My Computer** (or choose **Start > My Computer**), and then choose **Tools > Folder Options**.

Step 2.   Edit the **(NONE) URL:Telnet Protocol**.

Click the **File Types** tab, scroll down in the **Registered File Types** list and click the **(NONE) URL:Telnet Protocol** entry, as shown in Figure 1-12, and then click the **Advanced** button.

Figure 1-12   Folder Options Dialog Box

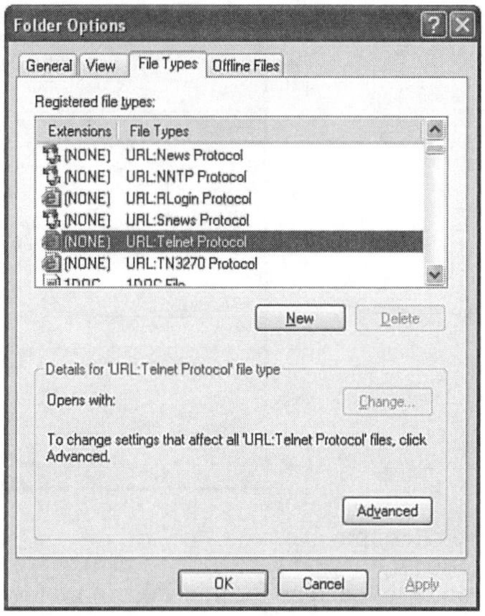

Step 3.   Edit the open action.

In the Edit File Type dialog box, click **Edit** to edit the **open** action, as shown in Figure 1-13.

Figure 1-13   Edit File Type Dialog Box

Step 4.   Change the application.

In the Editing Action for Type: URL: Telnet Protocol dialog box, the Application Used to Perform Action is currently set to HyperTerminal, as shown in Figure 1-14. Click **Browse** to change the application.

Figure 1-14   Editing Action for Type Dialog Box (Before Edit)

Step 5.   Open ttermpro.exe.

Browse to the Tera Term installation folder, as shown in Figure 1-15. Click **ttermpro.exe** to specify this program for the open action, and then click **Open**.

Step 6.   Confirm ttermpro.exe and close.

From the window shown in Figure 1-16, click **OK** twice and then click **Close** to close the Folder Options dialog box. The Windows default Telnet client is now set to Tera Term.

Figure 1-15   Open With Dialog Box

Figure 1-16   Editing Action for Type Dialog Box (After Edit)

Appendix 1C: Accessing and Configuring HyperTerminal

In most versions of Windows, you can open HyperTerminal by choosing **Start > Programs > Accessories > Communications > HyperTerminal**.

Step 1. Create a new connection.

Open HyperTerminal to create a new connection to the router. Enter an appropriate description in the Name field of the Connection Description dialog box, shown in Figure 1-17, and then click **OK**.

Step 2. Assign COM1 port.

In the Connect To dialog box, shown in Figure 1-18, make sure that the correct serial port is selected in the **Connect Using** field. Some PCs have more than one COM port. Click **OK**.

Figure 1-17   Connection Description Dialog Box

Figure 1-18   Connect To Dialog Box

Step 3.   Set COM1 properties.

In the COM1 Properties dialog box, on the Port Settings tab, if the properties are not set to the values shown in Figure 1-19, click **Restore Defaults**, which normally sets the correct properties. Then click **OK**.

Figure 1-19   COM1 Properties Dialog Box

Step 4.   Verify the connection.

You should now have a console connection to the router. Press **Enter** to get a router prompt.

Curriculum Lab 1-2: Review of Concepts from Exploration 1—Challenge (1.3.2)

Learning Objectives

Upon completion of this lab, you will be able to

- Create a logical topology given network requirements
- Create subnets to meet host requirements
- Configure the physical topology
- Configure the logical topology
- Verify network connectivity
- Configure and verify passwords

Scenario

In this lab, you will design and configure a small routed network and verify connectivity across multiple network devices. This requires creating and assigning two subnetwork blocks, connecting hosts and network devices, and configuring host computers and one Cisco router for basic network connectivity. Switch1 has a default configuration and does not require additional configuration. You will use common commands to test and document the network. The zero subnet is used.

Figure 1-20 shows the topology diagram for this lab.

Figure 1-20   Topology Diagram for Lab 1-2

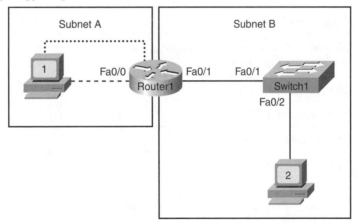

Task 1: Design a Logical LAN Topology

Step 1.   Design an IP addressing scheme.

Given the IP address block of 192.168.30.0/27, design an IP addressing scheme that satisfies the following requirements:

- Subnet A has 7 hosts.
- Subnet B has 14 hosts.
- Subnet zero is used.
- Create the smallest possible subnets that satisfy the requirements for hosts.
- Complete the calculations for Subnet A in Table 1-8.

- Complete the calculations for Subnet B in Table 1-9.

- No subnet calculators may be used.

Table 1-8   Subnet Calculations for Subnet A

Subnet Specification	Calculation
Number of bits in the subnet	
IP mask (binary)	
New IP mask (decimal)	
Maximum number of usable subnets (including the 0 subnet)	
Number of usable hosts per subnet	
IP subnetwork address	
First IP host address	
Last IP host address	

Table 1-9   Subnet Calculations for Subnet B

Subnet Specification	Calculation
Number of bits in the subnet	
IP mask (binary)	
New IP mask (decimal)	
Maximum number of usable subnets (including the 0 subnet)	
Number of usable hosts per subnet	
IP subnetwork address	
First IP host address	
Last IP host address	

Step 2.   Record the IP address information for each device:

- Assign the first usable IP address in the subnet to the hosts and record the information in Table 1-10.

- Assign the last usable IP address to the router interface and record the information in Table 1-10.

Table 1-10   IP Address Assignments

Device	IP Address	Mask	Gateway
Host1			
Router1-Fa0/0			
Host2			
Router1-Fa0/1			

Before proceeding, verify your IP addresses with the instructor.

Task 2: Configure the Physical Topology

Step 1.   Cable the network.

Refer to Figure 1-20 and in Table 1-11 indicate the necessary cables needed to connect the devices.

Table 1-11   Choosing the Correct Cable

Correct Cabling	Cable Type
LAN cable between Host1 and Router1 Fa0/0	
LAN cable between Switch1 and Router1 Fa0/1	
LAN cable between Switch1 and Host2	
Console cable between Host1 and Router1	

Step 2.   Physically connect lab devices.

Cable the network devices as shown in Figure 1-20 and power all devices.

Step 3.   Inspect the network connections.

After cabling the network devices, verify the connections.

Task 3: Configure the Logical Topology

Step 1.   Configure the host computers.

Configure the static IP address, subnet mask, and gateway for each host computer. After configuring each host computer, display and verify the host network settings with the **ipconfig** command.

Step 2.   Configure Router1.

From Host1, establish a console connection with Router1 and configure the following:

- Use **Router1** as the hostname
- Set the encrypted privileged EXEC password to **class**
- Set the console and Telnet access password to **cisco**
- Complete the description and IP addressing on both FastEthernet interfaces

Task 4: Verify Network Connectivity

Use the **ping** command to verify network connectivity.

In Table 1-12 record IP addresses and connectivity verification results for each network device. Take corrective action to establish connectivity if a test fails.

Table 1-12   Connectivity Verification

From	To	IP Address	Ping Results
Host1	NIC IP address		
Host1	Router1, Fa0/0		
Host1	Router1, Fa0/1		
Host1	Host2		
Host2	NIC IP address		
Host2	Router1, Fa0/1		
Host2	Router1, Fa0/0		
Host2	Host1		

Task 5: Verify Passwords

Step 1.   Telnet to Router1 from Host2 and verify the Telnet password.

You should be able to telnet to either Fast Ethernet interface of the router.

Step 2.   Verify that the enable secret password has been set.

From the Telnet session, enter privileged EXEC mode and verify that it is password protected.

Step 3.   Verify that the console is password protected.

Terminate and then re-establish the console connection from Host1 to the router to verify that the console is password protected.

Task 6: Clean Up

Unless directed otherwise by your instructor, erase the configurations and reload the switches. Disconnect and store the cabling. For PC hosts that are normally connected to other networks (such as the school LAN or to the Internet), reconnect the appropriate cabling and restore the TCP/IP settings.

Packet Tracer Companion: Review of Concepts from Exploration 1—Challenge (1.3.2)

You can now open the file LSG03-Lab132.pka on the CD-ROM that accompanies this book to repeat this hands-on lab using Packet Tracer. Remember, however, that Packet Tracer is not a substitute for a hands-on lab experience with real equipment.

Curriculum Lab 1-3: Troubleshooting a Small Network (1.3.3)

Learning Objectives

Upon completion of this lab, you will be able to

- Verify that a paper design meets stated network requirements
- Cable a network according to the topology diagram
- Erase the startup configuration and reload a router to the default state
- Load the routers with supplied scripts
- Discover where communication is not possible
- Gather information about the misconfigured portion of the network along with any other errors
- Analyze information to determine why communication is not possible
- Propose solutions to network errors
- Implement solutions to network errors

Scenario

In this lab, you are given a completed configuration for a small routed network. The configuration contains design and configuration errors that conflict with stated requirements and prevent end-to-end communication. You will examine the given design and identify and correct any design errors. You will then cable the network, configure the hosts, and load configurations onto the router. Finally, you will troubleshoot the connectivity problems to determine where the errors are occurring and correct them using the appropriate commands. When all errors have been corrected, each host should be able to communicate with all other configured network elements and with the other host.

Figure 1-21 shows the topology diagram for this lab.

Figure 1-21   Topology Diagram for Lab 1-3

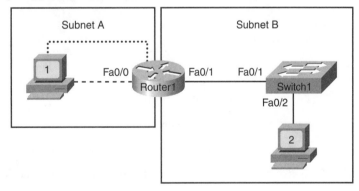

Task 1: Examine the Logical LAN Topology

Step 1.   Verify the IP addressing scheme.

The IP address block of 172.16.30.0/23 is already subnetted to meet the following requirements:

- Subnet A has 174 hosts.

- Subnet B has 54 hosts.

- Subnet zero is used.

- Created the smallest possible number of subnets that satisfy the requirements for hosts.

- Calculations for Subnet A are shown in Table 1-13.

- Calculations for Subnet B are shown in Table 1-14.

Table 1-13   Subnet Calculations for Subnet A

Subnet Specification	Calculated Value
IP mask (decimal)	255.255.255.0
IP address	172.16.30.0
First IP host address	172.16.30.1
Last IP host address	172.16.30.254

Table 1-14   Subnet Calculations for Subnet B

Subnet Specification	Calculated Value
IP mask (decimal)	255.255.255.128
IP address	172.16.31.0
First IP host address	172.16.31.1
Last IP host address	172.16.31.126

Examine each of the values in Tables 1-13 and 1-14 and verify that this topology meets all requirements and specifications.

Are any of the given values incorrect? _____

If yes, correct the values in Table 1-13 and/or Table 1-14.

Step 2.   Record the correct IP address information for each device:

- Assign the first usable IP address in the subnet to the hosts and record the information in Table 1-15.

- Assign the last usable IP address to the router interface and record the information in Table 1-15.

Table 1-15   IP Address Assignments

Device	IP Address	Mask	Gateway
Host1			
Router1–Fa0/0			
Host2			
Router1–Fa0/1			

Task 2: Cable, Erase, and Reload the Routers

Step 1.   Cable the network.

Step 2.   Clear the configuration on each router.

Task 3: Configure the Host Computers

Step 1.   Configure host computers with IP addressing.

Step 2.   Verify host computer configuration.

Task 4: Load the Router with the Supplied Scripts

Apply the following configurations to Router1. Alternatively, you can open the file LSG03-Lab133-Scripts.txt on the CD-ROM that accompanies this book and copy in the scripts for each of the switches.

```
enable
!
config term
!
hostname Router1
!
enable secret class
!
no ip domain-lookup
!
 interface FastEthernet0/0
 description connection to host1
 ip address 172.16.30.1 255.255.255.0
 duplex auto
 speed auto
!
interface FastEthernet0/1
 description connection to switch1
 ip address 192.16.31.1 255.255.255.192
 duplex auto
 speed auto
```

```
!
!
line con 0
 password cisco
 login
line vty 0
 login
line vty 1 4
 password cisco
 login
!
end
```

Task 5: Identify Connectivity Problems

Use the **ping** command to test network connectivity.

Use Table 1-16 to test the connectivity of each network device and record the initial results of your tests.

Table 1-16   Connectivity Verification

From	To	IP Address	Ping Results
Host1	NIC IP address	172.16.30.1	
Host1	Router1, Fa0/0	172.16.30.254	
Host1	Router1, Fa0/1	172.16.31.126	
Host1	Host2	172.16.31.1	
Host2	NIC IP address	172.16.30.1	
Host2	Router1, Fa0/1	172.16.31.126	
Host2	Router1, Fa0/0	172.16.30.254	
Host2	Host1	172.16.30.1	

Task 6: Troubleshoot Network Connections

Step 1.   Begin troubleshooting at PC1 (the host directly connected to Router1).

From host PC1, is it possible to ping PC2? _____

From host PC1, is it possible to ping the router Fa0/1 interface? _____

From host PC1, is it possible to ping the default gateway? _____

From host PC1, is it possible to ping itself? _____

Where is the most logical place to begin troubleshooting the PC1 connection problems?

_____

_____

Step 2.   Examine the router to find possible configuration errors.

Begin by viewing the summary of status information for each interface on the router.

Are there any problems with the status of the interfaces?

_____

_____

_____

If there are problems with the status of the interfaces, record any commands that are necessary to correct the configuration errors:

_____

_____

Step 3.   Use the necessary commands to correct the router configuration.

Step 4.   View a summary of the status information.

If any changes were made to the configuration in the previous step, view the summary of the status information for the router interfaces.

Does the information in the interface status summary indicate any configuration errors on Router1? _____

If the answer is yes, troubleshoot the interface status of the interfaces.

Has connectivity been restored? _____

Step 5.   Verify the logical configuration.

Examine the full status of Fa0/0 and Fa0/1. Is the IP address and subnet mask information in the interface status consistent with the configuration table? _____

If there are differences between the configuration table and the router interface configuration, record any commands that are necessary to correct the router configuration:

_____

_____

_____

Has connectivity been restored? _____

Why is it useful for a host to **ping** its own address?

_____

_____

Task 7: Clean Up

Unless directed otherwise by your instructor, erase the configurations and reload the switches. Disconnect and store the cabling. For PC hosts that are normally connected to other networks (such as the school LAN or to the Internet), reconnect the appropriate cabling and restore the TCP/IP settings.

Troubleshooting a Small Network (1.3.3)

You can now open the file LSG03-Lab133.pka on the CD-ROM that accompanies this book to repeat this hands-on lab using Packet Tracer. Remember, however, that Packet Tracer is not a substitute for a hands-on lab experience with real equipment.

Packet Tracer Skills Integration Challenge

Open the file LSG03-PTSkills1.pka on the CD-ROM that accompanies this book. You will use the topology in Figure 1-22 and the addressing table in Table 1-17 to document your design.

Figure 1-22   Packet Tracer Skills Integration Challenge Topology

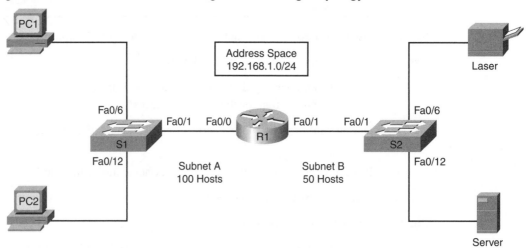

Table 1-17   Addressing Table for the Packet Tracer Skills Integration Challenge Activity

Device	Interface	IP Address	Subnet Mask	Default Gateway
R1	Fa0/0			
	Fa0/1			
PC1	NIC			
PC2	NIC			
Laser	NIC			
Server	NIC			

Learning Objectives

Upon completion of this lab, you will be able to

- Design the network
- Build the network
- Apply a basic configuration
- Test connectivity

Introduction

This activity reviews the skills you acquired in the Exploration: Network Fundamentals course. The skills include subnetting, building a network, applying an addressing scheme, and testing connectivity. You should review those skills before proceeding. In addition, this activity reviews the basics of using the Packet Tracer program. Packet Tracer is integrated throughout this course. You must know how to navigate the Packet Tracer environment to complete this course. Use the tutorials if you need a review of Packet Tracer fundamentals. The tutorials are located in the Packet Tracer **Help** menu.

Task 1: Design and Document an Addressing Scheme

Step 1.   Design an addressing scheme.

Using the 192.168.1.0/24 address space, design an addressing scheme according to the following requirements.

Subnet A:

- Subnet the address space to provide for 100 hosts.
- Assign the Fa0/0 interface the first useable IP address.
- Assign PC1 the second useable IP address.
- Assign PC2 the last useable IP address in the subnet.

Subnet B:

- Subnet the remaining address space to provide for 50 hosts.
- Assign the Fa0/1 interface the first useable IP address.
- Assign the laser printer the second useable IP address.
- Assign the server the last useable IP address in the subnet.

Step 2.   Document the addressing scheme.

Fill in the addressing information for the router and each end device in the network in Table 1-17.

Task 2: Add and Connect the Devices

Step 1.   Add the necessary equipment.

Add the following devices to the network. For placement of these devices, refer to the topology diagram in Figure 1-22.

- Two 2960-24TT switches
- One 1841 router
- Two generic PCs
- One generic server
- One generic printer

Step 2.   Name the devices.

Change the display name and hostname to match the device names shown in the topology diagram in Figure 1-22. Device names are case sensitive.

Step 3.   Connect the devices.

Use the following specifications for the connections between the devices:

- S1 Fa0/1 to R1 Fa0/0
- S1 Fa0/6 to PC1
- S1 Fa0/12 to PC2
- S2 Fa0/1 to R1 Fa0/1
- S2 Fa0/6 to Laser
- S2 Fa0/12 to Server

Step 4.   Check results.

Your completion percentage should be 46 percent. If not, click **Check Results** to see which required components are not yet completed.

Task 3: Apply Basic Configurations

Step 1.   Configure the router:

- Set the privileged EXEC secret password to **class**.
- Set the banner to **Authorized Access Only**.
- Set the line password to **cisco** for console and Telnet.
- Configure the appropriate interfaces. Use the following descriptions:
    - Link to PC LAN
    - Link to Server & Printer

Note: Remember that the banner and descriptions are case sensitive. Do not forget to activate the interfaces.

Step 2.   Configure the end devices.

Step 3.   Check results.

Your completion percentage should be 100 percent. If not, click **Check Results** to see which required components are not yet completed.

Task 4: Test Connectivity and Examine the Configuration

You should now have end-to-end connectivity, which means every end device should be reachable from any other end device. From PC1 and PC2, ping all end devices on the network. If you get an error, try pinging again to make sure ARP tables are updated. If you still receive an error, check your subnetting, the cables, and the IP addresses. Isolate problems and implement solutions.

CHAPTER 2

Basic Switch Concepts and Configuration

This chapter is a basic review of Ethernet concepts and the switching process—how a switch forwards a frame. In addition, you learn the basics of switch configuration and port security. You must master these skills before moving on to more complex switch configurations.

The Study Guide portion of this chapter uses a combination of matching, fill-in-the-blank, open-ended question, and Packet Tracer exercises to test your knowledge of basic switching concepts and configurations.

The Labs and Activities portion of this chapter includes all the online curriculum labs to ensure that you have mastered the hands-on skills needed to understand basic switch configuration.

As you work through this chapter, use Chapter 2 in *LAN Switching and Wireless, CCNA Exploration Companion Guide* or use the corresponding Chapter 2 in the Exploration LAN Switching and Wireless online curriculum for assistance.

Study Guide

Introduction to Ethernet/802.3 LANs

The exercises in this section review key components of the Ethernet standards and how a switch plays a role in the communication process.

Vocabulary Exercise: Matching

Match the definition on the left with a term on the right. All definitions and terms are used exactly one time.

Definitions

a. Bidirectional data flow.

b. A special set of rules used in Ethernet LANs operating in half-duplex mode.

c. Unidirectional data flow.

d. A frame is sent to a specific group of devices or clients.

e. The average amount of data that is actually transmitted as opposed to the rating of the port.

f. The time a frame or a packet takes to travel from the source to the destination.

g. Layer 2 identifier for the frame's originating NIC or interface.

h. A type of checksum used to detect errors in a transmitted frame.

i. Time it takes to place a frame on the wire (or read a frame off the wire).

j. Dedicated connection between two hosts.

k. Time it takes for a signal to travel through the media.

l. The network area where frames originate and collide.

m. A frame is sent from one host and addressed to one specific destination.

n. A frame is sent from one address to all other addresses.

o. Integrated circuits that control the data paths through the switch.

p. Layer 2 identifier for the intended recipient.

q. Bounded by a router or a switch with VLANs.

r. Automatically detects the required cable type for copper Ethernet connections.

Terms

_____ auto-MDIX

_____ broadcast domain

_____ broadcast transmission

_____ collision domain

_____ CSMA/CD

_____ cyclical redundancy check

_____ destination MAC address

_____ full-duplex communication

_____ half-duplex communication

_____ latency

_____ microsegment

_____ multicast transmission

_____ NIC delay

_____ propagation delay

_____ source MAC address

_____ switch fabric

_____ throughput

_____ unicast transmission

Basic Ethernet and Switching Concepts Exercise

Key Elements of Ethernet/802.3 Networks

Ethernet signals are transmitted to every host connected to the LAN using a special set of rules called _____ to determine which station can access the network. These rules are only used with _____ communication typically found in hubs.

Briefly describe the CSMA/CD access method:

_____

_____

_____

_____

_____

_____

_____

Ethernet communications in a switched LAN network occur in three ways: unicast, broadcast, and multicast. Briefly describe each.

Unicast communication:

_____

_____

What is an example of a unicast transmission?

_____

Broadcast communication:

_____

_____

What is an example of a broadcast transmission?

_____

Multicast communication:

_____

_____

What is an example of a multicast transmission?

_____

_____

As a review of the Ethernet frame structure, fill in the field names in Figure 2-1.

Figure 2-1   Ethernet Frame

IEEE 802.3							
7	1	6	6	2	46 to 1500	4	Bytes

The _____ (7 bytes) and _____ (SFD) (1 byte) fields are used for synchronization between the sending and receiving devices.

The _____ Address field (6 bytes) is the identifier for the intended recipient. This address is used by Layer ____ to assist a device in determining if a frame is addressed to it.

The _____ Address field (6 bytes) identifies the frame's originating NIC or interface.

The _____ field (2 bytes) defines the exact length of the frame's Data field. This field is used later as part of the _____ to ensure that the message was received properly. Only a frame length or a frame type can be entered here.

The Data field (46 to 1500 bytes) contains the _____ Layer 3 PDU, which is commonly an IPv4 _____. All frames must be at least ____ bytes long. If a smaller packet is encapsulated, the _____ field is used to increase the size of the frame to the minimum size.

The ____ (acronym) field (4 bytes) detects errors in a frame. It uses a _____ to calculate an error check. If the calculations do not match, the frame is _____.

An Ethernet MAC address is a two-part ____-bit binary value expressed as 12 _____ digits. The MAC address is permanently encoded into a _____ chip on a NIC. This type of MAC address is referred to as a _____.

The MAC address is made up of the _____ and the vendor assignment number. The ____ is the first part of a MAC address and is ____ bits long. It identifies the manufacturer of the NIC card.

The vendor-assigned part of the MAC address is ____ bits long and uniquely identifies the Ethernet hardware.

_____ communication relies on unidirectional data flow where sending and receiving data are not performed at the same time. This is similar to how walkie-talkies or two-way radios communicate.

In _____ communication, data flow is bidirectional, so data can be sent and received at the same time. The collision detect circuit is _____.

The Cisco Catalyst switches have three settings:

- The ____ option sets autonegotiation of duplex mode. With autonegotiation enabled, the two ports communicate to decide the best mode of operation.

- The ____ option sets full-duplex mode.

- The ____ option sets half-duplex mode.

For Fast Ethernet and 10/100/1000 ports, the default is ___. For 100BASE-FX ports, the default is ____.

Additionally, you can now use the _____ interface configuration command in the CLI to enable the automatic medium-dependent interface crossover (auto-MDIX) feature, which detects the required cable type for copper Ethernet connections and configures the interfaces accordingly.

Switches use MAC addresses to direct network communications through their _____ to the appropriate port toward the destination node. The _____ is the integrated circuits and the accompanying machine programming that allows the data paths through the switch to be controlled.

In Figure 2-2, PC1 is sending a frame to PC2. In the text that follows, fill in the missing information for the process the switch uses to populate its MAC address table.

Figure 2-2   MAC Address Table Population

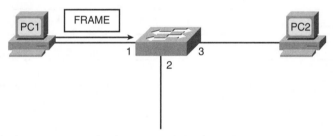

1. The switch receives a broadcast frame from PC1 on _____.

2. The switch enters the _____ MAC address and the _____ that received the frame into the address table.

3. Because the _____ address is a broadcast, the switch _____ the frame to all ports, except the port on which it received the frame.

4. The destination device replies to the broadcast with a _____ frame addressed to PC1.

5. The switch enters the _____ MAC address of PC2 and the _____ that received the frame into the address table. The destination address of the frame and its associated port is found in the MAC address table.

6. The switch can now forward frames between source and destination devices without _____, because it has entries in the address table that identify the associated ports.

Design Considerations for Ethernet/802.3 Networks

A major disadvantage of Ethernet 802.3 networks is _____ that occur when two hosts transmit frames simultaneously. The _____ of the port is considerably reduced as more nodes want to use the network.

To reduce the number of nodes on a given network segment, you can create separate physical network segments, called _____—the network area where frames originate and collide. All shared media environments, such as those created by using hubs, are _____. When a host is connected to a switch port, the switch creates a dedicated connection. When two connected hosts want to communicate with each other, the switch uses the switching table to establish a connection between the ports. This connection is referred to as a _____, which behaves as if the network has only two hosts sending and receiving simultaneously.

Switches reduce collisions and improve bandwidth use on network segments because they provide _____ bandwidth to each network segment.

Although switches filter most frames based on MAC addresses, they do not filter broadcast frames. A collection of interconnected switches forms a single _____ domain. Only a Layer 3 entity, such as a _____, or a _____, can bound a Layer 2 _____ domain. _____ and _____ are used to segment both _____ and _____ domains.

Latency is the time a frame or a packet takes to travel from the source to the destination.

Briefly explain the three sources of latency:

_____

_____

_____

_____

_____

_____

_____

_____

_____

List the three most common causes of network congestion:

- _____

- _____

- _____

LAN Design Considerations

There are two primary considerations when designing a LAN: controlling network _____ and removing _____.

Switches can introduce _____ on a network when _____ on a busy network. For example, if a core level switch has to support 48 ports, each one capable of running at 1000 Mbps full duplex, the switch should support around 96 Gbps internal throughput if it is to maintain full wire-speed across all ports simultaneously.

Higher-capacity links (for example, upgrading from 100-Mbps to 1000-Mbps connections) and using multiple links leveraging _____ technologies (for example, combining two links as if they were one to double a connection's capacity) can help to reduce the _____ created by inter-switch links and router links.

Building the MAC Address Table Exercise

Assume that the switch in Figure 2-3 was just installed and powered on. The MAC address table is empty. Answer the following questions and complete the table as the switch would build it.

Figure 2-3   Building the MAC Address Table

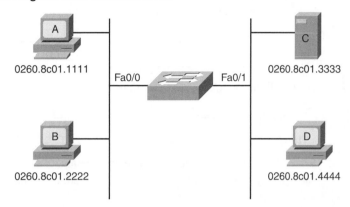

Port	MAC Address

1. Host A sends a unicast frame to Host B. What entry, if any, will the switch enter in its MAC address table?

   _____

   _____

   What will the switch do with the frame?

   _____

   _____

2. Host B responds to Host A with a unicast frame. What entry, if any, will the switch enter in its MAC address table?

   _____

   _____

   What will the switch do with the frame?

   _____

   _____

3. Host D attempts to log in to Server C. What entry, if any, will the switch enter in its MAC address table?

   _____

   _____

   What will the switch do with the frame?

   _____

   _____

4. Server C responds to the login attempt by Host D. What entry, if any, will the switch enter in its MAC address table?

_____

_____

What will the switch do with the frame?

_____

_____

5. Server C sends out a broadcast frame announcing its services to all potential clients. What entry, if any, will the switch enter in its MAC address table?

_____

What will the switch do with the frame?

_____

_____

Collision and Broadcast Domain Exercises

Using Figure 2-4, circle all the collision domains with a solid line and all the broadcast domains with a dashed line.

Figure 2-4   Collision and Broadcast Domains: Topology 1

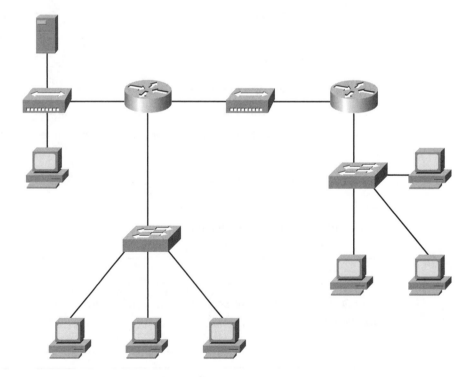

Using Figure 2-5, circle all the collision domains with a solid line and all the broadcast domains with a dashed line.

Figure 2-5   Collision and Broadcast Domains: Topology 2

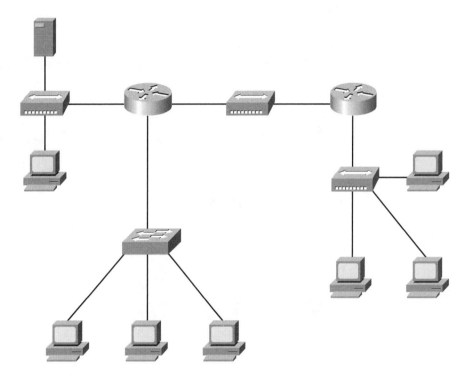

Using Figure 2-6, circle all the collision domains with a solid line and all the broadcast domains with a dashed line.

Figure 2-6   Collision and Broadcast Domains: Topology 3

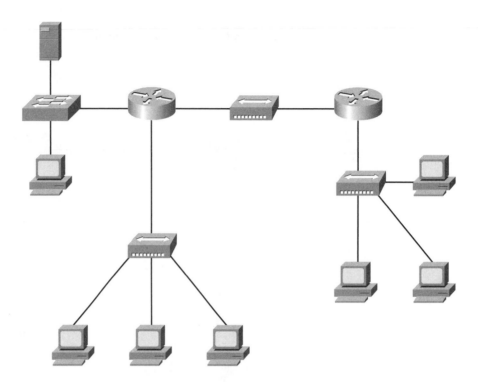

Forwarding Frames Using a Switch

The vocabulary exercise in this section reviews concepts related to forwarding frames with a switch, including: switch forwarding methods; symmetric and asymmetric switching; memory buffering; and Layer 3 switching.

Vocabulary Exercise: Completion

Switch Forwarding Methods

In store-and-forward switching, when the switch receives the frame, it stores the data in _____ until the complete frame has been received. During the storage process, the switch performs an error check using the _____ trailer portion of the Ethernet frame. After confirming the integrity of the frame, the frame is _____. If an error is detected, the frame is _____.

In cut-through switching, the switch buffers just enough of the frame to read the _____ MAC address so that it can determine to which port to forward the data.

There are two variants of cut-through switching:

- _____ switching immediately forwards a packet after reading the destination address.

- _____ switching stores the first ___ bytes of the frame before forwarding to ensure that a collision has not occurred before forwarding the frame.

Symmetric and Asymmetric Switching

LAN switching may be classified as symmetric or asymmetric based on the way in which bandwidth is allocated to the switch ports.

_____ switching provides switched connections between ports with the same bandwidth, such as all 100-Mbps ports or all 1-Gbps ports. An _____ LAN switch provides switched connections between ports of unlike bandwidth, such as a combination of 100-Mbps and 1-Gbps ports.

Memory Buffering

A switch stores packets briefly in a memory buffer before forwarding to the destination host. There are two methods of memory buffering. In _____ memory buffering, frames are stored in queues that are linked to specific incoming ports. _____ buffering deposits all frames into a common memory buffer that all the ports on the switch share.

Layer 2 and Layer 3 Switching

A Layer 2 LAN switch performs switching and filtering based only on the _____ address. A Layer 3 switch can also use _____ address information and the need for dedicated _____ on a LAN.

Switch Management Configuration

The exercises in this section review CLI skills you learned in Exploration Network Fundamentals. You will answer questions based on a scenario and then implement those answers in Packet Tracer.

Basic Switch Configuration Exercise

In this exercise, use Figure 2-7 and Table 2-1 to answer the following questions.

Figure 2-7   Basic Switch Configuration Topology

Table 2-1   Addressing Table for Chapter 2 Topology

Device	Interface	IP Address	Subnet Mask	Default Gateway
R1	Fa0/0	10.1.1.1	255.255.255.0	N/A
	Fa0/1	10.2.2.1	255.255.255.0	N/A
S1	VLAN 99	10.1.1.11	255.255.255.0	10.1.1.1
PC1	NIC	10.1.1.21	255.255.255.0	10.1.1.1
TFTP server	NIC	10.2.2.254	255.255.255.0	10.2.2.1

Note: The Fa0/1 interface on R1 and the TFTP server will be configured later during the "Basic Switch Management Exercise."

When configuring a switch, there are certain basic tasks that are performed, including

- Naming the switch
- Setting passwords
- Configuring a banner
- Configuring the VLAN interface
- Saving changes on a switch
- Verifying basic configuration

The first prompt is at _____ mode and allows you to view the state of the switch. What major limitation does this mode have?

_____

What is the switch prompt for this mode?

_____

The _____ command is used to enter _____ mode. What is the major difference between this mode and the previous mode?

_____

What is the switch prompt for this mode?

_____

Basic Configuration Tasks

Table 2-2 lists the basic switch configuration tasks in the left column. Fill in the right column with the correct command syntax for each of the tasks. Do not enter the actual values for command parameters at this point. Only record the syntax. The first one is done for you as an example.

Table 2-2   Basic Switch Configuration Command Syntax

Configuration Task	Command Syntax
Naming the switch	`Switch(config)#`**`hostname`** `name`
Setting the privileged mode password	`Switch(config)#`
Entering console line configuration	`Switch(config)#`
Setting the console password	`Switch(config-line)#`
Requiring users to log in	`Switch(config-line)#`
Entering vty line configuration mode	`Switch(config)#`
Setting the vty passwords	`Switch(config-line)#`
Requiring users to log in	`Switch(config-line)#`
Configuring a message-of-the-day banner	`Switch(config)#`
Configuring the VLAN interface	`Switch(config)#`
Configuring addressing on an interface	`Switch(config-if)#`
Configuring a port for access mode	`Switch(config-if)#`
Assigning an access VLAN to a port	`Switch(config-if)#`
Setting the port speed to 100 Mbps	`Switch(config-if)#`
Setting the duplex mode to full	`Switch(config-if)#`
Setting the port speed to autoconfigure	`Switch(config-if)#`
Setting the duplex mode to autoconfigure	`Switch(config-if)#`
Activating an interface	`Switch(config-if)#`
Configuring the default gateway	`Switch(config)#`
Enabling HTTP authentication to use a local user database	`Switch(config)#`
Configuring the HTTP service on the switch	`Switch(config)#`
Creating a static mapping in the MAC address table	`Switch(config)#`
Saving changes on a router	`Switch#`

Applying a Basic Configuration

The following exercise walks you through a basic configuration.

First, enter global configuration mode for the switch:

`Switch#`_____

Next, apply a unique hostname to the switch. Use S1 for this example.

`Switch(config)#`_____

Now, configure the password that is to be used to enter privileged EXEC mode. Use **class** as the password.

`S1 (config)#`_____

Next, configure the console and Telnet lines with the password **cisco**. The console commands follow:

`S1(config)#`_____

`S1(config-line)#`_____

`S1(config-line)#`_____

The Telnet lines use similar commands:

`S1(config-line)#`_____

`S1(config-line)#`_____

`S1(config-line)#`_____

Return to global configuration mode:

`S1(config-line)#`_____

From global configuration mode, configure the message-of-the-day banner. Use the following text: **Authorized Access Only**. A delimiting character such as a # is used at the beginning and at the end of the message.

`S1(config)#`_____

What is the purpose of the message of the day?

_____

_____

Refer to Table 2-1 for the VLAN interface configuration information. What is the command to enter VLAN interface configuration mode for S1?

`S1(config)#`_____

Enter the command to configure the IP address using the address specified in Table 2-1:

`S1(config-if)#`_____

VLAN interfaces on the 2960 switch do not need to be manually activated. However, if you are using a 2950 switch, you need to activate the interface. Enter the command to activate the VLAN interface:

```
S1(config-if)#_____
```

Enter interface configuration mode for the Fa0/5 interface connected to PC1:

```
S1(config)#_____
```

Set the interface for access mode:

```
S1(config-if)#_____
```

Assign the access VLAN 99 to the interface:

```
S1(config-if)#_____
```

Enter the command to set the interface to 100 Mbps:

```
S1(config-if)#_____
```

Enter the command to force full-duplex operation:

```
S1(config-if)#_____
```

Enter the command to activate the interface:

```
S1(config-if)#_____
```

Return to global configuration mode:

```
S1(config-if)#_____
```

Enter the command to statically configure the MAC address for the FastEthernet 0/0 interface on R1. The MAC address is 00d0.d306.1401.

```
S1(config)#_____
```

Use the address in Table 2-1 to configure S1 with a default gateway:

```
S1(config)#_____
```

Return to the privileged EXEC prompt:

```
S1(config)#_____
```

What command will save the current configuration?

```
S1#_____
```

Verifying Basic Switch Configuration

Basic configurations can be verified using the four basic **show** commands in Table 2-3. The second four basic **show** commands in the table do not necessarily verify the configuration but might also be helpful to the network administrator. List the command in the left column that fits the description in the right column.

Table 2-3   Basic Router Configuration Verification Commands

Command	Description
	Displays interface status and configuration for a single interface or all interfaces available on the switch
	Displays the startup configuration file stored in NVRAM
	Displays the current running configuration that is stored in RAM
	Displays information about the flash file system
	Displays system hardware and software status
	Displays the session command history
	Displays the MAC forwarding table
	Displays abbreviated interface configuration information, including IP address and interface status

Packet Tracer Exercise 2-1: Basic Switch Configuration

Now you are ready to use Packet Tracer to apply your documented addressing scheme. Open file LSG03-0201.pka on the CD-ROM that accompanies this book to perform this exercise using Packet Tracer.

Note: The following instructions are also contained within the Packet Tracer Exercise.

Learning Objectives

Upon completion of this Packet Tracer Exercise, you will be able to

- Add devices and connect cables
- Configure the PC
- Configure S1
- Save the Packet Tracer file

Scenario

In this exercise, you will practice configuring the Chapter 2 Study Guide Topology (see Figure 2-7) using your answers to the questions in the section "Basic Switch Configuration Exercise."

Task 1: Add Devices and Connect Cables

Step 1.   Add PC1. Make sure that you name it PC1. Attach PC1 to the correct interface on S1. The link will not be active at this point.

Step 2.   Attach R1 to the correct interface on S1. The link will not be active at this point.

Step 3.   Your completion percentage should be 15 percent. If not, click **Check Results** to see which required components are not yet completed.

Task 2: Configure the PC

Step 1.   Configure PC1 according to Table 2-1.

Step 2.   Your completion percentage should be 26 percent. If not, click **Check Results** to see which required components are not yet completed.

Task 3: Configure S1

Step 1.   Configure the hostname, banner, enable secret password, lines, and default gateway according to the following guidelines:

- To avoid incorrect grading, make sure that all names and text strings are case sensitive, with no spacing before or after the name or text string.

- Use the hostname **S1**.

- Use the following text for the banner: **Authorized Access Only**.

- For the secret password, use **class**.

- For the console and Telnet lines, configure login access with the password **cisco**.

- Configure the default gateway.

- Your completion percentage should be 56 percent. If not, click **Check Results** to see which required components are not yet completed.

Step 2.   Configure the VLAN interface:

- Use the IP address and subnet mask according to Table 2-1.

- Your completion percentage should be 63 percent. If not, click **Check Results** to see which required components are not yet completed.

Step 3.   Configure interface Fa0/1 for access:

- Set interface Fa0/1 to access mode.

- Assign access VLAN 99 to the interface.

- Set the duplex mode to full.

- Set the speed to 100 Mbps.

- Activate the interface.

- Your completion percentage should be 81 percent. If not, click **Check Results** to see which required components are not yet completed.

Step 4. Configure interface Fa0/5 for access:

- Set interface Fa0/5 to access mode.

- Assign access VLAN 99 to the interface.

- Activate the interface.

- Your completion percentage should be 93 percent. If not, click **Check Results** to see which required components are not yet completed.

Step 5. Enter a static MAC address:

- Configure the MAC address for the Fa0/0 interface on R1 as a static entry in the MAC forwarding table for S1. The MAC address is 00d0.d306.1401.

- Your completion percentage should be 96 percent. If not, click **Check Results** to see which required components are not yet completed.

Step 6. Save the configuration to S1. Your completion percentage should be 100 percent. If not, click **Check Results** to see which required components are not yet completed.

Step 7. Test connectivity. PC1 should be able to ping R1 and S1. S1 should be able to ping R1.

Task 4: Save the Packet Tracer File

Save your Packet Tracer file as LSG03-0201-end.pka.

Basic Switch Management Exercise

Once a switch is up and running in a LAN, a switch administrator must still maintain the switch. This includes backing up and restoring switch configuration files, clearing configuration information, and deleting configuration files. The exercises in this section review basic switch management.

If you want to maintain multiple distinct startup-config files on the device, you can copy the configuration to different filenames.

What command would you enter to save the startup configuration file as the name **config2.text** to flash?

_____

Storing multiple startup-config versions allows you to roll back to a point in time if your configuration has problems.

What command would you enter to replace the current startup configuration with the **config2.text** saved in flash?

_____

Once the configuration has been restored to the startup-config, you restart the switch with the _____ command.

If the system prompts you to save the configuration, what would be your answer and why?

_____

_____

You can use TFTP to back up your configuration files over the network. Cisco IOS software comes with a built-in TFTP client that allows you to connect to a TFTP server on your network.

The chapter topology in Figure 2-8 now has a TFTP server attached to R1. As shown in Table 2-1, the IP address for the TFTP server is 10.2.2.254.

Figure 2-8   Basic Switch Management Topology

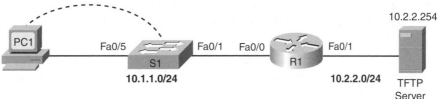

Enter the commands to upload the startup configuration to the TFTP server:

1. Test connectivity to the TFTP server:

    S1#_____

2. Enter the command to copy the startup configuration file to the TFTP server:

    S1#_____

    Address or name of remote host []? _____

3. Change the name to **config2.text:**

    Destination filename [S1-confg]? _____

    !!

    [OK - 1614 bytes]

Now assume the switch has lost its configuration. Enter the commands to restore the configuration from the TFTP server:

1. Configure the VLAN 99 interface:

    Switch(config)#_____

    Switch(config-if)#_____

2. Set the FastEthernet 0/1 interface to access mode and assign VLAN 99 as the access VLAN:

    Switch(config)#_____

    Switch(config-if)#_____

    Switch(config-if)#_____

3. Configure the switch default gateway:

    Switch(config)#_____

4. Test connectivity to the TFTP server:

    Switch#_____

5. Enter the command to download **config2.text** as the switch's startup configuration:

    Switch#_____

    Address or name of remote host []? _____

    Source filename []? _____

    Destination filename [startup-config]?

    Accessing tftp://10.2.2.254/config2.text...

    Loading config2.text from 10.2.2.254: !

    [OK - 1614 bytes]

6. Restart the switch so that the restored startup configuration will become the current running configuration:

Switch#_____

Packet Tracer Exercise 2-2: Basic Switch Management

Now you are ready to use Packet Tracer to apply your documented addressing scheme. Open file LSG03-0202.pka on the CD-ROM that accompanies this book to perform this exercise using Packet Tracer.

Note: The following instructions are also contained within the Packet Tracer Exercise.

Learning Objectives

Upon completion of this Packet Tracer Exercise, you will be able to:

■ Upload a configuration to a TFTP server

■ Restore a configuration from a TFTP server

■ Save the Packet Tracer file

Scenario

In this exercise, you will practice uploading and downloading a configuration to and from a TFTP server using your answers to the questions in the section "Basic Switch Management Exercise." Refer to Figure 2-8 for the topology and Table 2-1 for addressing information.

Note: The tasks for this exercise are not graded by Packet Tracer. The activity opens with the completion percentage at 100 percent.

Task 1: Upload a Configuration to a TFTP Server

Step 1. You cannot access the console for S1 by clicking it. You must use the console connection on PC1. Click **PC1**, then the **Desktop** tab, then **Terminal** to access S1 through the console port. Passwords are **cisco** and **class**.

Step 2. From the S1 command line, test connectivity to the TFTP server. You may need to wait for the link lights on S1 to turn green. Alternatively, you can switch back and forth between Realtime and Simulation mode to expedite convergence.

Step 3. Copy the startup configuration to the TFTP server. Use the name **config2.text**.

Task 2: Download a Configuration from a TFTP Server

Step 1. To simulate the restoration of a configuration, erase the startup configuration stored in NVRAM and reload the switch.

Step 2. When the switch reboots, configure the VLAN 99 interface.

Step 3. Set the FastEthernet 0/1 interface to access mode and assign VLAN 99 as the access VLAN.

Step 4. Configure the default gateway.

Step 5. Test connectivity to the TFTP server. The ping may fail at first while the Fa0/1 interface on S1 transitions to the "up" state and S1 builds the MAC address table.

Step 6.   Enter the command to download **config2.text** as the switch's startup configuration.

Step 7.   Restart the switch so that the restored startup configuration will become the current running configuration. Once reloaded, the switch should prompt you for the **cisco** password and the switch prompt should be **S1**. Once the interfaces are "up," pings from S1 to the TFTP server should be successful.

Task 3: Save the Packet Tracer File

Save your Packet Tracer file as LSG03-0202-end.pka.

Configuring Switch Security

In modern networks, security is integral to implementing any device, protocol, or technology. You should already have strong skills in configuring passwords on a switch. The exercises in this section review configuring SSH, common security attacks, and configuring port security.

Configuring SSH Exercise

Older switches may not support secure communication with _____ (SSH). Why is Telnet a popular protocol used for terminal access?

_____

Why is Telnet an insecure way of accessing a network device?

_____

_____

_____

What command will re-enable the Telnet protocol on a Cisco 2960 switch: _____
_____.

SSH supports the _____ (DES) algorithm, the Triple DES (3DES) algorithm, and password-based user authentication. DES offers ____-bit encryption, and 3DES offers ____-bit encryption.

To implement SSH, you need to generate RSA keys. RSA involves a public key, kept on a public RSA server, and a private key, kept only by the sender and receiver.

_____

Note: Neither Packet Tracer nor the basic image on the Catalyst 2960 switch supports SSH configuration.

_____

To configure a Catalyst 2960 switch as an SSH server, fill in the blanks in the following steps:

Step 1.   Configure a host domain for S1. Use the domain **mydomain.com**.

```
S1(config)#_____
```

Step 2. Enter the command to generate an encrypted RSA key pair. Use 1024 as the modulus size.

```
S1(config)#_____
The name for the keys will be: S1.mydomain.com
Choose the size of the key modulus in the range of 360 to 2048 for your
   General Purpose Keys. Choosing a key modulus greater than 512 may take
   a few minutes.

How many bits in the modulus [512]: _____
% Generating 1024 bit RSA keys, keys will be non-exportable...[OK]
%SSH-5-ENABLED: SSH 1.99 has been enabled
```

Step 3. Enter the command to verify the current SSH configuration:

```
S1#_____
SSH Enabled - version 1.99
Authentication timeout: 120 secs; Authentication retries: 3
```

Step 4. Enter the commands to configure SSH version 2, change the timeout to 30 seconds, and change the authentication retries to 5:

```
S1(config)#_____
S1(config)#_____
S1(config)#_____
```

Step 5. Enter the command to configure all vty lines to allow only SSH access:

```
S1(config)#_____
S1(config-line)#_____
```

Common Security Attacks Exercise

Explain how a MAC address flooding attack works:

_____

_____

_____

_____

Explain how DHCP spoofing works:

_____

_____

_____

_____

_____

Explain how a DHCP starvation attack works:

_____

_____

_____

Explain how you prevent DHCP attacks on a Cisco Catalyst switch:

_____

_____

_____

_____

Explain what CDP is and how it can be used to attack Cisco devices:

_____

_____

_____

_____

_____

_____

Explain how Telnet can be used by an attacker:

_____

_____

_____

_____

_____

_____

_____

Configuring Port Security Exercise

A switch that does not provide port security allows an attacker to attach a system to an unused, enabled port and to perform information gathering or to launch attacks.

All switch ports or interfaces should be secured before the switch is deployed. Port security can limit the number of valid MAC addresses allowed on a port to one and automatically shut down a port if a security violation occurs. In addition, all unused ports should be administratively shut down.

List the three ways a switch can learn the MAC addresses allowed on a port:

- _____

- _____

- _____

List and explain the three violation modes you can configure:

- _____

- _____

  _____

  _____

  _____

■ _____

_____

_____

_____

_____

In Table 2-4, list the violation mode and answer "yes" or "no" to each of the different effects listed.

Table 2-4   Port Security Violation Modes

Violation Mode	Forwards Traffic	Sends SNMP Trap	Sends Syslog Message	Displays Error Message	Increases Violation Counter	Shuts Down Port

In Table 2-5, list the default security settings for ports.

Table 2-5   Port Security Default Settings

Feature	Default Setting
Port security	
Maximum number of secure MAC addresses	
Violation mode	
Sticky address learning	

Use Figure 2-9 as reference when answering the following port security questions.

Figure 2-9   Configuring Port Security Topology

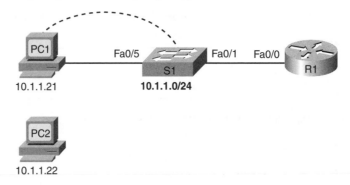

Enter the commands to enable port security on interface FastEthernet 0/5:

S1(config)#_____

S1(config-if)#_____

Although 1 is the default setting, enter the command to explicitly configure the maximum number of secure MAC addresses to one:

S1(config-if)#_____

Enter the command to enable dynamically learned MAC addresses to be added to the running configuration:

S1(config-if)#_____

Enter the command to set the violation mode to **shutdown**:

S1(config-if)#_____

What command can you use to verify port security on the entire switch?

_____

What command do you use to verify port security on interface FastEthernet 0/5?

_____

Assume a new PC is attached to FastEthernet 0/5 after another MAC address has already been learned. What steps must you take to enable the new PC to gain access to the network?

1. _____

   _____

2. _____

   _____

   _____

   _____

Packet Tracer Exercise 2-3: Configuring Port Security

Now you are ready to use Packet Tracer to apply your port security configuration. Open file LSG03-0203.pka on the CD-ROM that accompanies this book to perform this exercise using Packet Tracer.

Note: The following instructions are also contained within the Packet Tracer Exercise.

Learning Objectives

Upon completion of this Packet Tracer Exercise, you will be able to

- Configure port security
- Test port security
- Save the Packet Tracer file

Scenario

All switch ports or interfaces should be secured before the switch is deployed. Port security can limit the number of valid MAC addresses allowed on a port to one and automatically shut down a port if a security violation occurs. In addition, all unused ports should be administratively shut down. In this exercise, you will configure port security and disable all other unused ports.

Task 1: Configure Port Security

Step 1.   You cannot access the console for S1 by clicking it. You must use the console connection on PC1. Click **PC1**, then the **Desktop** tab, then **Terminal** to access S1 through the console port. Passwords are **cisco** and **class**.

Step 2.   From the S1 command line, enter the commands necessary to enable port security on FastEthernet 0/5 using the following guidelines:

- The maximum allowed secure MAC addresses is 1.

- The learned MAC address should automatically be added to the running configuration.

- The port should automatically shut down if there is a security violation.

Step 3.   To ensure S1 learns the MAC address for PC1, ping from PC1 to R1 at 10.1.1.1.

Step 4.   The MAC address table on S1 should now have two entries:

```
S1#show mac-address-table
          Mac Address Table
— — — — — — — — — — — — — — — — — — — — — .


Vlan    Mac Address        Type        Ports
— —     — — — — — .        — — — —      — — .


  99    0005.5ee7.416d     STATIC      Fa0/5
  99    00d0.d306.1401     DYNAMIC     Fa0/1
```

Step 5.   Examine the current interface status with the **show ip interface brief** command. Secure any unused ports.

Step 6.   Your completion percentage should be 70 percent. If not, click **Check Results** to see which required components are not yet completed.

Task 2: Test Port Security

Step 1.   Disconnect PC1 from S1 and connect PC2 to the same FastEthernet 0/5 interface.

Step 2.   When the link lights turn green, attempt to ping from PC2 to R1 at 10.1.1.1. The port should immediately shut down.

Step 3.   Verify the port security shutdown action with the appropriate command:

```
S1#_____
Port Security                : Enabled
Port Status                  : Secure-shutdown
Violation Mode               : Shutdown
Aging Time                   : 0 mins
Aging Type                   : Absolute
SecureStatic Address Aging   : Disabled
Maximum MAC Addresses        : 1
Total MAC Addresses          : 1
Configured MAC Addresses     : 1
Sticky MAC Addresses         : 0
Last Source Address:Vlan     : 0060.5C91.AA22:99
Security Violation Count     : 1
```

Note that the port status is Shutdown and that the last source address learned was from PC2.

Step 4.   Assume that PC2 is a legitimate user and will now be using interface FastEthernet 0/5 to access network resources. Enter the necessary commands to enable S1 to learn only the MAC address for PC2 and allow access through FastEthernet 0/5.

Step 5.   To ensure S1 learns the MAC address for PC2, ping from PC2 to R1 at 10.1.1.1. You may need to wait until the link light on S1 turns green.

Step 6.   Your completion percentage should be 100 percent. If not, click **Check Results** to see which required components are not yet completed.

Task 3: Save the Packet Tracer File

Save your Packet Tracer file as LSG03-0203-end.pka.

Labs and Activities

Command Reference

In Table 2-6, record the command, *including the correct prompt*, that fits the description. Fill in any blanks with the appropriate missing information.

Table 2-6   Commands for Basic Switch Configuration

Command	Description
	Displays the command history, which by default shows the last _____ commands entered
	Enables the storing of command history; on by default
	Sets the command history buffer to 50
	Restores the command history buffer to the default
	Disables the storing of command history
	Displays the current VLAN configuration
	Removes VLAN database from flash memory
	Enters virtual interface configuration mode for VLAN 99
	Configures the VLAN interface IP address as 192.168.1.11/24
	Activates the VLAN interface
	Configures a gateway to allow IP packets an exit
	Enters interface configuration mode for Fa0/5
	Configures the interface as an access port
	Assigns VLAN 99 to the access port
	Forces full-duplex operation on an interface
	Enables auto-duplex configuration
	Forces half-duplex operation on an interface
	Enables auto detection of the cable type connected to the interface
	Forces 10-Mbps operation on an interface

Table 2-6   Commands for Basic Switch Configuration

Command	Description
	Forces 100-Mbps operation on an interface
	Enables autospeed configuration
	Enables web-based configuration of the switch
	Requires users to enter the enable password before managing the switch through web-based configuration tools
	Displays the current MAC address forwarding table
	Deletes all entries from the current MAC address forwarding table
	Sets a static address of *aaaa.aaaa.aaaa* in the MAC address table for Fa0/1
	Displays information about the flash system file
	Displays system hardware and software status
	Displays HTTP information about device manager running on the switch; has many options
	Displays the ARP table on the switch
	Copies the startup configuration to flash with the name **config.bak1**
	Copies the stored configuration in flash named **config.bak1** to the startup configuration
	Uploads the running configuration as **config.bak1** to the TFTP server at 192.168.1.254
	Downloads the configuration file named **config.bak1** from the TFTP server at 192.168.1.254 and stores it in NVRAM as the startup-config
	Clears the contents of the startup configuration
	Deletes a stored file config.bak1 in flash
	Enables a weak type 7 encryption of clear-text passwords
	Re-enables the default Telnet protocol after it has been disabled
	Permits both Telnet and SSH protocols to access the switch

continues

Table 2-6   Commands for Basic Switch Configuration   *continued*

Command	Description
	Configures SSH as the only allowed protocol for remote access to the switch
	Configures the host domain as mydomain.com
	Enables version 2 of the SSH protocol
	Generates an RSA key pair
	Changes the SSH timeout value from the default _____ seconds to 60 seconds
	Changes the number of times a client can reauthenticate to the SSH server from the default of _____ to 5
	Displays the status of the SSH server connections on the switch
	Enables DHCP snooping for all VLANs
	Enables DHCP snooping only for VLAN 10
	Defines the port as trusted to receive DHCP responses
	Limits the rate to 1 for bogus DHCP requests sent through untrusted ports to the DHCP server
	Enables port security on the interface
	Sets the maximum MAC addresses that a port can learn to 1
	Configures the port to dynamically learn MAC addresses and "stick" them to the configuration
	Configures the port to be disabled if there is a security violation
	Configures the port to send a SNMP trap if a security violation is detected, but does not shut down the port
	Configures the port to drop all frames from unknown source MAC addresses after the maximum configured MAC addresses have been learned

Lab 2-1: Basic Switch Configuration (2.5.1)

Figure 2-10 shows the topology diagram for this lab.

Figure 2-10   Topology Diagram for Lab 2-1

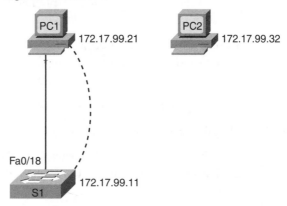

Table 2-7 shows the addressing scheme used in this lab.

Table 2-7   Addressing Table for Lab 2-1

Device	Interface	IP Address	Subnet Mask	Default Gateway
PC1	NIC	172.17.99.21	255.255.255.0	172.17.99.11
PC2	NIC	172.17.99.32	255.255.255.0	172.17.99.11
S1	VLAN 99	172.17.99.11	255.255.255.0	172.17.99.1

[handwritten: ← use sw for default Gateway if router not available]

Learning Objectives

Upon completion of this lab, you will be able to

- Cable a network according to the topology diagram
- Clear an existing configuration on a switch
- Examine and verify the default configuration
- Create a basic switch configuration, including a name and an IP address
- Configure passwords to ensure that access to the CLI is secured
- Configure switch port speed and duplex properties for an interface
- Configure basic switch port security
- Manage the MAC address table
- Assign static MAC addresses
- Add and move hosts on a switch

Scenario

In this lab, you will examine and configure a standalone LAN switch. Although a switch performs basic functions in its default out-of-the-box condition, there are a number of parameters that a network administrator should modify to ensure a secure and optimized LAN. This lab introduces you to the basics of switch configuration.

Task 1: Cable, Erase, and Reload the Switch

Step 1.   Cable a network.

Cable a network that is similar to the one shown in Figure 2-10. Create a console connection to the switch. If necessary, refer to Lab 1.3.1 for instructions on how to create a console connection.

You can use any current switch in your lab as long as it has the required interfaces shown in the topology. The output shown in this lab is from a 2960 switch. If you use other switches, the switch outputs and interface descriptions may appear different.

PC2 is not initially connected to the switch. It is only used in Task 5.

Step 2.   Clear the configuration on the switch.

Clear the configuration on the switch using the procedure in the section "Appendix 1: Erasing and Reloading the Switch" at the end of this lab.

Task 2: Verify the Default Switch Configuration

Step 1.   Enter privileged mode.

You can access all the switch commands in privileged mode. However, because many of the privileged mode commands configure operating parameters, privileged access should be password-protected to prevent unauthorized use. You will set passwords in Task 3.

The privileged EXEC command set includes those commands contained in user EXEC mode, as well as the **configure** command through which access to the remaining command modes is gained. Enter privileged EXEC mode by entering the **enable** command:

```
Switch>enable
Switch#
```

Notice that the prompt changed in the configuration to reflect privileged EXEC mode.

Step 2.   Examine the current switch configuration.

Examine the current running configuration file:

```
Switch#show running-config
```

How many Fast Ethernet interfaces does the switch have? ___24___

How many Gigabit Ethernet interfaces does the switch have? ___2___

What is the range of values shown for the vty lines? ___5 – 15___

Examine the current contents of NVRAM:

```
Switch#show startup-config
startup-config is not present
```

Why does the switch give this response?

Because we have not save running config

Examine the characteristics of the virtual interface VLAN 1:

```
Switch#show interface vlan1
```

Is there an IP address set on the switch? _No_

What is the MAC address of this virtual switch interface? _0013.7f36.5a40_

Is this interface up?

No.   admns down , line down

_____

_____

_____

Now view the IP properties of the interface:

```
Switch#show ip interface vlan1
```

What output do you see?

admns down , line protocol is down.

_____

Step 3.   Display Cisco IOS information.

Examine the following version information that the switch reports:

```
Switch#show version
```

What is the Cisco IOS version that the switch is running? _12.1 (22)EA2_

What is the system image filename? _flash:/c 2950-16q412-mz.121-22. EA2.bin_

What is the base MAC address of this switch? _00:13:7F:36:5A:40_

Step 4.   Examine the Fast Ethernet interfaces.

Examine the default properties of the Fast Ethernet interface used by PC1:

```
Switch#show interface fastethernet 0/18
```

Is the interface up or down? _up_

What event would make an interface go up? _by default is up_

What is the MAC address of the interface? _0013.7f36.5a52_

What is the speed and duplex setting of the interface? _100Mb/s_

Step 5.   Examine VLAN information.

Examine the default VLAN settings of the switch:

```
Switch#show vlan
```

What is the name of VLAN 1? _default_

Which ports are in this VLAN? _fas 0/1 to 0/24_

Is VLAN 1 active? _yes_

What type of VLAN is the default VLAN? _enet_

Step 6.   Examine flash memory.

Issue one of the following commands to examine the contents of the flash directory:

Switch#**dir flash:**

or

Switch#**show flash**

Which files or directories are found?

Info, env-var, image, html

Files have a file extension, such as .bin, at the end of the filename. Directories do not have a file extension. To examine the files in a directory, issue the following command using the filename displayed in the output of the previous command:

Switch#**dir flash:c2960-lanbase-mz.122-25.SEE3**

```
Directory of flash:/c2960-lanbase-mz.122-25.SEE3/
    6   drwx       4480    Mar 1 1993 00:04:42 +00:00   html
  618   -rwx    4671175    Mar 1 1993 00:06:06 +00:00
   c2960-lanbase-mz.122-25.SEE3.bin
  619   -rwx        457    Mar 1 1993 00:06:06 +00:00   info
32514048 bytes total (24804864 bytes free)
```

What is the name of the Cisco IOS image file?

C2950-i6g 412-mz.121-22.EA2.bin

Step 7.   Examine the startup configuration file.

To view the contents of the startup configuration file, issue the **show startup-config** command in privileged EXEC mode:

```
Switch#show startup-config
startup-config is not present
```

Why does this message appear?

Running file has not been save.

Make one configuration change to the switch and then save it. Type the following commands:

```
Switch#configure terminal
Enter configuration commands, one per line.  End with CNTL/Z.
Switch(config)#hostname S1
S1(config)#exit
S1#
```

To save the contents of the running configuration file to NVRAM, issue the command **copy running-config startup-config**:

```
Switch#copy running-config startup-config
Destination filename [startup-config]?  [Enter]
Building configuration...
[OK]
```

Note: This command is easier to enter by using the **copy run start** abbreviation.

Now display the contents of NVRAM using the **show startup-config** command:

```
S1#show startup-config
Using 1170 out of 65536 bytes
!
version 12.2
no service pad
service timestamps debug uptime
service timestamps log uptime
no service password-encryption
!
hostname S1
!
<output omitted>
```

The current configuration has been written to NVRAM.

Task 3: Create a Basic Switch Configuration

Step 1.   Assign a name to the switch.

In the last step of the previous task, you configured the hostname. Here's a review of the commands used:

```
S1#configure terminal
S1(config)#hostname S1
S1(config)#exit
```

Step 2.   Set the access passwords.

Enter config-line mode for the console. Set the login password to **cisco**. Also configure the vty lines 0 to 15 with the password **cisco**.

```
S1#configure terminal
Enter the configuration commands, one for each line. When you are finished,
return to global configuration mode by entering the exit command or press-
ing Ctrl-Z.

S1(config)#line console 0
S1(config-line)#password cisco
S1(config-line)#login
S1(config-line)#line vty 0 15
S1(config-line)#password cisco
S1(config-line)#login
S1(config-line)#exit
```

Why is the login command required?

_____ require password at per line _____

Step 3.   Set the command mode passwords.

Set the enable secret password to **class**. This password protects access to privileged EXEC mode.

```
S1(config)#enable secret class
```

Step 4.   Configure the Layer 3 address of the switch.

Before you can manage S1 remotely from PC1, you need to assign the switch an IP address. The default configuration on the switch is to have the management of the switch controlled through VLAN 1. However, a best practice for basic switch configuration is to change the management VLAN to a VLAN other than VLAN 1. The implications and reasoning behind this action are explained in Chapter 3, "VLANs."

For management purposes, we will use VLAN 99. The selection of VLAN 99 is arbitrary and in no way implies you should always use VLAN 99.

First, you will create the new VLAN 99 on the switch. Then you will set the IP address of the switch to 172.17.99.11 with a subnet mask of 255.255.255.0 on the internal virtual interface VLAN 99.

[handwritten: Creat vlan 99 -]
[handwritten: addition pg 80]

```
S1(config)#vlan 99
S1(config-vlan)#exit
S1(config)#interface vlan99
%LINEPROTO-5-UPDOWN: Line protocol on Interface Vlan99, changed state to
 down

S1(config-if)#ip address 172.17.99.11 255.255.255.0
S1(config-if)#no shutdown
S1(config-if)#exit
S1(config)#
```

[handwritten: make this layer 3 interface operational.]

[handwritten: VL99 is up but line protocol is down]

Notice that the VLAN 99 interface is in the down state even though you entered the command **no shutdown**. The interface is currently down because no switchports are assigned to VLAN 99.

Assign all user ports to VLAN 99:

```
S1#configure terminal
S1(config)#interface range fa0/1 - 24
S1(config-if-range)#switchport access vlan 99
S1(config-if-range)#exit
S1(config-if-range)#
%LINEPROTO-5-UPDOWN: Line protocol on Interface Vlan1, changed state to
 down
%LINEPROTO-5-UPDOWN: Line protocol on Interface Vlan99, changed state to up
```

[handwritten: Assign Vlan 99 to the port by allowing all ports interfaces to act as member of Vlan 99]

[handwritten: take 30sec.]

Note: To execute the **switchport access vlan 99** command on multiple interfaces at the same time, you can use the **interface range** command as shown here. You can also specify a list of nonconsecutive interfaces using a comma separator as follows:

```
S1(config)#interface range fa0/1 , fa0/3, fa0/5
```

You can also mix consecutive and nonconsecutive ranges of interfaces as follows:

```
S1(config)#interface range fa0/1, fa0/3 , fa0/5 - 10
```

It is beyond the scope of this lab to fully explore VLANs. This subject is discussed in greater detail in Chapter 3. However, to establish connectivity between the host and the switch, the ports used by the host must be in the same VLAN as the switch. Notice in the preceding output that the VLAN 1 interface goes down because none of the ports are assigned to VLAN 1. After a few seconds, VLAN 99 will come up because at least one port is now assigned to VLAN 99.

Step 5.   Set the switch default gateway.

S1 is a Layer 2 switch, so it makes forwarding decisions based on the Layer 2 header. If multiple networks are connected to a switch, you need to specify how the switch forwards the internetwork frames, because the path must be determined at Layer 3. This is done by specifying a default gateway address that points to a router or Layer 3 switch. Although this activity does not include an external IP gateway, assume that you will eventually connect the LAN to a router for external access. Assuming that the LAN interface on the router is 172.17.99.1, set the default gateway for the switch:

```
S1(config)#ip default-gateway 172.17.99.1
S1(config)#exit
```

Step 6.   Verify the management LANs settings.

Verify the interface settings on VLAN 99:

```
S1#show interface vlan 99
Vlan99 is up, line protocol is up
  Hardware is EtherSVI, address is 001b.5302.4ec1 (bia 001b.5302.4ec1)
  Internet address is 172.17.99.11/24
  MTU 1500 bytes, BW 1000000 Kbit, DLY 10 usec,
     reliability 255/255, txload 1/255, rxload 1/255
  Encapsulation ARPA, loopback not set
  ARP type: ARPA, ARP Timeout 04:00:00
  Last input 00:00:06, output 00:03:23, output hang never
  Last clearing of "show interface" counters never
  Input queue: 0/75/0/0 (size/max/drops/flushes); Total output drops: 0
  Queueing strategy: fifo
  Output queue: 0/40 (size/max)
  5 minute input rate 0 bits/sec, 0 packets/sec
  5 minute output rate 0 bits/sec, 0 packets/sec
     4 packets input, 1368 bytes, 0 no buffer
     Received 0 broadcasts (0 IP multicast)
     0 runts, 0 giants, 0 throttles
     0 input errors, 0 CRC, 0 frame, 0 overrun, 0 ignored
     1 packets output, 64 bytes, 0 underruns
     0 output errors, 0 interface resets
     0 output buffer failures, 0 output buffers swapped out
```

What is the bandwidth on this interface? _____1G_____

What are the VLAN states? VLAN 1 is __up__ Line protocol is ____up____

What is the queuing strategy? ____fifo____

Step 7.   Configure the IP address and default gateway for PC1.

Set the IP address of PC1 to 172.17.99.21, with a subnet mask of 255.255.255.0. Configure a default gateway of 172.17.99.11. (If needed, refer to Lab 1.3.1 to configure the PC NIC.)

1?

Step 8.   Verify connectivity.

To verify the host and switch are correctly configured, ping the IP address of the switch (172.17.99.11) from PC1.

Was the ping successful?

_____ *Yes* _____

If not, troubleshoot the switch and host configuration. Note that this may take a couple of tries for the pings to succeed while the switch and PC build their ARP tables.

Step 9.   Configure the port speed and duplex settings for a Fast Ethernet interface.

Configure the duplex and speed settings on Fast Ethernet 0/18. Use the **end** command to return to privileged EXEC mode when finished.

By default the speed was 100M & duplex full, why we need to set them?

```
S1#configure terminal
S1(config)#interface fastethernet 0/18
S1(config-if)#speed 100
S1(config-if)#duplex full
S1(config-if)#end
%LINEPROTO-5-UPDOWN: Line protocol on Interface FastEthernet0/18, changed
  state to down
%LINEPROTO-5-UPDOWN: Line protocol on Interface Vlan99, changed state to
  down
%LINK-3-UPDOWN: Interface FastEthernet0/18, changed state to down
%LINK-3-UPDOWN: Interface FastEthernet0/18, changed state to up
%LINEPROTO-5-UPDOWN: Line protocol on Interface FastEthernet0/18, changed
  state to up
%LINEPROTO-5-UPDOWN: Line protocol on Interface Vlan99, changed state to up
```

The line protocol for both interface FastEthernet 0/18 and interface VLAN 99 will temporarily go down while the interface hardware resets to the manual configuration.

Verify the new duplex and speed settings on the Fast Ethernet interface:

```
S1#show interface fastethernet 0/18
FastEthernet0/18 is up, line protocol is up (connected)
  Hardware is Fast Ethernet, address is 001b.5302.4e92 (bia 001b.5302.4e92)
  MTU 1500 bytes, BW 100000 Kbit, DLY 100 usec,
      reliability 255/255, txload 1/255, rxload 1/255
  Encapsulation ARPA, loopback not set
  Keepalive set (10 sec)
  Full-duplex, 100Mb/s, media type is 10/100BaseTX
  input flow-control is off, output flow-control is unsupported
  ARP type: ARPA, ARP Timeout 04:00:00
  Last input never, output 00:00:01, output hang never
  Last clearing of "show interface" counters never
  Input queue: 0/75/0/0 (size/max/drops/flushes); Total output drops: 0
  Queueing strategy: fifo
  Output queue: 0/40 (size/max)
```

```
 5 minute input rate 0 bits/sec, 0 packets/sec
 5 minute output rate 0 bits/sec, 0 packets/sec
    265 packets input, 52078 bytes, 0 no buffer
    Received 265 broadcasts (0 multicast)
    0 runts, 0 giants, 0 throttles
    0 input errors, 0 CRC, 0 frame, 0 overrun, 0 ignored
    0 watchdog, 32 multicast, 0 pause input
    0 input packets with dribble condition detected
    4109 packets output, 342112 bytes, 0 underruns
    0 output errors, 0 collisions, 1 interface resets
    0 babbles, 0 late collision, 0 deferred
    0 lost carrier, 0 no carrier, 0 PAUSE output
    0 output buffer failures, 0 output buffers swapped out
```

The default on the Ethernet interface of the switch is auto-sensing, so it automatically negotiates optimal settings. You should set duplex and speed manually only if a port must operate at a certain speed and duplex mode. Manually configuring ports can lead to duplex mismatches, which can significantly degrade performance.

Because auto-sensing is the desired configuration for our purposes, let's restore the configuration for FastEthernet 0/18:

```
S1#configure terminal
S1(config)#interface fastethernet 0/18
S1(config-if)#speed auto
S1(config-if)#duplex auto
S1(config-if)#end
```

Again, verify the restored settings with the **show interface** command:

```
S1#show interface fastethernet 0/18
FastEthernet0/18 is up, line protocol is up (connected)
  Hardware is Fast Ethernet, address is 001b.5302.4e92 (bia 001b.5302.4e92)
  MTU 1500 bytes, BW 100000 Kbit, DLY 100 usec,
     reliability 255/255, txload 1/255, rxload 1/255
  Encapsulation ARPA, loopback not set
  Keepalive set (10 sec)
  Auto-duplex, Auto-speed, media type is 10/100BaseTX
<output omitted>
```

Step 10.   Save the configuration.

You have completed the basic configuration of the switch. Now back up the running configuration file to NVRAM to ensure that the changes made will not be lost if the system is rebooted or loses power:

```
S1#copy running-config startup-config
Destination filename [startup-config]?[Enter]
Building configuration...
[OK]
S1#
```

Step 11.   Examine the startup configuration file.

To see the configuration that is stored in NVRAM, issue the **show startup-config** command from privileged EXEC mode:

```
S1#show startup-config
```

Are all the changes that were entered recorded in the file? ___yes___

Task 4: Manage the MAC Address Table

Step 1.   Record the MAC addresses of the hosts.

Determine and record the Layer 2 (physical) addresses of the PC network interface cards using the following commands:

```
Start > Run > cmd > ipconfig /all
```

PC1: ___00-1C-C0-BE-9A-DD___

PC2: ___00-1C-C0-BE-9A-C9___

Step 2.   Determine the MAC addresses that the switch has learned.

Display the MAC addresses using the **show mac-address-table** command in privileged EXEC mode:

```
S1#show mac-address-table
```

How many dynamic addresses are there? ___1___

How many MAC addresses are there in total? ___5___

Do the dynamic MAC addresses match the host MAC addresses? ___yes___

Step 3.   List the **show mac-address-table** options:

```
S1#show mac-address-table ?
```

How many options are available for the **show mac-address-table** command? ___10___

Show only the MAC addresses from the table that were learned dynamically:

```
S1#show mac-address-table address PC1-MAC-here
```

How many dynamic addresses are there? ___1___

Step 4.   Clear the MAC address table.

To remove the existing MAC addresses, use the **clear mac-address-table** command from privileged EXEC mode:

```
S1#clear mac-address-table dynamic
```

Step 5.   Verify the results.

Verify that the MAC address table was cleared:

```
S1#show mac-address-table
```

How many static MAC addresses are there?

4

How many dynamic addresses are there?

0

Step 6. Examine the MAC table again.

More than likely, an application running on your PC1 has already sent a frame out the NIC to S1. Look at the MAC address table again in privileged EXEC mode to see if S1 has relearned the MAC address for PC1:

```
S1#show mac-address-table
```

How many dynamic addresses are there? ____1____

Why did this change from the last display?

If S1 has not yet relearned the MAC address for PC1, ping the VLAN 99 IP address of the switch from PC1 and then repeat Step 6.

Step 7. Set up a static MAC address.

To specify which ports a host can connect to, one option is to create a static mapping of the host MAC address to a port.

Set up a static MAC address on Fast Ethernet interface 0/18 using the address that was recorded for PC1 in Step 1 of this task. The MAC address 00e0.2917.1884 is used here as an example only. You must use the MAC address of your PC1, which is different from the one given here as an example.

```
S1(config)#mac-address-table static 00e0.2917.1884 interface fastethernet
   0/18 vlan 99
```

Step 8. Verify the results.

Verify the MAC address table entries:

```
S1#show mac-address-table
```

How many total MAC addresses are there? ____5____

How many static addresses are there?

5

Step 9. Remove the static MAC entry.

To complete the next task, it is necessary to remove the static MAC address table entry. Enter configuration mode and remove the command by putting a **no** in front of the command string:

```
S1(config)#no mac-address-table static 00e0.2917.1884 interface
   fastethernet 0/18 vlan 99
```

Step 10.   Verify the results.

Verify that the static MAC address has been cleared:

```
S1#show mac-address-table
```

How many total static MAC addresses are there? _____4_____

Task 5: Configure Port Security

Step 1.   Configure a second host.

A second host is needed for this task. Set the IP address of PC2 to 172.17.99.32, with a subnet mask of 255.255.255.0 and a default gateway of 172.17.99.11. Do not connect this PC to the switch yet.

Step 2.   Verify connectivity.

Verify that PC1 and the switch are still correctly configured by pinging the VLAN 99 IP address of the switch from the host.

Were the pings successful? ____yes____

If the answer is no, troubleshoot the host and switch configurations.

Step 3.   Determine which MAC addresses the switch has learned.

Display the learned MAC addresses using the **show mac-address-table** command in privileged EXEC mode:

```
S1#show mac-address-table
```

How many dynamic addresses are there? ____1____

Do the MAC addresses match the host MAC addresses? ____yes____

Step 4.   List the port security options.

Explore the options for setting port security on interface Fast Ethernet 0/18:

```
S1#configure terminal
S1(config)#interface fastethernet 0/18
S1(config-if)#switchport port-security ?
  aging        Port-security aging commands
  mac-address  Secure mac address
  maximum      Max secure addresses
  violation    Security violation mode
  <cr>
```

Notice the last option is a carriage return, <cr>, which means the command **switchport port-security** can be entered without specifying any additional options. In fact, you must enter the **switchport port-security** command before port security is active and any remaining port security commands are evaluated by the IOS.

In addition, a port must be in access mode before you can enable port security. Otherwise, you will get the following error message:

```
S1(config)#interface fastethernet 0/18                    reason.
S1(config-if)#switchport port-security
Command rejected: FastEthernet0/18 is a dynamic port.
```

Step 5. Configure port security on an access port.

In the following series of commands, the FastEthernet 0/18 switch port is set to access mode and port security is enabled. Then the following port security options are enabled:

- The port only accepts two devices (**maximum 2**).

- The port learns these two device MAC addresses dynamically (**mac-address sticky**).

- The port blocks traffic from invalid hosts if a violation occurs (**violation protected**).

```
S1(config-if)#switchport mode access
S1(config-if)#switchport port-security
S1(config-if)#switchport port-security maximum 2
S1(config-if)#switchport port-security mac-address sticky
S1(config-if)#switchport port-security violation protect
S1(config-if)#exit
```

Step 6. Verify the results.

Show the port security settings:

```
S1#show port-security
```

How many secure addresses are allowed on Fast Ethernet 0/18? _____2_____

What is the security action for this port? ___protect___

Step 7. Examine the running configuration file:

```
S1#show running-config
```

Are there statements listed that directly reflect the security implementation of the running configuration? ___yes___

Step 8. Modify the post security settings on a port.

On interface Fast Ethernet 0/18, change the port security maximum MAC address count to 1 and to shut down if a violation occurs:

```
S1(config-if)#switchport port-security maximum 1
S1(config-if)#switchport port-security violation shutdown
```

Step 9. Verify the results.

Show the port security settings:

```
S1#show port-security
```

Have the port security settings changed to reflect the modifications in Step 8? ___yes___

Ping the VLAN 99 address of the switch from PC1 to verify connectivity and to refresh the MAC address table. You should now see the MAC address for PC1 "stuck" to the running configuration.

```
S1#show run
Building configuration...

<output omitted>
!
interface FastEthernet0/18
```

```
switchport access vlan 99
switchport mode access
switchport port-security
switchport port-security mac-address sticky
switchport port-security mac-address sticky 00e0.2917.1884
speed 100
duplex full
!
<output omitted>
```

Step 10.   Introduce a rogue host.

Now that S1 has learned the MAC address for PC1, it will not allow any inbound traffic on FastEthernet 0/18 for any other source MAC address. If another MAC address is detected, the port will automatically shut down.

To test this, disconnect PC1 and connect PC2 to FastEthernet 0/18. Watch for the amber link light to turn green. Once it turns green, it should almost immediately turn off. If not, ping the VLAN 99 address 172.17.99.11 from PC2. This action will ensure that S1 receives a frame from PC2. The link light should now be off.

What messages did S1 send to your console connection?

_____

_____

_____

_____

_____

Step 11.   Show port configuration information.

To see the configuration information for just FastEthernet port 0/18, issue the following command in privileged EXEC mode:

```
S1#show interface fastethernet 0/18
```

What is the state of this interface?

Fast Ethernet 0/18 is ____*down*____ and line protocol is ____*down*____

Step 12.   Reactivate the port.

If a security violation occurs and the port is shut down, you can use the **no shutdown** command to reactivate it. However, as long as the rogue host is attached to FastEthernet 0/18, any traffic from the host disables the port. Reconnect PC1 to FastEthernet 0/18, and enter the following commands on the switch:

```
S1#configure terminal
S1(config)#interface fastethernet 0/18
```
shut -
```
S1(config-if)#no shutdown
S1(config-if)#exit
```

Note: Some IOS versions may require a manual **shutdown** command before entering the **no shutdown** command.

Task 6: Clean Up

Unless directed otherwise by your instructor, erase the configurations and reload the switches. Disconnect and store the cabling. For PC hosts that are normally connected to other networks (such as the school LAN or to the Internet), reconnect the appropriate cabling and restore the TCP/IP settings.

Packet Tracer Companion: Basic Switch Configuration (2.5.1)

You can now open the file LSG03-Lab251.pka on the CD-ROM that accompanies this book to repeat this hands-on lab using Packet Tracer. Remember, however, that Packet Tracer is not a substitute for a hands-on lab experience with real equipment.

Appendix 1: Erasing and Reloading the Switch

For the majority of the labs in *LAN Switching and Wireless, CCNA Exploration Labs and Study Guide* (2nd Edition), it is necessary to start a lab with a switch without a configuration or VLAN database. Using a switch with an existing configuration may produce unpredictable results. These instructions show you how to prepare the switch prior to starting the lab. These instructions are for the 2960 switch; however, the procedure for the 2900 and 2950 switches is the same.

Step 1.   Enter privileged EXEC mode by typing the **enable** command.

If prompted for a password, enter **class**. If that does not work, ask the instructor.

```
Switch>enable
```

Step 2.   Remove the VLAN database information file:

```
Switch#delete flash:vlan.dat
Delete filename [vlan.dat]?[Enter]
Delete flash:vlan.dat? [confirm] [Enter]
```

If there is no VLAN file, this message is displayed:

```
%Error deleting flash:vlan.dat (No such file or directory)
```

Step 3.   Remove the switch startup configuration file from NVRAM:

```
Switch#erase startup-config
```

The responding line prompt will be

```
Erasing the nvram filesystem will remove all files! Continue? [confirm]
```

Step 4.   Press **Enter** to confirm. The response should be:

```
Erase of nvram: complete
```

Step 5.   Reload the switch.

At the privileged EXEC mode prompt, enter the **reload** command. If prompted to save the configuration, you must answer **no**. Otherwise, if any VLAN configurations remain in the running configuration, they will be rewritten to a new **vlan.dat** file once the switch loads the saved configuration file.

```
S2#reload

System configuration has been modified. Save? [yes/no]: no
Proceed with reload? [confirm][Enter]

10:00:12: %SYS-5-RELOAD: Reload requested by console. Reload Reason: Reload
  Command.
```

After the switch has reloaded, you may be prompted to terminate autoinstall. Press the **Enter** key. Then, when asked if you would like to enter the initial configuration dialog (setup mode), answer **no**. Then press **Enter** when prompted to do so.

```
Would you like to terminate autoinstall? [yes]:[Enter]



        —- System Configuration Dialog —-

Would you like to enter the initial configuration dialog? [yes/no]: no
Press RETURN to get started! [Enter]
```

Lab 2-2: Managing Switch Operating System and Configuration Files (2.5.2)

Figure 2-11 shows the topology diagram for this lab.

Figure 2-11   Topology Diagram for Lab 2-2

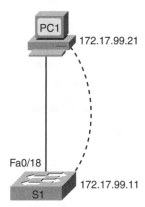

Table 2-8 shows the addressing scheme used in this lab.

Table 2-8   Addressing Table for Lab 2-2

Device	Interface	IP Address	Subnet Mask	Default Gateway
PC1	NIC	172.17.99.21	255.255.255.0	172.17.99.11
S1	VLAN 99	172.17.99.11	255.255.255.0	172.17.99.1

Learning Objectives

Upon completion of this lab, you will be able to

- Create and save a basic switch configuration
- Set up a TFTP server on the network
- Back up the switch Cisco IOS software to a TFTP server and then restore it
- Back up the switch configuration to a TFTP server
- Configure a switch to load a configuration from a TFTP server
- Upgrade the Cisco IOS software from a TFTP server
- Recover the password for a 2960 switch (2900 series)

Scenario

In this lab, you will practice file management skills and password recovery procedures. You will set up a TFTP server and then back up the configuration and IOS image to the server. You will then configure a switch to automatically retrieve and load its configuration from a TFTP server and upgrade the IOS. Finally, you will recover a lost password on a 2960 switch.

Task 1: Cable and Initialize the Network

Step 1.   Cable a network.

Cable a network that is similar to the one shown in Figure 2-11. Create a console connection to the switch. If necessary, refer to Lab 1.3.1. The output shown in this lab is from a 2960 switch. If you use other switches, the switch outputs and interface descriptions may appear different.

Step 2.   Clear the configuration on the switch.

Set up a console connection to the switch and erase the existing configuration. If necessary, refer to "Appendix 1: Erasing and Reloading the Switch" in Lab 2-1.

Step 3.   Create a basic configuration.

Use the following commands to configure a hostname, line access passwords, and the enable secret password:

```
Switch#configure terminal
Switch(config)#hostname S1
S1(config)#enable secret class
S1(config)#line con 0
S1(config-line)#password cisco
S1(config-line)#login
S1(config-line)#line vty 0 15
S1(config-line)#password cisco
S1(config-line)#login
S1(config-line)#exit
```

Create interface VLAN 99 and assign it IP addressing according to Table 2-8. Then assign VLAN 99 to the FastEthernet 0/18 interface so that PC1 can manage S1 through its network connection as well as the console connection.

```
S1(config)#interface vlan 99
%LINEPROTO-5-UPDOWN: Line protocol on Interface Vlan99, changed state to
    down
S1(config-if)#ip address 172.17.99.11 255.255.255.0
S1(config-if)#interface fa0/18
S1(config-if)#switchport access vlan 99
% Access VLAN does not exist. Creating vlan 99
%LINEPROTO-5-UPDOWN: Line protocol on Interface Vlan99, changed state to up
S1(config-if)#end
S1#
```

this command will creat vlan 99

similar pg 68

Note: Creating VLANs is covered in Chapter 3. However, notice that the IOS created VLAN 99 automatically when you assigned it to the FastEthernet 0/18 interface. Also notice that the VLAN 99 interface changed its state to **up** without you having to enter the **no shutdown** command.

Step 4.   Configure the host attached to the switch.

PC1 acts as the TFTP server in this lab, so make sure TFTP server software is already installed. If not, you can download the SolarWinds TFTP Server used in this lab at

http://www.solarwinds.com/downloads/

If this URL is out of date, then use your favorite search engine and search for SolarWinds' free TFTP download.

Configure PC1 to use the IP address, mask, and default gateway identified in Table 2-8.

Step 5.   Verify connectivity.

To verify that the host and switch are correctly configured, ping the switch IP address that was configured for VLAN 99 from the host.

Was the ping successful? _____yes_____

If the answer is no, troubleshoot the host and switch configurations.

Task 2: Start and Configure the TFTP Server

Step 1.   Start up and configure the TFTP server.

The screenshots and instructions in this lab assume you are using SolarWinds TFTP Server. If your classroom uses a different TFTP server, please check with your instructor for the operating instructions.

Start the server on the host: **Start > Programs > SolarWinds TFTP Server > TFTP Server**. Once open, the server acquires the IP address of the Ethernet interface and uses the C:\TFTP-Root directory by default. As shown in the status bar in Figure 2-12, the server opens in the stopped state.

Figure 2-12   TFTP Server Open But Not Started

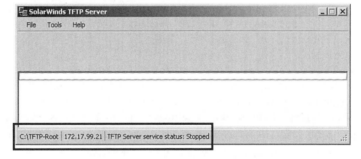

To start the server, choose **File > Configure**. The dialog box shown in Figure 2-13 opens.

Figure 2-13   TFTP Server Configuration Dialog Box

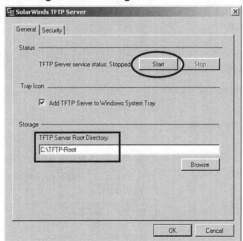

Note the server's storage location is C:\TFTP-Root by default. Make sure this directory actually exists (or browse to a location specified by your instructor) and then click the **Start** button. The status changes to *Started*. Click **OK** to close the dialog box. The server window should now display the start message, as shown in Figure 2-14.

Figure 2-14   TFTP Server Service Is Started

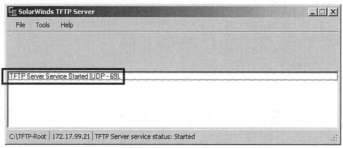

Step 2.   Verify connectivity to the TFTP server.

Verify that the TFTP server is running and that it can be pinged from the switch. You did this in Task 1, but check again to make sure the link between S1 and PC1 is still operational.

```
S1#ping 172.17.99.21

Type escape sequence to abort.
Sending 5, 100-byte ICMP Echos to 172.17.99.21 , timeout is 2 seconds:
!!!!!
Success rate is 100 percent (5/5), round-trip min/avg/max = 1/202/1006 ms
S1#
```

Note: If the ping fails from S1 to PC1 but succeeds from PC1 to S1, then security measures are blocking inbound ping requests to PC1. In addition, you may not be able to send the IOS image to PC1. If the security is the Windows Firewall, choose **Start > Settings > Control Panel > Windows Firewall** and make sure it is turned off.

PC1 may also have other security software installed that needs to be disabled. If so, consult the documentation for the installed software or ask your instructor for directions.

You are now ready to copy the Cisco IOS file from S1 to the TFTP server running on PC1.

Task 3: Save the Cisco IOS File to a TFTP Server

Step 1.   Identify the Cisco IOS filename.

Determine the exact name of the image file that is to be saved. From the console session, enter **show flash**:

```
S1#show flash

Directory of flash:/

    2  -rwx    616  Mar 1 1993 00:43:53 +00:00  vlan.dat
    6  drwx    192  Mar 1 1993 00:06:16 +00:00  c2960-lanbase-mz.122-25.SEE2

32514048 bytes total (24803840 bytes free)
```

The image on your switch will probably have a different name from what is shown in the **show flash** output.

✓ If the file is in a subdirectory indicated by the **drwx** highlighted in the **show flash** output, then you are not seeing the actual Cisco IOS filename. To see the filename, use the **cd** command to change the directory to the Cisco IOS directory. Then display the contents of the directory with the **show flash** command:

```
S1#cd flash:/c2960-lanbase-mz.122-25.SEE2
S1#show flash

Directory of flash:/c2960-lanbase-mz.122-25.SEE2/

    7   drwx        4480    Mar 1 1993 00:04:51 +00:00   html
  619   -rwx     4670535    Mar 1 1993 00:06:16 +00:00   c2960-lanbase-mz.
   122-25.SEE2.bin
  620   -rwx         457    Mar 1 1993 00:06:16 +00:00   info

32514048 bytes total (24801792 bytes free)
S1#
```

What is the name and size of the Cisco IOS image stored in flash?

_____

What attributes can be identified from the codes in the Cisco IOS filename?

_____

From privileged EXEC mode, enter the **copy flash tftp** command. Enter the filename of the Cisco IOS image file. Because you are already in the IOS subdirectory, you do not need to enter the directory path. Next, enter the IP address of the TFTP server. When asked for a destination filename, accept the default by pressing **Enter**.

```
S1#copy flash tftp
Source filename [/c2960-lanbase-mz.122-25.SEE2/]? c2960-lanbase-mz.122-
   25.SEE2.bin
Address or name of remote host []? 172.17.99.21
Destination filename [c2960-lanbase-mz.122-25.SEE2.bin]? [Enter]
!!!!!!!!!!!!!!!!!!!!!!!!!!!!!!!!!!!!!!!!!!!!!!!!!!!!!!!!!!!!!!!!!!!!!!!!!!!!!
!!!!!!!!!!!!!!!!!!!!!!!!!!!!!!!!!!!!!!!!!!!!!!!!!!!!!!!!!!!!!!!!!!!!!!!!!!!!!
<output omitted>
!!!!!!!!!!!!!!!
4670535 bytes copied in 11.291 secs (413651 bytes/sec)
S1#
```

Step 2.   Verify the transfer to the TFTP server.

Verify the IOS transfer by checking the TFTP server on PC1, as shown in Figure 2-15. SolarWinds TFTP Server shows the most recent message at the top of the list.

Figure 2-15   TFTP Server Message Window Shows IOS Transfer

Verify the IOS image is now stored in the server root directory, as shown in Figure 2-16.

Figure 2-16   TFTP-Root Directory on PC1 Shows Stored IOS Image

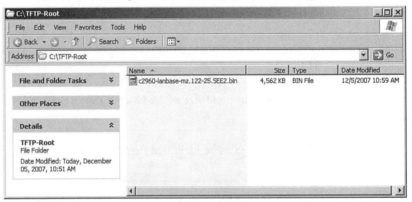

Task 4: Restore the Cisco IOS File to the Switch from a TFTP Server

skip

Step 1.   Verify connectivity.

Verify that the TFTP server is running, and ping the TFTP server IP address from the switch:

```
S1#ping 172.17.99.21
```

```
Type escape sequence to abort.
Sending 5, 100-byte ICMP Echos to 172.17.99.21, timeout is 2 seconds:
!!!!!
Success rate is 100 percent (5/5), round-trip min/avg/max = 1/1/1 ms
S1#
```

If the pings fail, troubleshoot the switch and server configurations.

Step 2.   Identify the Cisco IOS filename on the server and the entire pathname of the destination for the switch.

What is the name of the file on the TFTP server root directory that will be copied to the switch?

Step 3.   Upload the Cisco IOS software from the server to the switch.

Caution: Do not interrupt the process once the copy routine has started.

If necessary, change to the flash root directory with the **cd ..** command. Then, when asked for the destination filename, enter the full path as shown here:

```
S1#cd ..
S1#copy tftp flash
Address or name of remote host []? 172.17.99.21
Source filename []? c2960-lanbase-mz.122-25.SEE2.bin
Destination filename [c2960-lanbase-mz.122-25.SEE2.bin]? c2960-lanbase-
   mz.122-25.SEE2/c2960-lanbase-mz.122-25.SEE2.bin
%Warning:There is a file already existing with this name
Do you want to over write? [confirm] [Enter]
Accessing tftp://172.17.99.21/c2960-lanbase-mz.122-25.SEE2.bin...
Loading c2960-lanbase-mz.122-25.SEE2.bin from 172.17.99.21 (via Vlan99):
!!!!!!!!!!!!!!!!!
!!!!!!!!!!!!!!!!!!!!!!!!!!!!!!!!!!!!!!!!!!!!!!!!!!!!!!!!!!!!!!!!!!!!!!!!!!!!
<output omitted>
!!!!!!!!!!!!!!!!!!!!!!!!!!!!!!!!!!!!!!!!!!!!!!!!!!!!!!!!!!!!!!!!!!!!!!!!!!!!
[OK - 4670535 bytes]

4670535 bytes copied in 47.018 secs (99335 bytes/sec)
S1#
```

The TFTP server message window displays a *Completed* message, as shown in Figure 2-17.

Figure 2-17   TFTP Server Message Window Displays Completed Message IOS Transfer

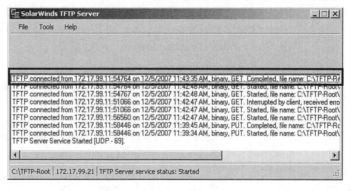

Step 4.   Test the restored Cisco IOS image.

Verify that the switch image is correct. To do this, reload the switch and observe the start-up process. The Cisco IOS software should load properly. To further verify the Cisco IOS image in flash, issue the **show version** command, which will show output similar to the following:

```
S1#show version
Cisco IOS Software, C2960 Software (C2960-LANBASE-M), Version 12.2(25)SEE2,
RELEASE SOFTWARE (fc1)
```

```
Copyright  1986-2006 by Cisco Systems, Inc.
Compiled Fri 28-Jul-06 04:33 by yenanh
Image text-base: 0x00003000, data-base: 0x00AA2F34

ROM: Bootstrap program is C2960 boot loader
BOOTLDR: C2960 Boot Loader (C2960-HBOOT-M) Version 12.2(25r)SEE1, RELEASE
SOFTWARE (fc1)

S1 uptime is 1 minute
System returned to ROM by power-on
System image file is "flash:c2960-lanbase-mz.122-25.SEE2/c2960-lanbase-
  mz.122-25.SEE2.bin"
<output omitted>
```

Task 5: Back Up and Restore a Configuration File from a TFTP Server

Step 1.   Copy the startup configuration file to the TFTP server.

Copying configuration files to a TFTP server is similar to copying the Cisco IOS software. First, verify that the TFTP server is running and that it can be pinged from the switch.

Then, in privileged EXEC mode, enter the **copy running-config startup-config** command to make sure that the running configuration file is saved to the startup configuration file:

```
S1#copy running-config startup-config
Destination filename [startup-config]? [Enter]
Building configuration...
[OK]
```

Back up the saved configuration file to the TFTP server with the command **copy startup-config tftp**. At the prompt, enter the IP address of the TFTP server and then press **Enter** to confirm the destination filename.

```
S1#copy startup-config tftp
Address or name of remote host []? 172.17.99.21
Destination filename [s1-confg]? [Enter]
!!
1452 bytes copied in 0.445 secs (3263 bytes/sec)
S1#
```

Step 2.   Verify the transfer to the TFTP server.

Verify the transfer to the TFTP server by checking the message window on the TFTP server. In Figure 2-18, the message window was scrolled to the right so you can see the filename.

Figure 2-18   TFTP Server Message Window Shows Completed Message for Configuration Transfer

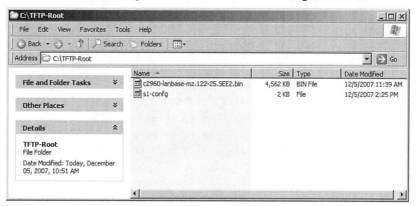

Verify that the **s1-confg** file is in the TFTP server directory C:\TFTP-root, as shown in Figure 2-19.

Figure 2-19   TFTP-Root Directory on PC1 Shows Stored Configuration File

Step 3.   Restore the startup configuration file from the TFTP server.

Erase the existing startup configuration file in NVRAM and reload the switch:

```
S1#erase nvram
Erasing the nvram filesystem will remove all configuration files! Continue?
[confirm]
[OK]
Erase of nvram: complete
S1#
S1#reload
Proceed with reload? [confirm] [Enter]
```

When the switch has reloaded, you must reestablish connectivity between the switch and the TFTP server before the configuration can be restored. To do this, configure VLAN 99 with the correct IP address and assign port FastEthernet 0/18 to VLAN 99. When you are finished, return to privileged EXEC mode.

```
Switch>enable
Switch#configure terminal
Enter configuration commands, one per line.  End with CNTL/Z.
```

```
Switch(config)#interface vlan 99
Switch(config-if)#ip address 172.17.99.11 255.255.255.0
Switch(config-if)#interface fastethernet 0/18
Switch(config-if)#switchport access vlan 99
Switch(config-if)#end
Switch#
%LINEPROTO-5-UPDOWN: Line protocol on Interface Vlan99, changed state to up
```

Wait until the link light for FastEthernet 0/18 turns green and you receive the VLAN 99 is up message, as shown here. After VLAN 99 is up, verify connectivity by pinging the server from the switch.

```
Switch#ping 172.17.99.21

Type escape sequence to abort.
Sending 5, 100-byte ICMP Echos to 172.17.99.21, timeout is 2 seconds:
!!!!!
Success rate is 100 percent (5/5), round-trip min/avg/max = 1/202/1007 ms
Switch#
```

If the ping is unsuccessful, troubleshoot the switch and server configuration. Restore the configuration from the TFTP server with the **copy tftp startup-config** command:

```
Switch#copy tftp startup-config
Address or name of remote host []? 172.17.99.21
Source filename []? s1-confg
Destination filename [startup-config]? [Enter]
Accessing tftp://172.17.99.21/s1-confg...
Loading s1-confg from 172.17.99.21 (via Vlan99): !
[OK - 1476 bytes]
[OK]
1476 bytes copied in 9.060 secs (163 bytes/sec)
00:16:50: %SYS-5-CONFIG_NV_I: Nonvolatile storage configured from
   tftp://172.17.99.21/s1-confg by console
Switch#
```

Was the operation successful? _____

Step 4. Copy the startup configuration to the running configuration.

In privileged EXEC mode, enter the command **copy startup-config running-config** to copy the stored configuration into RAM and make it the active configuration. Alternatively, you could simply reload the switch. If reloading, make sure you do *not* save the running configuration to NVRAM.

```
Switch#copy startup-config running-config
Destination filename [running-config]?

1476 bytes copied in 0.201 secs (7343 bytes/sec)
S1#
```

Notice that the switch prompt changes to S1.

Task 6: Upgrade the Cisco IOS Software of the Switch

Note: This task requires that a combination of a Cisco IOS image and the HTML archive (tar) file be placed in the default TFTP server directory by the instructor or student. This file should be downloaded by the instructor from the Cisco.com Software Center. In this lab, the c2960-lanbase-mz.122-25.SEE2.tar file is referenced for instructional purposes only. This has the same filename stem as the current image. However, for the purpose of the lab, assume that this is an update. The Cisco IOS software update release includes the binary image and new HTML files to support changes to the web interface.

This lab also requires a saved copy of the current configuration file as a backup.

Step 1.   Determine the current boot sequence for the switch.

Use the **show boot** command to display the settings of the boot environment variables:

```
S1#show boot
BOOT path-list          : flash:c2960-lanbase-mz.122-25.SEE2/c2960-lanbase-
mz.122-25.SEE2.bin
Config file             : flash:/config.text
Private Config file     : flash:/private-config.text
Enable Break            : no
Manual Boot             : no
HELPER path-list        :
Auto upgrade            : yes
NVRAM/Config file
        buffer size:    65536
```

Determine whether there is sufficient memory to hold multiple image files:

```
S1#show flash

Directory of flash:/

    2  -rwx     616   Mar 1 1993 00:43:53 +00:00  vlan.dat
    3  -rwx       5   Mar 1 1993 00:47:11 +00:00  private-config.text
    4  -rwx    1476   Mar 1 1993 00:47:11 +00:00  config.text
    6  drwx     192   Mar 1 1993 00:06:16 +00:00  c2960-lanbase-mz.122-25.SEE2

32514048 bytes total (24801792 bytes free)
S1#
```

Note that on this platform, about 32 MB are in use and approximately 25 MB are free. So there is plenty of memory for multiple images. If there is insufficient space for multiple images, you must overwrite the existing image with the new one, so make sure there is a backup of the existing Cisco IOS file on the TFTP server before beginning the upgrade.

Step 2.   Prepare for the new image.

If the switch has enough free memory, as shown in the last step, use the **rename** command to rename the existing Cisco IOS file to the same name with the .old extension:

```
S1#rename flash:/c2960-lanbase-mz.122-25.SEE2/c2960-lanbase-mz.122-25.SEE2.bin
   flash:/c2960-lanbase-mz.122-25.SEE2/c2960-lanbase-mz.122-25.SEE2.old
```

Verify that the renaming was successful:

```
S1#dir flash:/c2960-lanbase-mz.122-25.SEE2
Directory of flash:/c2960-lanbase-mz.122-25.SEE2/

    7   drwx     4480   Mar 1 1993 00:04:51 +00:00   html
  619   -rwx   4670535   Mar 1 1993 14:06:01 +00:00   c2960-lanbase-mz.122-
    25.SEE2.old
  620   -rwx      457   Mar 1 1993 00:06:16 +00:00   info

32514048 bytes total (24801792 bytes free)
S1#
```

Enter the following to place the new Cisco IOS image and HTML files into the flash memory target directory:

```
S1#archive tar /x tftp://172.17.99.21/c2960-lanbase-mz.122-25.SEE2.tar
  flash:/c2960-lanbase-mz.122-25.SEE2
```

Step 3. Configure the new file as the boot image.

Enter the **boot** command with the name of the new image filename at the global configuration mode prompt. When you are finished, return to privileged EXEC mode and save the configuration.

```
S1(config)#boot system flash:/c2960-lanbase-mz.122-25.SEE2/ c2960-lanbase-
  mz.122-25.SEE2.bin
S1(config)#end
S1#copy running-config startup-config
```

Step 4. Restart the switch.

Restart the switch using the **reload** command to verify that the new Cisco IOS software loaded. You should see the Loading message display the path and IOS filename as the file is decompressed into RAM.

```
S1#reload

Proceed with reload? [confirm] [Enter]

%SYS-5-RELOAD: Reload requested by console. Reload Reason: Reload Command.
<output omitted>
Loading "flash:/c2960-lanbase-mz.122-25.SEE2/c2960-lanbase-mz.122-
  25.SEE2.bin"...@@@@@@@@
@@@@@@@@@@@@@@@@@@@@@@@@@@@@@@@@@@@@@@@@@@@@@@@@@@@@@@@@@@@@@@@@@@@@@@@@@@@@@@@@@
<output omitted>
```

Once loaded, you can verify the correct IOS loaded with the **show version** command:

```
S1#show version
Cisco IOS Software, C2960 Software (C2960-LANBASE-M), Version 12.2(25)SEE2,
RELEASE SOFTWARE (fc1)
Copyright  1986-2006 by Cisco Systems, Inc.
Compiled Fri 28-Jul-06 04:33 by yenanh
Image text-base: 0x00003000, data-base: 0x00AA2F34
```

```
ROM: Bootstrap program is C2960 boot loader
BOOTLDR: C2960 Boot Loader (C2960-HBOOT-M) Version 12.2(25r)SEE1, RELEASE
SOFTWARE (fc1)

S1 uptime is 6 minutes
System returned to ROM by power-on
System image file is "flash:/c2960-lanbase-mz.122-25.SEE2/c2960-lanbase-
  mz.122-25.SEE2.bin"
<output omitted>
```

Remove the backup file from flash memory using the **delete** command from privileged
EXEC mode:

```
S1(config)#delete flash:/c2960-lanbase-mz.122-25.SEE2/c2960-lanbase-mz.122-
  25.SEE2.old
```

Task 7: Recover Passwords on the Catalyst 2960

Step 1.   Reset the console password.

Have a classmate change the console and vty passwords on the switch. Save the changes
to the startup-config file and reload the switch.

Step 2.   Recover access to the switch.

Now, without knowing the passwords, try to gain access to the switch. Make sure that a
PC is connected to the console port and a HyperTerminal window is open. Turn the switch
off by unplugging the cable. Then reattach the power cable and hold down the **MODE**
button on the front of the switch. Release the **MODE** button after the SYST LED stops
blinking and stays lit.

*you can release w/o having
to waiting unit it stop.*

The following output should be displayed:

```
Base ethernet MAC Address: 00:1b:53:02:4e:80
Xmodem file system is available.
The password-recovery mechanism is enabled.

The system has been interrupted prior to initializing the
flash filesystem.  The following commands will initialize
the flash filesystem, and finish loading the operating
system software:

    flash_init
    load_helper
    boot


switch:
```

To initialize the file system and finish loading the operating system, enter the following
commands:

```
switch: flash_init
Initializing Flash...
```

```
flashfs[0]: 600 files, 19 directories
flashfs[0]: 0 orphaned files, 0 orphaned directories
flashfs[0]: Total bytes: 32514048
flashfs[0]: Bytes used: 7712256
flashfs[0]: Bytes available: 24801792
flashfs[0]: flashfs fsck took 9 seconds.
...done Initializing Flash.
Boot Sector Filesystem (bs) installed, fsid: 3
Setting console baud rate to 9600...

switch: load_helper
```

List the contents of flash using the **dir flash:** command. Do not forget to type the colon (:).

```
switch: dir flash:
Directory of flash:/

2      -rwx   616      <date>          vlan.dat
4      -rwx   5        <date>          private-config.text
6      drwx   192      <date>          c2960-lanbase-mz.122-25.SEE2
622    -rwx   1496     <date>          config.text

24801792 bytes available (7712256 bytes used)
```

To make sure the switch does not load with the configuration file with the unknown password (config.text), change the filename using the **rename** command and then verify the name change with the **dir flash:** command:

```
switch: rename flash:config.text flash:config.old

switch: dir flash:
Directory of flash:/

2      -rwx   616      <date>          vlan.dat
4      -rwx   5        <date>          private-config.text
6      drwx   192      <date>          c2960-lanbase-mz.122-25.SEE2
622    -rwx   1496     <date>          config.old

24801792 bytes available (7712256 bytes used)

switch:
```

Now when the system reboots, it will load without a configuration.

Step 3. Restart the system.

Type the **boot** command to boot the system:

```
switch: boot
Loading "flash:/c2960-lanbase-mz.122-25.SEE2/c2960-lanbase-mz.122-
  25.SEE2.bin"...@@@@@@@@
@@@@@@@@@@@@@@@@@@@@@@@@@@@@@@@@@@@@@@@@@@@@@@@@@@@@@@@@@@@@@@@@@@@@@@@@@@@@@@@@@@@
<output omitted>
```

At the switch prompt, enter the **enable** command. Notice you were not asked for a password.

```
Switch>enable
Switch#
```

Now rename the configuration file back to its original name and copy the configuration file into RAM:

```
Switch#rename flash:config.old flash:config.text
Destination filename [config.text]? [Enter]
Switch#copy flash:config.text system:running-config
Destination filename [running-config]? [Enter]

1496 bytes copied in 0.218 secs (6862 bytes/sec)
S1#
%LINEPROTO-5-UPDOWN: Line protocol on Interface Vlan1, changed state to
  down
%LINEPROTO-5-UPDOWN: Line protocol on Interface Vlan99, changed state to
  down
%LINK-5-CHANGED: Interface Vlan1, changed state to administratively down
%LINEPROTO-5-UPDOWN: Line protocol on Interface Vlan99, changed state to up
S1#
```

The configuration file is now reloaded. The switch prompt changes to S1 and interface VLAN 99 comes up. Now you can change the privileged EXEC password to **class** and the vty and console passwords to **cisco**:

```
S1#configure terminal
S1(config)#enable secret class
S1(config)#line console 0
S1(config-line)#password cisco
S1(config-line)#line vty 0 15
S1(config-line)#password cisco
S1(config-line)#end
S1#copy running-config startup-config
Destination filename [startup-config]?[Enter]
Building configuration...
[OK]
S1#
```

Task 8: Clean Up

Unless directed otherwise by your instructor, erase the configurations and reload the switches. Disconnect and store the cabling. For PC hosts that are normally connected to other networks (such as the school LAN or to the Internet), reconnect the appropriate cabling and restore the TCP/IP settings.

Lab 2-3: Managing Switch Operating System and Configuration Files Challenge (2.5.3)

Learning Objectives

Upon completion of this lab, you will be able to

- Create and save a basic switch configuration
- Set up a TFTP server on the network
- Back up the switch Cisco IOS software to a TFTP server and then restore it
- Back up the switch configuration to a TFTP server
- Configure a switch to load a configuration from a TFTP server
- Upgrade the Cisco IOS software from a TFTP server
- Recover the password for a Cisco 2960 switch (2900 series)

Scenario

In this lab, you will complete file management and password recovery procedures on a Cisco Catalyst switch with little or no assistance from the instructions. Try to complete the tasks without asking for help from your instructor, referring to the curriculum, or revisiting "Lab 2-2: Managing Switch Operating System and Configuration Files (2.5.2)."

Figure 2-20 shows the topology diagram for this lab.

Figure 2-20   Topology Diagram for Lab 2-3

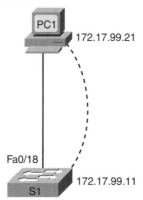

Table 2-9 shows the addressing scheme used in this lab.

Table 2-9   Addressing Table for Lab 2-3

Device	Interface	IP Address	Subnet Mask	Default Gateway
PC1	NIC	172.17.99.21	255.255.255.0	172.17.99.11
S1	VLAN 99	172.17.99.11	255.255.255.0	172.17.99.1

Task 1: Cable and Initialize the Network

Step 1.   Cable the network.

Step 2.   Clear the configuration on the switch.

Step 3.   Create a basic configuration:

- Use **cisco** for the console and vty password, and use **class** for the privileged EXEC mode password:

- Configure the VLAN 99 interface and assign VLAN 99 to FastEthernet 0/18:

Step 4.   Configure the host attached to the switch.

Step 5.   Verify connectivity from PC1 to S1.

Task 2: Start and Configure the TFTP Server

Step 1.   Start up and configure the TFTP server.

Step 2.   Verify connectivity from S1 to the TFTP server running on PC1.

Task 3: Save the Cisco IOS File to the TFTP Server

Step 1.   Identify the Cisco IOS filename.

Step 2.   In privileged EXEC mode, copy the image file to the TFTP server.

Step 3.   Verify the transfer to the TFTP server.

Task 4: Restore the Cisco IOS File to the Switch from a TFTP Server

Step 1.   Identify the Cisco IOS filename on the server and the entire pathname of the destination for the switch.

Step 2.   Upload the Cisco IOS software from the server to the switch.

Step 3.   Test the restored Cisco IOS image.

Task 5: Back Up and Restore a Configuration File from a TFTP Server

Step 1.   Copy the startup configuration file to the TFTP server.

Step 2.   Verify the transfer to the TFTP server.

Step 3.   Restore the startup configuration file from the TFTP server.

Step 4.   Verify the restored startup configuration file.

Task 6: Upgrade the Cisco IOS Software of the Switch

Step 1.   Determine the current boot sequence for the switch and check memory availability.

Step 2.   Rename the current IOS image.

Step 3.   Extract the new Cisco IOS image and HTML files into flash memory.

Step 4.   Configure the new file as the boot image.

Step 5.   Restart the switch.

Task 7: Recover Passwords on the Catalyst 2960

Step 1.   Reset the console password.

Have a classmate change the console and vty passwords on the switch. Save the changes to the startup-config file and reload the switch.

Step 2.   Recover access to the switch.

Task 8: Clean Up

Unless directed otherwise by your instructor, erase the configurations and reload the switches. Disconnect and store the cabling. For PC hosts that are normally connected to other networks (such as the school LAN or to the Internet), reconnect the appropriate cabling and restore the TCP/IP settings.

Packet Tracer Skills Integration Challenge

Open the file LSG03-PTSkills2.pka on the CD-ROM that accompanies this book. You will use the topology in Figure 2-21 and the addressing table in Table 2-10 to document your design.

Figure 2-21   Packet Tracer Skills Integration Challenge Topology

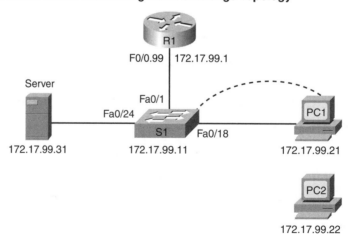

Table 2-10   Addressing Table for the Packet Tracer Skills Integration Challenge Activity

Device	Interface	IP Address	Subnet Mask
R1	Fa0/0	172.17.99.1	255.255.255.0
S1	Fa0/1	172.17.99.11	255.255.255.0
PC1	NIC	172.17.99.21	255.255.255.0
PC2	NIC	172.17.99.22	255.255.255.0
Server	NIC	172.17.99.31	255.255.255.0

Learning Objectives

Upon completion of this lab, you will be able to

- Establish a console connection to a switch
- Configure the hostname and VLAN 99
- Configure the clock using Help
- Modify the history buffer
- Configure passwords and console/Telnet access
- Configure the login banner
- Configure the router
- Configure the boot sequence
- Solve a mismatch between duplex and speed
- Manage the MAC address table
- Configure port security
- Secure unused ports
- Manage the switch configuration file

Introduction

In this activity, you will configure basic switch management, including general maintenance commands, passwords, and port security. This activity provides you an opportunity to review previously acquired skills.

Task 1: Establish a Console Connection to a Switch

Step 1.   Connect a console cable to S1.

For this activity, direct access to S1 Config and CLI tabs is disabled. You must establish a console session through PC1. Connect a console cable from PC1 to S1.

Step 2.   Establish a terminal session.

From PC1, open a terminal window and use the default terminal configuration. You should now have access to the CLI for S1.

Step 3.   Check results.

Your completion percentage should be 6 percent. If not, click **Check Results** to see which required components are not yet completed.

Task 2: Configure the Hostname and VLAN 99

Step 1.   Configure the switch hostname as S1.

Step 2.   Configure port Fa0/1 and interface VLAN 99.

Assign VLAN 99 to FastEthernet 0/1 and set the mode to access mode. These commands are discussed further in Chapter 3.

```
S1(config)#interface fastethernet 0/1
S1(config-if)#switchport access vlan 99
S1(config-if)#switchport mode access

```

Configure IP connectivity on S1 using VLAN 99:

```
S1(config)#interface vlan 99
S1(config-if)#ip address 172.17.99.11 255.255.255.0
S1(config-if)#no shutdown
```

Step 3.   Configure the default gateway for S1.

Configure the default gateway and then test connectivity. S1 should be able to ping R1.

Step 4.   Check results.

Your completion percentage should be 26 percent. If not, click **Check Results** to see which required components are not yet completed. Also, make sure that interface VLAN 99 is active.

Task 3: Configure the Clock Using Help

Step 1.   Configure the clock to the current time.

At the privileged EXEC prompt, enter **clock ?**. Use Help to discover each additional step required to set the current time. Packet Tracer does not grade this command, so the completion percentage does not change.

Step 2.   Verify that the clock is set to the current time.

Use the **show clock** command to verify that the clock is now set to the current time. Packet Tracer may not correctly simulate the time you entered.

Task 4: Modify the History Buffer

Step 1.   Set the history buffer to 50 for the console line.

Step 2.   Set the history buffer to 50 for the vty lines.

Step 3.   Check results.

Your completion percentage should be 32 percent. If not, click **Check Results** to see which required components are not yet completed.

Task 5: Configure Passwords and Console/Telnet Access

Step 1.   Configure the privileged EXEC password.

Use the encrypted form of the privileged EXEC mode password and set the password to **class**.

Step 2.   Configure the passwords for console and Telnet.

Set the console and vty password to **cisco** and require users to log in.

Step 3.   Encrypt passwords.

View the current configuration on S1. Notice that the line passwords are shown in clear text. Enter the command to encrypt these passwords.

Step 4.   Check results.

Your completion percentage should be 41 percent. If not, click **Check Results** to see which required components are not yet completed.

Task 6: Configure the Login Banner

If you do not enter the banner text exactly as specified, Packet Tracer does not grade your command correctly. These commands are case sensitive. Also make sure that you do not include any spaces before or after the text.

Step 1.   Configure the message-of-the-day banner on S1.

Configure the message-of-the-day as **Authorized Access Only.**

Step 2.   Check results.

Your completion percentage should be 44 percent. If not, click **Check Results** to see which required components are not yet completed.

Task 7: Configure the Router

Step 1.   Configure the router with the same basic commands you used on S1.

Routers and switches share many of the same commands. Access the CLI for R1 by clicking the device. Do the following on R1:

- Configure the hostname.

- Set the history buffer to 50 for both console and vty.

- Configure the encrypted form of the privileged EXEC mode password and set the password to **class**.

- Set the console and vty password to **cisco** and require users to log in.

- Encrypt the console and vty passwords.

- Configure the message-of-the-day as **Authorized Access Only**.

Step 2.   Check results.

Your completion percentage should be 65 percent. If not, click **Check Results** to see which required components are not yet completed.

Task 8: Configure the Boot Sequence

Step 1. View current files stored in flash.

On S1, enter the command **show flash**. You should see the following files listed:

```
S1#show flash
Directory of flash:/

    1  -rw-    4414921    <no date>  c2960-lanbase-mz.122-25.FX.bin
    3  -rw-    4670455    <no date>  c2960-lanbase-mz.122-25.SEE1.bin
    2  -rw-        616    <no date>  vlan.dat

32514048 bytes total (23428056 bytes free)
```

Step 2. Configure S1 to boot using the second image listed.

Make sure your command includes the file system, which is **flash**.

Note: Packet Tracer does not show this command in the running configuration. In addition, if you reload the switch, Packet Tracer does not load the image you specified.

Step 3. Check results.

Your completion percentage should be 68 percent. If not, click **Check Results** to see which required components are not yet completed.

Task 9: Solve a Mismatch Between Duplex and Speed

Step 1. Change the duplex and speed on S1.

PC1 and Server currently do not have access through S1 because of a mismatch between duplex and speed. Enter commands on S1 to solve this problem.

Step 2. Verify connectivity.

Both PC1 and Server should now be able to ping S1, R1, and each other.

Step 3. Check results.

Your completion percentage should be 74 percent. If not, click **Check Results** to see which required components are not yet completed.

Task 10: Manage the MAC Address Table

Step 1. View the current MAC address table.

What command would you use to display the MAC address table?

```
S1#_____

              Mac Address Table
  --------------------------------------------.

  Vlan    Mac Address       Type        Ports
  --      -----.            ----        --.

    99    0001.637b.b267    DYNAMIC     Fa0/24
    99    0004.9a32.8e01    DYNAMIC     Fa0/1
    99    0060.3ee6.1659    DYNAMIC     Fa0/18
```

The list of MAC addresses in your output may be different depending on how long it has been since you sent any packets across the switch.

Step 2. Configure a static MAC address.

Network policy may dictate that all server addresses be statically configured. Enter the command to statically configure the MAC address of Server.

Step 3. Check results.

Your completion percentage should be 76 percent. If not, click **Check Results** to see which required components are not yet completed.

Task 11: Configure Port Security

Step 1. Configure port security for PC1.

Use the following policy to establish port security on the port used by PC1:

- Enable port security.

- Allow only one MAC address.

- Configure the first learned MAC address to "stick" to the configuration.

- Set the port to shut down if there is a security violation.

Note: Only the enable port security step is graded by Packet Tracer and counted toward the completion percentage. However, all the port security tasks listed above are required to complete this activity successfully.

Step 2. Verify port security.

Verify that port security is enabled for Fa0/18. Your output should look like the following output. Notice that S1 has not yet learned a MAC address for this interface.

What command generated the following output?

```
S1#_____
Port Security              : Enabled
Port Status                : Secure-up
Violation Mode             : Shutdown
Aging Time                 : 0 mins
Aging Type                 : Absolute
SecureStatic Address Aging : Disabled
Maximum MAC Addresses      : 1
Total MAC Addresses        : 0
Configured MAC Addresses   : 0
Sticky MAC Addresses       : 0
Last Source Address:Vlan   : 0000.0000.0000:0
Security Violation Count   : 0
```

Step 3. Force S1 to learn the MAC address for PC1.

Send a ping from PC1 to S1. Then verify that S1 has added the MAC address for PC1 to the running configuration.

```
!
interface FastEthernet0/18
 <output omitted>
 switchport port-security mac-address sticky 0060.3EE6.1659
 <output omitted>
!
```

Step 4.   Test port security.

Remove the FastEthernet connection between S1 and PC1. Connect PC2 to Fa0/18. Wait for the link lights to turn green. If necessary, send a ping from PC2 to S1 to cause the port to shut down. Port security should show the following results:

```
Port Security                 : Enabled
Port Status                   : Secure-shutdown
Violation Mode                : Shutdown
Aging Time                    : 0 mins
Aging Type                    : Absolute
SecureStatic Address Aging    : Disabled
Maximum MAC Addresses         : 1
Total MAC Addresses           : 1
Configured MAC Addresses      : 1
Sticky MAC Addresses          : 0
Last Source Address:Vlan      : 00D0.BAD6.5193:99
Security Violation Count      : 1
```

Viewing the Fa0/18 interface shows that **line protocol is down (err-disabled)**, which also indicates a security violation.

```
S1#show interface fa0/18
FastEthernet0/18 is down, line protocol is down (err-disabled)
<output omitted>
```

Step 5.   Reconnect PC1 and reenable the port.

To reenable the port, disconnect PC2 from Fa0/18 and reconnect PC1. Interface Fa0/18 must be manually configured before returning to the active state.

Step 6.   Check results.

Your completion percentage should be 82 percent. If not, click **Check Results** to see which required components are not yet completed.

Task 12: Secure Unused Ports

Step 1.   Disable all unused ports on S1.

Disable all ports that are currently not used on S1. Packet Tracer grades the status of the following ports: Fa0/2, Fa0/3, Fa0/4, Gig1/1, and Gig1/2.

Step 2.   Check results.

Your completion percentage should be 97 percent. If not, click **Check Results** to see which required components are not yet completed.

Task 13: Manage the Switch Configuration File

Step 1.   Save the current configuration to NVRAM for R1.

Step 2.   Back up the startup configuration files for S1 and R1 to Server.

Back up the startup configuration file on S1 and R1 by uploading them to Server. Once complete, verify the server has the R1-confg and S1-confg files.

Step 3.   Check results.

Your completion percentage should be 100 percent. If not, click **Check Results** to see which required components are not yet completed.

CHAPTER 3

VLANs

One of the contributing technologies to excellent network performance is the separation of large broadcast domains into smaller ones with virtual local-area networks (VLANs). Smaller broadcast domains limit the number of devices participating in broadcasts and allow devices to be separated into functional groups. This chapter offers exercises to help you review how to configure, manage, and troubleshoot VLANs and Ethernet trunk links.

The Study Guide portion of this chapter uses a combination of fill-in-the-blank, open-ended question, and Packet Tracer exercises to test your knowledge of VLAN concepts and configurations.

The Labs and Activities portion of this chapter includes all the online curriculum labs to ensure that you have mastered the hands-on skills needed to understand VLAN configuration.

As you work through this chapter, use Chapter 3 in *LAN Switching and Wireless, CCNA Exploration Companion Guide* or use the corresponding Chapter 3 in the Exploration LAN Switching and Wireless online curriculum for assistance.

Study Guide

Introducing VLANs

VLANs give network administrators flexibility in LAN design. VLANs extend the traditional router-bounded broadcast domain to a VLAN-bounded broadcast domain; VLANs make it possible to sculpt a broadcast domain into any shape that can be defined and bounded by the switches within the network. The exercise in this section reviews basic VLAN concepts.

VLAN Concepts Exercise

Defining VLANs

A VLAN allows a network administrator to create groups of _____ networked devices based on _____, _____, or _____ teams.

For computers to communicate on the same VLAN, each must have an _____ and a _____ that belong to the same subnet and are consistent for that VLAN. The switch has to be configured with the VLAN, and each port in the VLAN must be assigned to the VLAN. A switch port with a singular VLAN configured on it is called an _____ port. Remember that just because two computers are physically connected to the same switch does not mean that they can communicate. Devices on two separate subnets must communicate via a _____, whether or not VLANs are used.

Benefits of VLANs

Implementing VLAN technology enables a network to more flexibly support business goals. The primary benefits of using VLANs are

- _____
- _____
- _____
- _____
- _____
- _____

VLAN ID Ranges

VLANs are divided numerically into a normal range and an extended range. Normal range VLANs are identified by a VLAN ID between _____ and _____. Configurations are stored within a VLAN database file, called _____, which is the _____ memory of the switch.

Extended range VLANs are identified by a VLAN ID between _____ and _____ and are saved in the _____ file. _____ does not learn extended range VLANs.

One Cisco Catalyst 2960 switch can support up to _____ VLANs. Why is the number of VLANs that can be configured on a switch limited?

_____

Types of VLANs

Today there is essentially one way of implementing VLANs: port-based VLANs. Among the port-based VLANs, there are a number of different types of VLANs.

A _____ VLAN is a VLAN that is configured to carry only user-generated traffic. These VLANs are sometimes referred to as _____ VLANs.

All switch ports are members of the _____ VLAN after the initial, out-of-the-box bootup of the switch. In this VLAN, which is numbered VLAN _____, all switch ports are part of the same _____ domain.

Briefly define and explain the purpose of a black hole VLAN:

_____

_____

_____

_____

_____

A _____ VLAN is assigned to an IEEE _____ trunk port, which supports traffic coming from many VLANs (_____ traffic) as well as traffic that does not come from a VLAN (_____ traffic).

You assign the _____ VLAN an _____ and _____ so that the switch can be managed via HTTP, Telnet, SSH, or SNMP. VLAN ___ would serve as the _____ VLAN if you did not proactively define a unique VLAN to serve this purpose. It is a security best practice to define this VLAN to be a VLAN distinct from *all* other VLANs defined in the switched LAN.

Note: For simplicity and for our purposes in this book, we most often use VLAN 99 for both the management VLAN and the native VLAN. However, some activities and labs may require you to use a different number so that you do not get in the habit of always using 99 as the VLAN number.

Voice VLANs

It is easy to appreciate why a separate VLAN is needed to support Voice over IP (VoIP). List four requirements for VoIP traffic:

- _____
- _____
- _____
- _____

Network Application Traffic Types

In CCNA Exploration: Network Fundamentals, you learned about the different kinds of traffic a LAN handles. Because a VLAN has all the characteristics of a LAN, a VLAN must accommodate the same network traffic as a LAN.

List three different types of network management and control traffic that can be present on the LAN:

- _____
- _____
- _____

IP telephony traffic consists of _____ traffic and _____ traffic. _____ traffic is responsible for call setup, progress, and teardown, and traverses the network end to end.

_____ traffic is sent from a particular source address to a multicast group that is identified by a single IP address.

Normal _____ traffic is related to file creation and storage, print services, e-mail database access, and other shared network applications that are common to business uses.

The _____ class is intended to provide less-than-best-effort services to certain applications. Applications assigned to this class have little or no contribution to the organizational objectives of the enterprise and are typically entertainment oriented in nature.

Switch Port Membership Options

A port can be configured to support these VLAN options:

- **_____ VLAN:** Ports on a switch are manually assigned to a VLAN. Enter the commands to configure FastEthernet 0/5 as an access port using VLAN 15:

   ```
   S1(config)#_____

   S1(config-if)#_____

   S1(config-if)#_____
   ```

- **_____ VLAN:** Configured using a special server called a _____ that can assign switch ports to VLANs automatically based on the _____ of the device connected to the port.

- **_____ VLAN:** A port is configured with the voice VLAN feature enabled so that it can support an IP phone attached to it. To configure voice support on the port, you need to configure a VLAN for voice and a VLAN for data. Enter the commands to configure FastEthernet 0/5 as an access port using data VLAN 15 and voice VLAN 115:

   ```
   S1(config)#_____

   S1(config-if)#_____

   S1(config-if)#_____

   S1(config-if)#_____

   S1(config-if)#_____
   ```

   What command generated the following output?

```
S1#_____

Name: Fa0/5

Switchport: Enabled

Administrative Mode: static access

Operational Mode: down

Administrative Trunking Encapsulation: dot1q

Negotiation of Trunking: Off

Access Mode VLAN: 15 (VLAN0015)

Trunking Native Mode VLAN: 1 (default)

Administrative Native VLAN tagging: enabled

Voice VLAN: 115 (VLAN0115)

<output omitted>
```

The switch port configuration supporting voice and data has the following characteristics:

- The configuration command _____ ensures that voice traffic is identified as priority traffic.

- The _____ command identifies VLAN 115 as the voice VLAN.

- The _____ command configures VLAN 15 as the access mode (data) VLAN.

Controlling Broadcast Domains with VLANs

Communicating with a device in the same VLAN is called _____-VLAN communication. Using the topology in Figure 3-1, answer the following questions to explain how traffic is forwarded in the network when PC2 attempts to ping PC5. Assume that all PCs and switches start with empty ARP and MAC address tables.

Figure 3-1   Intra-VLAN Communications

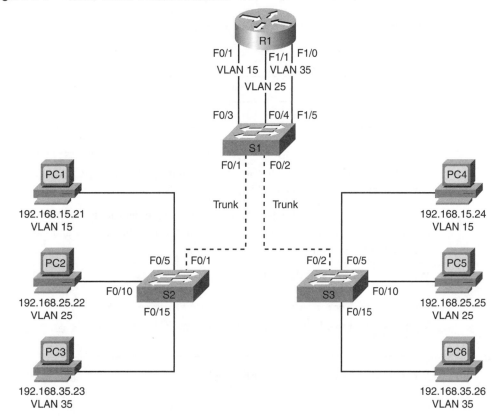

What type of frame will PC2 send?

_____

What does S2 do with the frame it receives from PC2?

_____

_____

S2 did not send the frame to PC1 or PC3. Why not?

_____

_____

What does S1 do with the frame it receives from S2?

_____

What does R1 do with the frame it receives from S1?

_____

_____

What does S3 do with the frame it receives from S1?

_____

Explain the rest of the process until PC2 receives a successful ping reply from PC5:

_____

_____

_____

_____

_____

_____

_____

_____

Next, assume PC2 in VLAN 15 wants to communicate with PC6 in VLAN 35. Communicating with a device in another VLAN is called _____-VLAN communication.

Using the topology in Figure 3-1, answer the following questions to explain how traffic is forwarded in the network when PC2 attempts to ping PC6. Assume that all PCs and switches have empty ARP and MAC address tables.

What type of frame will PC2 send?

_____

What does S2 do with the frame it receives from PC2?

_____

What does S1 do with the frame it receives from S2?

_____

What does R1 do with the frame it receives from S1?

_____

_____

What does S3 do with the frame it receives from S1?

_____

What does PC5 do with the frame it receives from S3?

_____

What does S1 do with the frame it receives from R1?

_____

What does S2 do with the frame it receives from S1?

_____

Explain the rest of the process until PC2 receives a successful ping reply from PC6. Include all the details such as port numbers and type of frame (unicast or broadcast), and whether the device drops, forwards, or processes the frame. Do not forget to include R1's responsibility for traffic forwarding.

_____

_____

1. _____

2. _____

3. _____

4. _____

   _____

5. _____

   _____

6. _____

7. _____

8. _____

9. _____

10. _____

11. _____

    _____

12. _____

13. _____

14. _____

    _____

15. _____

    _____

16. _____

17. _____

    _____

18. _____

VLAN Trunking

VLANs and VLAN trunks are inextricably linked. VLANs in a modern switched LAN would be practically useless without VLAN trunks. The exercise in this section reviews the concepts necessary for understanding the role of trunks in a switched LAN.

Understanding VLAN Trunking Exercise

VLAN Trunks

Briefly define a VLAN trunk:

_____

_____

_____

Explain what a switch does with a frame received on an access port assigned to one VLAN before placing the frame on a trunk link for all VLANs:

_____

_____

_____

The VLAN tag field consists of an _____ field and a _____ field. Also, the _____ is recalculated for tagged frames.

The _____ field is set to the hexadecimal value of _____. This value is called the _____ value. This is how the switch receiving the frame knows to look for information in the tag control information field for VLAN information.

In Figure 3-2, fill in the missing field descriptions.

Figure 3-2   IEEE 802.1Q VLAN Tag Fields

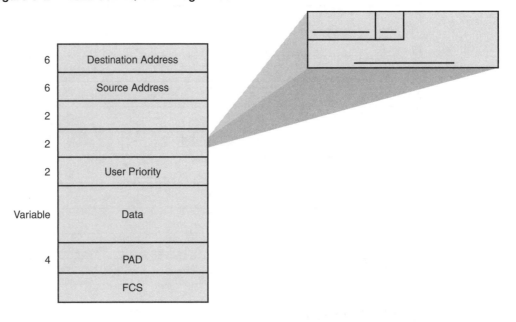

When a Cisco switch trunk port receives untagged frames, it forwards those frames to the _____ VLAN, which by default is VLAN number _____. Remember that it is a security best practice to change the native VLAN to a different number. Because trunk links will use VLAN 1 by default, it is necessary to configure trunks with the administrator-defined native VLAN. Enter the command to assign VLAN 99 as the native VLAN to a trunking port:

S1(config-if)#_____

Trunking Modes

Although most Cisco Catalyst switches can be configured to support two types of trunk ports, _____ _____ and _____, today only _____ is used in practice. However, legacy networks may still use _____.

_____ is a Cisco proprietary protocol that negotiates both the _____ of trunk ports and the trunk _____ of trunk ports.

A switch port on a Cisco Catalyst switch supports a number of trunking modes. The trunking mode defines how the port negotiates using DTP to set up a trunk link with its peer port. Identify the commands used to configure the trunking mode:

- The command _____ configures the local switch port to advertise to the remote port that it is dynamically changing to a trunking state. The local port is considered to be in an unconditional (always on) trunking state.

- The command _____ configures the local switch port to advertise to the remote switch port that it is able to trunk but does not request to go to the trunking state. The local port transitions to the trunking state only if the remote port trunk mode has been configured to be _____ or _____. If both ports on the switches are set to _____, they do not negotiate to be in a trunking state. They negotiate to be in an _____ state.

- The command _____ configures the local switch port to advertise to the remote switch port that it is able to trunk and asks the remote switch port to go to the trunking state. If the local port detects that the remote has been configured in _____, _____, or _____ mode, the local port ends up in a trunking state. If the remote switch port is in the _____ mode, the local switch port remains as a nontrunking port.

- You can turn off DTP for the trunk so that the local port does not send out DTP frames to the remote port. The command _____ disables DTP. The local port is then considered to be in an unconditional _____ state. Why would you use this command instead of the **switchport mode trunk** command?

_____

In Table 3-1, the arguments for the **switchport mode** command are listed for the local side of the link down the first column and for the remote side of the link across the first row. Indicate whether the link will transition to **access** mode or **trunk** mode after the two switches have sent DTP messages.

Table 3-1   Trunk Negotiation Combinations

	Dynamic Auto	Dynamic Desirable	Trunk	Access
Dynamic Auto				
Dynamic Desirable				
Trunk				Not recommended
Access			Not recommended	

Configure VLANs and Trunks

The exercises in this section review commands for configuring VLANs and trunks. You will use your answers in the "VLAN Configuration Exercise" to complete "Packet Tracer Exercise 3-1: VLAN Configuration."

VLAN Configuration Exercise

Configuring VLANs

Use the information in Figure 3-3 and Table 3-2 to answer the following questions related to configuring VLANs and trunks.

Figure 3-3   VLAN Configuration Topology

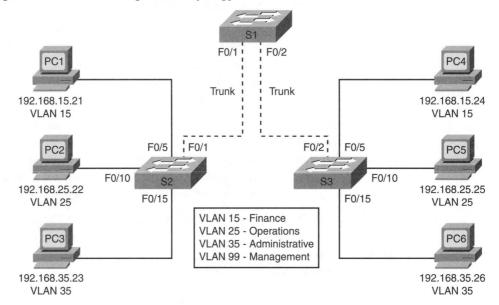

Table 3-2   VLAN Configuration Addressing Table

Device	Interface	IP Address	Subnet Mask	Default Gateway
S1	VLAN 99	192.168.99.11	255.255.255.0	—
S2	VLAN 99	192.168.99.12	255.255.255.0	—
S3	VLAN 99	192.168.99.13	255.255.255.0	—
PC1	NIC	192.168.15.21	255.255.255.0	192.168.15.1
PC2	NIC	192.168.25.22	255.255.255.0	192.168.25.1
PC3	NIC	192.168.35.23	255.255.255.0	192.168.35.1
PC4	NIC	192.168.15.24	255.255.255.0	192.168.15.1
PC5	NIC	192.168.25.25	255.255.255.0	192.168.25.1
PC6	NIC	192.168.35.26	255.255.255.0	192.168.35.1

Enter the commands, including the switch prompts, to configure the management interface on each switch:

_____

_____

_____

_____

_____

_____

_____

_____

Enter the commands, including the switch prompts, to configure the VLANs on each switch (the commands are the same on each switch, so you only need to enter the commands for S1 here):

_____

_____

_____

_____

_____

_____

_____

_____

_____

Enter the commands, including the switch prompts, to establish trunking between S1, S2, and S3 (VLAN 99 is the native VLAN):

_____

_____

_____

_____

_____

_____

_____

_____

_____

_____

_____

_____

_____

_____

_____

Enter the commands, including the switch prompts, to configure access ports and assign VLANs for the PCs that are attached to S2 and S3 (because the commands are the same on both switches, you only need to record them once):

_____

_____

_____

_____

_____

_____

_____

_____

_____

_____

Managing VLANs

After you configure a VLAN, you can validate the VLAN configurations using Cisco IOS **show** commands. Enter the command used to display the following output:

S1#_____

```
VLAN Name                             Status    Ports
-- ------------------             ----- ------------------.

1    default                          active    Fa0/3, Fa0/4, Fa0/5, Fa0/6
                                                Fa0/7, Fa0/8, Fa0/9, Fa0/10
                                                Fa0/11, Fa0/12, Fa0/13, Fa0/14
                                                Fa0/15, Fa0/16, Fa0/17, Fa0/18
                                                Fa0/19, Fa0/20, Fa0/21, Fa0/22
                                                Fa0/23, Fa0/24, Gig1/1, Gig1/2
15   Finance                          active
25   Operations                       active
35   Administrative                   active
99   Management                       active
1002 fddi-default                     active
1003 token-ring-default               active
1004 fddinet-default                  active
1005 trnet-default                    active
S1#
```

Enter the command used to display the information for only one VLAN, specifying the VLAN number:

S1#_____

```
VLAN Name                             Status    Ports
-- ------------------             ----. ------------------.

15   Finance                          active


VLAN Type  SAID    MTU   Parent RingNo BridgeNo Stp  BrdgMode Trans1 Trans2
-- --.  ----- --. --- --- ---- -- ---- --- ---

15   enet  100015  1500  -      -      -        -    -        0      0

S1#
```

Enter the command used to display the information for only one VLAN, specifying the VLAN name:

S1#_____

```
VLAN Name                         Status    Ports
———  ————————————————————————    ————·  ————————————————————·

25   Operations                   active


VLAN Type  SAID     MTU   Parent RingNo BridgeNo Stp  BrdgMode Trans1 Trans2
———  ——·  —————  ——·  ———  ———  ————  ——  ————  ———  ———

25   enet  100025   1500  -      .      .        .  -  .        0      0


S1#
```

Enter the command that will display the following output:

S1#_____

```
Number of existing VLANs          : 9
Number of existing VTP VLANs      : 9
Number of existing extended VLANs : 0
```

Enter the command that will display the following output:

S2#_____

```
Name: Fa0/5
Switchport: Enabled
Administrative Mode: static access
Operational Mode: static access
Administrative Trunking Encapsulation: dot1q
Operational Trunking Encapsulation: native
Negotiation of Trunking: On
Access Mode VLAN: 15 (Finance)
Trunking Native Mode VLAN: 1 (default)
Voice VLAN: none
Administrative private-vlan host-association: none
Administrative private-vlan mapping: none
Administrative private-vlan trunk native VLAN: none
Administrative private-vlan trunk encapsulation: dot1q
Administrative private-vlan trunk normal VLANs: none
Administrative private-vlan trunk private VLANs: none
Operational private-vlan: none
Trunking VLANs Enabled: ALL
Pruning VLANs Enabled: 2-1001
Capture Mode Disabled
Capture VLANs Allowed: ALL
Protected: false
Appliance trust: none
```

Packet Tracer Exercise 3-1: VLAN Configuration

Now you are ready to use Packet Tracer to apply your answers to the "VLAN Configuration Exercise." Open file LSG03-0301.pka on the CD-ROM that accompanies this book to perform this exercise using Packet Tracer.

Note: The following instructions are also contained within the Packet Tracer Exercise.

Learning Objectives

Upon completion of this Packet Tracer Exercise, you will be able to

- Configure VLANs
- Configure the management interface
- Configure trunking
- Assign VLANs to access ports
- Verify connectivity
- Save the Packet Tracer file

Scenario

In this exercise, you will practice configuring VLANs and establishing trunk links. In addition, you will assign VLANs to access ports and then test connectivity between devices on the same VLAN. The PCs are already configured with IP addressing. The switches have a basic configuration. The passwords are **cisco** for user EXEC mode and **class** for privileged EXEC mode.

Task 1: Configure VLANs

Step 1.   Configure VLANs on S1, S2, and S3. VLAN names are case sensitive.

Step 2.   Your completion percentage should be 32 percent. If not, click **Check Results** to see which required components are not yet completed.

Task 2: Configure the Management Interface

Step 1.   Create the VLAN 99 interface and assign it an IP address on each of the switches.

Step 2.   Your completion percentage should be 47 percent. If not, click **Check Results** to see which required components are not yet completed.

Task 3: Configure Trunking

Step 1.   Configure trunking between S1, S2, and S3 and assign VLAN 99 as the native VLAN. The mode must be set for trunking.

Step 2.   Wait for the link lights between S1, S2, and S3 to transition to green, then test connectivity between the switches.

Step 3.   Your completion percentage should be 68 percent. If not, click **Check Results** to see which required components are not yet completed.

Task 4: Assign VLANs to Access Ports

Step 1.   Configure access ports and assign VLANs for the PCs that are attached to S2 and S3.

Step 2.   Your completion percentage should be 100 percent. If not, click **Check Results** to see which required components are not yet completed.

Task 5: Verify Connectivity

S1, S2, and S3 should now be able to ping each other. PCs belonging to the same VLAN should be able to ping each other. You can test connectivity using the **ping** command or by creating simple PDUs between devices. Alternatively, you can click **Check Results** and then the **Connectivity Tests** tab. The status of all six connectivity tests should be listed as "Correct."

Task 6: Save the Packet Tracer File

Save your Packet Tracer file as LSG03-00301-end.pka.

Troubleshooting VLANs and Trunks

Common VLAN and trunking issues are usually associated with incorrect configurations. The exercise in this section reviews basic troubleshooting knowledge and skills.

Troubleshooting VLANs and Trunks Exercise

List and briefly explain four common VLAN and trunk configuration errors:

- _____
  _____
  _____

- _____
  _____
  _____

- _____
  _____
  _____

- _____
  _____
  _____

For practice troubleshooting VLAN and trunk configurations, Complete "Lab 3-3: Troubleshooting VLAN Configurations (3.5.3)."

Labs and Activities

Command Reference

In Table 3-3, record the command, *including the correct prompt*, that fits the description. Fill in any blanks with the appropriate missing information.

Table 3-3   Commands for VLAN Configuration

Command	Description
	Displays switchport information for Fa0/5
	Configures a port as an access port
	Assigns VLAN 10 to an access port
	Configures prioritization so that voice traffic is identified on the port and given preference over other port traffic
	Assigns the voice VLAN 110 to the access port
	Configures a port as a trunk port
	Assigns the native VLAN 99 to a trunk port
	Configures the local port to advertise that it is able to trunk but does not configure the port to request the remote port to go into the trunking state
	Configures the local port to advertise that it is able to trunk and requests that the remote port go into the trunking state
	Disables DTP on the port
	Displays DTP information and statistics for Fa0/1
	Global configuration command that creates VLAN 10
	Assigns the name Marketing to a VLAN
	Displays the contents of the vlan.dat file
	Displays information about VLAN 10 only
	Displays information about the Marketing VLAN only
	Displays a count of the number of existing VLANs

Command	Description
	Removes VLAN 10 for the vlan.dat file
	Removes all previously configured VLANs
	Configures a trunk port to permit trunking for VLANs 10, 20, and 30
	Displays trunking information for the switch

Lab 3-1: Basic VLAN Configuration (3.5.1)

Learning Objectives

Upon completion of this lab, you will be able to

- Cable a network according to the topology diagram
- Erase the startup configuration and reload a switch to the default state
- Perform basic configuration tasks on a switch
- Create VLANs
- Assign switch ports to a VLAN
- Add, move, and change ports
- Verify VLAN configuration
- Enable trunking on inter-switch connections
- Verify trunk configuration
- Save the VLAN configuration

Figure 3-4 shows the topology diagram for this lab.

Figure 3-4   Topology Diagram for Lab 3-1

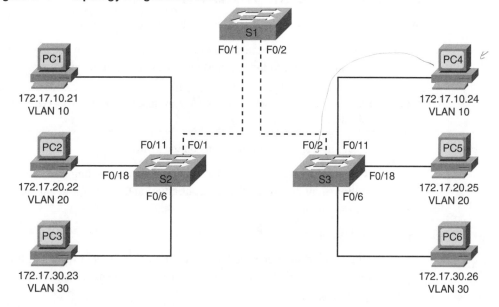

Table 3-4 shows the addressing scheme used in this lab.

Table 3-4   Addressing Table for Lab 3-1

Device	Interface	IP Address	Subnet Mask	Default Gateway
S1	VLAN 99	172.17.99.11	255.255.255.0	—
S2	VLAN 99	172.17.99.12	255.255.255.0	—
S3	VLAN 99	172.17.99.13	255.255.255.0	—
PC1	NIC	172.17.10.21	255.255.255.0	172.17.10.1
PC2	NIC	172.17.20.22	255.255.255.0	172.17.20.1
PC3	NIC	172.17.30.23	255.255.255.0	172.17.30.1
PC4	NIC	172.17.10.24	255.255.255.0	172.17.10.1
PC5	NIC	172.17.20.25	255.255.255.0	172.17.20.1
PC6	NIC	172.17.30.26	255.255.255.0	172.17.30.1

Table 3-5 shows the port assignments used in this lab.

Table 3-5   Initial Port Assignments (Switches 2 and 3)

Ports	Assignment	Network
Fa0/1–0/5	802.1Q Trunks (Native VLAN 99)	172.17.99.0 /24
Fa0/6–0/10	VLAN 30—Guest (Default)	172.17.30.0 /24
Fa0/11–0/17	VLAN 10—Faculty/Staff	172.17.10.0 /24
Fa0/18–0/24	VLAN 20—Students	172.17.20.0 /24

Task 1: Prepare the Network

Step 1.   Cable a network that is similar to the one shown in Figure 3-4.

You do not need to connect any PCs at this time. You can use any current switch in your lab as long as it has the required interfaces shown in the topology.

Note: If you use 2900 or 2950 switches, the outputs may appear different. Also, certain commands may be different or unavailable.

Step 2.   Clear any existing configurations on the switches.

If necessary, refer to "Appendix 1: Erasing and Reloading the Switch" in the Chapter 2 section "Lab 2-1: Basic Switch Configuration (2.5.1)" for the procedure to clear switch configurations.

Step 3.   Disable all ports.

Unlike routers, Cisco switch ports are in the "up" state by default. It is a good practice to disable any unused ports on the switches with the **shutdown** command:

```
Switch#config term
Switch(config)#interface range fa0/1-24
```

```
Switch(config-if-range)#shutdown
Switch(config-if-range)#interface range gi0/1-2
Switch(config-if-range)#shutdown
```

Task 2: Perform Basic Switch Configurations

Step 1.   Configure the switches according to the following guidelines:

- Configure the switch hostname.

- Disable DNS lookup.

- Configure an EXEC mode password of **class**.

- Configure a password of **cisco** for console connections.

- Configure a password of **cisco** for vty connections.

Step 2. ✓ Reenable the user ports ^FOR ALL CCS^ on S2 and S3:

```
S2(config)#interface range fa0/6, fa0/11, fa0/18
S2(config-if-range)#switchport mode access
S2(config-if-range)#no shutdown
```

```
S3(config)#interface range fa0/6, fa0/11, fa0/18
S3(config-if-range)#switchport mode access
S3(config-if-range)#no shutdown
```

Task 3: Configure and Activate Ethernet Interfaces

Configure the PCs. You can complete this lab using only two PCs by simply changing the IP addressing for the two PCs specific to a test you want to conduct. For example, if you want to test connectivity between PC1 and PC2, then configure the IP addresses for those PCs by referring to the addressing table at the beginning of the lab. Alternatively, you can configure all six PCs with the IP addresses and default gateways.

Task 4: Configure VLANs on the Switch

Step 1.   Create VLANs on S1.

Use the **vlan** *vlan-id* command in global configuration mode to add a VLAN to switch S1. There are four VLANs configured for this lab:

- VLAN 10 (Faculty/Staff)

- VLAN 20 (Students)

- VLAN 30 (Guest)

- VLAN 99 (Management)

After you create the VLAN, you will be in VLAN configuration mode, where you can assign a name to the VLAN with the **name** *vlan-name* command:

```
S1(config)#vlan 10
S1(config-vlan)#name faculty/staff
S1(config-vlan)#vlan 20
```

```
S1(config-vlan)#name students
S1(config-vlan)#vlan 30
S1(config-vlan)#name guest
S1(config-vlan)#vlan 99
S1(config-vlan)#name management
S1(config-vlan)#end
S1#
```

Step 2.   Verify that the VLANs have been created on S1.

Use the **show vlan brief** command to verify that the VLANs have been created:

```
S1#show vlan brief

VLAN Name                 Status    Ports
---- -------------------- --------- ---------------

1    default              active    Fa0/1, Fa0/2, Fa0/4, Fa0/5
                                    Fa0/6, Fa0/7, Fa0/8, Fa0/9
                                    Fa0/10, Fa0/11, Fa0/12, Fa0/13
                                    Fa0/14, Fa0/15, Fa0/16, Fa0/17
                                    Fa0/18, Fa0/19, Fa0/20, Fa0/21
                                    Fa0/22, Fa0/23, Fa0/24, Gi0/1
                                    Gi0/2
10   faculty/staff        active
20   students             active
30   guest                active
99   management           active
```

Step 3.   Configure and name VLANs on switches S2 and S3.

Create and name VLANs 10, 20, 30, and 99 on S2 and S3 using the commands from Step 1. Verify the correct configuration with the **show vlan brief** command.

What ports are currently assigned to the four VLANs you have created?

_____

Step 4. — Assign switch ports to VLANs on S2 and S3.

Refer to the port assignments in Table 3-5. Ports are assigned to VLANs in interface configuration mode, using the **switchport access vlan** *vlan-id* command. You can assign each port individually or you can use the **interface range** command to simplify this task, as shown here. The commands are shown for S3 only. Configure S2 with the same commands. Save your configurations when done.

```
S3(config)#interface range fa0/6-10
S3(config-if-range)#switchport mode access
S3(config-if-range)#switchport access vlan 30
S3(config-if-range)#interface range fa0/11-17
S3(config-if-range)#switchport mode access
S3(config-if-range)#switchport access vlan 10
S3(config-if-range)#interface range fa0/18-24
S3(config-if-range)#switchport mode access
S3(config-if-range)#switchport access vlan 20
S3(config-if-range)#end
```

```
S3#copy running-config startup-config
Destination filename [startup-config]? [enter]
Building configuration...
[OK]
```

Step 5.   Determine which ports have been added.

Use the **show vlan id** *vlan-number* command on S2 to see which ports are assigned to VLAN 10.

Which ports are assigned to VLAN 10?

_____ *Fa 0/11* _____

Note: The **show vlan id** *vlan-name* command displays the same output. You can also view VLAN assignment information using the **show interfaces** *interface* **switchport** command.

Step 6.   Assign the management VLAN.

A management VLAN is any VLAN that you configure to access the management capabilities of a switch. VLAN 1 serves as the management VLAN if you did not specifically define another VLAN. You assign to the management VLAN an IP address and subnet mask. A switch can be managed via HTTP, Telnet, SSH, or SNMP. Because the out-of-the-box configuration of a Cisco switch has VLAN 1 as the default VLAN, VLAN 1 is a bad choice as the management VLAN. You do not want an arbitrary user who is connecting to a switch to default to the management VLAN. Recall that you configured the management VLAN as VLAN 99 earlier in this lab.

From interface configuration mode, use the **ip address** command to assign the management IP address to the switches:

```
S1(config)#interface vlan 99
%LINEPROTO-5-UPDOWN: Line protocol on Interface Vlan99, changed state to
 down
S1(config-if)#ip address 172.17.99.11 255.255.255.0
```

```
S2(config)#interface vlan 99
%LINEPROTO-5-UPDOWN: Line protocol on Interface Vlan99, changed state to
 down
S2(config-if)#ip address 172.17.99.12 255.255.255.0
```

```
S3(config)#interface vlan 99
%LINEPROTO-5-UPDOWN: Line protocol on Interface Vlan99, changed state to
 down
S3(config-if)#ip address 172.17.99.13 255.255.255.0
```

Note: The **no shutdown** command is not necessary on 2960 switches. However, depending on the equipment you are using, you may need to add this command.

Assigning a management address allows IP communication between the switches, and also allows any host connected to a port assigned to VLAN 99 to connect to the switches. Because VLAN 99 is configured as the management VLAN, any ports assigned to this VLAN are considered management ports and should be secured to control which devices can connect to these ports.

Optional: Configure port security on all access ports by defining one as the maximum number of allowed MAC addresses, setting the switch to dynamically "stick" the MAC addresses to the running configuration, and setting the switch to automatically shut down the port if there is a security violation.

Step 7.   Configure trunking and the native VLAN for the trunking ports on all switches.

Trunks are connections between the switches that allow the switches to exchange information for all VLANs. By default, a trunk port belongs to all VLANs, as opposed to an access port, which can only belong to a single VLAN. If the switch supports both ISL and 802.1Q VLAN encapsulation, the trunks must specify which method is being used. Because the 2960 switch only supports 802.1Q trunking, it is not specified in this lab.

A native VLAN is assigned to an 802.1Q trunk port. In the topology, the native VLAN is VLAN 99. An 802.1Q trunk port supports traffic coming from many VLANs (tagged traffic) and traffic that does not come from a VLAN (untagged traffic). The 802.1Q trunk port places untagged traffic on the native VLAN. Untagged traffic is generated by a computer attached to a switch port that is configured with the native VLAN. One of the IEEE 802.1Q specifications for native VLANs is to maintain backward compatibility with untagged traffic common to legacy LAN scenarios. For the purposes of this lab, a native VLAN serves as a common identifier on opposing ends of a trunk link. It is a best practice to use a VLAN other than VLAN 1 as the native VLAN.

Use the **interface range** command in global configuration mode to simplify configuring trunking:

```
S1(config)#interface range fa0/1-5
S1(config-if-range)#switchport mode trunk
S1(config-if-range)#switchport trunk native vlan 99
S1(config-if-range)#no shutdown
S1(config-if-range)#end
```

```
S2(config)#interface range fa0/1-5
S2(config-if-range)#switchport mode trunk
S2(config-if-range)#switchport trunk native vlan 99
S2(config-if-range)#no shutdown
S2(config-if-range)#end
```

```
S3(config)#interface range fa0/1-5
S3(config-if-range)#switchport mode trunk
S3(config-if-range)#switchport trunk native vlan 99
S3(config-if-range)#no shutdown
S3(config-if-range)#end
```

Verify that the trunks have been configured with the **show interface trunk** command:

```
S1#show interface trunk
```

Port	Mode	Encapsulation	Status	Native vlan
Fa0/1	on	802.1q	trunking	99
Fa0/2	on	802.1q	trunking	99

```
Port            Vlans allowed on trunk
Fa0/1           1-4094
Fa0/2           1-4094


Port            Vlans allowed and active in management domain
Fa0/1           1,10,20,30,99
Fa0/2           1,10,20,30,99


Port            Vlans in spanning tree forwarding state and not pruned
Fa0/1           1,10,20,30,99
Fa0/2           1,10,20,30,99
```

Step 8. Verify that the switches can communicate.

From S1, ping the management address on both S2 and S3:

```
S1#ping 172.17.99.12
Type escape sequence to abort.
Sending 5, 100-byte ICMP Echos to 172.17.99.12, timeout is 2 seconds:
!!!!!
Success rate is 100 percent (5/5), round-trip min/avg/max = 1/2/9 ms
S1#ping 172.17.99.13
Type escape sequence to abort.
Sending 5, 100-byte ICMP Echos to 172.17.99.13, timeout is 2 seconds:
.!!!!
Success rate is 80 percent (4/5), round-trip min/avg/max = 1/1/1 ms
```

Step 9. Ping several hosts from PC2.

Ping from host PC2 to host PC1 (172.17.10.21). Is the ping attempt successful? _____No_____

Ping from host PC2 to the switch VLAN 99 IP address 172.17.99.12. Is the ping attempt successful? _____No_____

Because these hosts are on different subnets and in different VLANs, they cannot communicate without a Layer 3 device to route between the separate subnetworks.

Ping from host PC2 to host PC5. Is the ping attempt successful? _____Yes_____

Because PC2 is in the same VLAN and the same subnet as PC5, the ping is successful

Step 10. Move PC1 into the same VLAN as PC2.

The port connected to PC2 (S2 Fa0/18) is assigned to VLAN 20, and the port connected to PC1 (S2 Fa0/11) is assigned to VLAN 10. Reassign the S2 Fa0/11 port to VLAN 20. You do not need to first remove a port from a VLAN to change its VLAN membership. After you reassign a port to a new VLAN, that port is automatically removed from its previous VLAN.

```
S2#configure terminal
Enter configuration commands, one per line.  End with CNTL/Z.
S2(config)#interface fastethernet 0/11
S2(config-if)#switchport access vlan 20
S2(config-if)#end
```

Ping from host PC2 to host PC1. Is the ping attempt successful? ___No___

Why or why not?

Bec these host are on difference subnet, and in different VLAN. They can not communicate w/o Layer 3 betw seperate NT

Even though the ports used by PC1 and PC2 are in the same VLAN, they are still in different subnetworks, so they cannot communicate directly.

Step 11.   Change the IP address and network on PC1.

because .22 already exist.

Change the IP address on PC1 to **172.17.20.22**. The subnet mask and default gateway can remain the same. Once again, ping from host PC2 to host PC1, using the newly assigned IP address.

Is the ping attempt successful? ___Yes___

Task 5: Document the Switch Configurations

On each switch, capture the running configuration to a text file and save it for future reference. These scripts can be edited to expedite configuring switches in future labs.

Task 6: Clean Up

Unless directed otherwise by your instructor, erase the configurations and reload the switches. Disconnect and store the cabling. For PC hosts that are normally connected to other networks (such as the school LAN or to the Internet), reconnect the appropriate cabling and restore the TCP/IP settings.

Packet Tracer Companion: Basic VLAN Configuration (3.5.1)

You can now open the file LSG03-Lab351.pka on the CD-ROM that accompanies this book to repeat this hands-on lab using Packet Tracer. Remember, however, that Packet Tracer is not a substitute for a hands-on lab experience with real equipment.

- If the OSI image file is older version, you use command below to create VLAN.
S3#VLan data base
S3(VLAN)# Vlan 30 name Guest

Lab 3-2: Challenge VLAN Configuration (3.5.2)

Learning Objectives

Upon completion of this lab, you will be able to

- Cable a network according to the topology diagram
- Erase the startup configuration and reload a switch to the default state
- Perform basic configuration tasks on a switch
- Create VLANs
- Assign switch ports to a VLAN
- Add, move, and change ports
- Verify VLAN configuration
- Enable trunking on inter-switch connections
- Verify trunk configuration
- Save the VLAN configuration

Figure 3-5 shows the topology diagram for this lab.

Figure 3-5   Topology Diagram for Lab 3-2

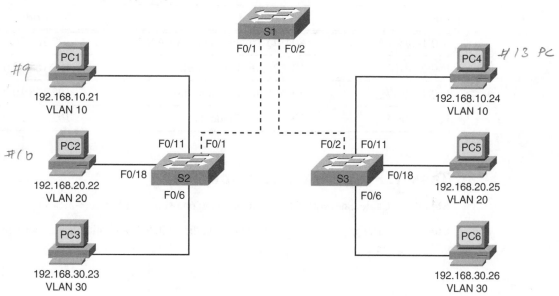

Table 3-6 shows the addressing scheme used in this lab.

Table 3-6   Addressing Table for Lab 3-2

Device	Interface	IP Address	Subnet Mask	Default Gateway
S1	VLAN 56	192.168.56.11	255.255.255.0	—
S2	VLAN 56	192.168.56.12	255.255.255.0	—
S3	VLAN 56	192.168.56.13	255.255.255.0	—
PC1	NIC	192.168.10.21	255.255.255.0	192.168.10.1
PC2	NIC	192.168.20.22	255.255.255.0	192.168.20.1
PC3	NIC	192.168.30.23	255.255.255.0	192.168.30.1
PC4	NIC	192.168.10.24	255.255.255.0	192.168.10.1
PC5	NIC	192.168.20.25	255.255.255.0	192.168.20.1
PC6	NIC	192.168.30.26	255.255.255.0	192.168.30.1

Table 3-7 shows the port assignments used in this lab.

Table 3-7   Initial Port Assignments (Switches 2 and 3)

Ports	Assignment	Network
Fa0/1–0/5	802.1Q Trunks (Native VLAN 56)	192.168.56.0 /24
Fa0/6–0/10	VLAN 30—Guest (Default)	192.168.30.0 /24
Fa0/11–0/17	VLAN 10—Faculty/Staff	192.168.10.0 /24
Fa0/18–0/24	VLAN 20—Students	192.168.20.0 /24

Task 1: Prepare the Network

Step 1.   Cable a network that is similar to the one shown in Figure 3-5.

Step 2.   Clear any existing configurations on the switches, and initialize all ports in the shutdown state.

Task 2: Perform Basic Switch Configurations

Step 1.   Configure the switches according to the following guidelines:

- Configure the switch hostname.

- Disable DNS lookup.

- Configure an EXEC mode password of **class**.

- Configure a password of **cisco** for console connections.

- Configure a password of **cisco** for vty connections.

Step 2.   Reenable the user ports on S2 and S3.

Task 3: Configure and Activate Ethernet Interfaces

Configure the PCs. You can complete this lab using only two PCs by simply changing the IP addressing for the two PCs specific to a test you want to conduct. Alternatively, you can configure all six PCs with the IP addresses and default gateways.

Task 4: Configure VLANs on the Switch

Step 1.   Create VLANs on switch S1.

Step 2.   Verify that the VLANs have been created on S1.

Step 3.   Configure, name, and verify VLANs on switches S2 and S3.

Step 4.   Assign switch ports to VLANs on S2 and S3.

Step 5.   Configure management VLAN 56 on each of the switches.

Step 6.   Configure trunking and the native VLAN for the trunking ports on all three switches. Verify that the trunks have been configured.

Step 7.   Verify that S1, S2, and S3 can communicate.

Step 8.   Ping several hosts from PC2 and record the results:

PC2 can ping to PC5 because they are on the same vlan

PC2 can not ping any other pcs because of difference Vlan.

Step 9.   Move PC1 into the same VLAN as PC2.

Can PC1 successfully ping PC2? ___No___

Why or why not?

because the PC1 was assigned to difference subnet
as 192.168.10.21

Step 10.   Change the IP address on PC1 to **192.168.10.22**. Can PC1 successfully ping PC2? Yes.
20.21

Task 5: Document the Switch Configurations

On each switch, capture the running configuration to a text file and save it for future reference. These scripts can be edited to expedite configuring switches in future labs.

Task 6: Clean Up

Unless directed otherwise by your instructor, erase the configurations and reload the switches. Disconnect and store the cabling. For PC hosts that are normally connected to other networks (such as the school LAN or to the Internet), reconnect the appropriate cabling and restore the TCP/IP settings.

Packet Tracer Companion: Challenge VLAN Configuration (3.5.2)

You can now open the file LSG03-Lab352.pka on the CD-ROM that accompanies this book to repeat this hands-on lab using Packet Tracer. Remember, however, that Packet Tracer is not a substitute for a hands-on lab experience with real equipment.

Lab 3-3: Troubleshooting VLAN Configurations (3.5.3)

Learning Objectives

Upon completion of this lab, you will be able to

- Cable a network according to the topology diagram

- Erase the startup configuration and vlan.dat files and reload switches to the default state

- Load the switches with supplied scripts

- Find and correct all configuration errors

- Document the corrected network

Scenario

In this lab, you will practice troubleshooting a misconfigured VLAN environment. Your objective is to locate and correct any and all errors in the configurations and establish end-to-end connectivity. Your final configuration should match the topology diagram shown in Figure 3-6 and addressing table shown in Table 3-8. All passwords are set to **cisco**, except the enable secret password, which is set to **class**.

Figure 3-6   Topology Diagram for Lab 3-3

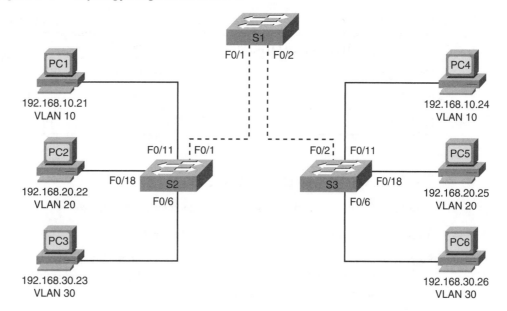

Table 3-8   Addressing Table for Lab 3-3

Device	Interface	IP Address	Subnet Mask	Default Gateway
S1	VLAN 56	192.168.56.11	255.255.255.0	—
S2	VLAN 56	192.168.56.12	255.255.255.0	—
S3	VLAN 56	192.168.56.13	255.255.255.0	—
PC1	NIC	192.168.10.21	255.255.255.0	192.168.10.1
PC2	NIC	192.168.20.22	255.255.255.0	192.168.20.1
PC3	NIC	192.168.30.23	255.255.255.0	192.168.30.1
PC4	NIC	192.168.10.24	255.255.255.0	192.168.10.1
PC5	NIC	192.168.20.25	255.255.255.0	192.168.20.1
PC6	NIC	192.168.30.26	255.255.255.0	192.168.30.1

Table 3-9 shows the port assignments used in this lab.

Table 3-9   Initial Port Assignments (Switches 2 and 3)

Ports	Assignment	Network
Fa0/1–0/5	~~Management & Native~~ 802.1Q Trunks (Native VLAN 56)	192.168.56.0 /24
Fa0/6–0/10	VLAN 30—Guest (Default)	192.168.30.0 /24
Fa0/11–0/17	VLAN 10—Faculty/Staff	192.168.10.0 /24
Fa0/18–0/24	VLAN 20—Students	192.168.20.0 /24

Task 1: Prepare the Network

Step 1.   Cable a network that is similar to the one shown in Figure 3-6.

Step 2.   Clear any existing configurations on the switches.

Step 3.   Apply the following configurations to each switch. Alternatively, you can open the file LSG03-Lab353-Scripts.txt on the CD-ROM that accompanies this book and copy in the scripts for each of the switches.

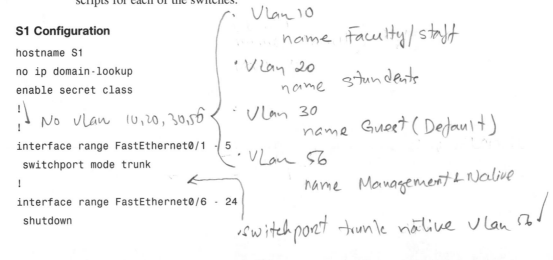

S1 Configuration

```
hostname S1
no ip domain-lookup
enable secret class
!
!
interface range FastEthernet0/1 - 5
 switchport mode trunk
!
interface range FastEthernet0/6 - 24
 shutdown
```

[Handwritten annotations:]
No vlan 10,20,30,56

- Vlan 10
  name Faculty/staff
- Vlan 20
  name stundents
- Vlan 30
  name Guest (Default)
- Vlan 56
  name Management & Native
  switchport trunk native vlan 56

```
!
interface Vlan1
 no ip address
 no ip route-cache
!
interface Vlan56
 ip address 192.168.56.11 255.255.255.0
 no ip route-cache
!
line con 0
 logging synchronous          ← password CISCO
                                Login
line vty 0 4
 no login                     ← password cisco
line vty 5 15                   Login
 password cisco
 login
!
end
```

S2 Configuration

```
hostname S2
no ip domain-lookup
enable secret class
!
vlan 10,20,30,56
!
interface range FastEthernet0/1-5
 switchport trunk native vlan 56
 switchport mode access  ←   switchport mode trunk
!
interface range FastEthernet0/6-10
 switchport access vlan 30
 switchport mode access
!
interface range FastEthernet0/11-17
 switchport access vlan 10
 switchport mode access
!
interface range FastEthernet0/18-24
 switchport access vlan 20
 switchport mode access
!
interface GigabitEthernet0/1
!
interface GigabitEthernet0/2
```

```
!
interface Vlan1
 ip address 192.168.56.12 255.255.255.0
 no ip route-cache
 shutdown
!
line con 0
 password cisco
 login
line vty 0 4
 password cisco
 login
line vty 5 15
 password cisco
 login
!
end
```

← • Remove ip address
  • place in to Vlan 56

← no shut

S3 Configuration

```
hostname S3
no ip domain-lookup
enable secret class
!
vlan 10,20,30
!
interface range FastEthernet0/1-5
 switchport trunk native vlan 56
 switchport mode trunk
!
interface range FastEthernet0/6-10
 switchport mode access
!
interface range FastEthernet0/11-17
 switchport mode access
!
interface range FastEthernet0/18-24
 switchport mode access
!
interface GigabitEthernet0/1
!
interface GigabitEthernet0/2
!
interface Vlan1
```

← Vlan 56
  name Management & Native

← switchport access Vlan 30

← switchport access vlan 10

← switchport access vlan 20

```
 no ip address
 no ip route-cache
 shutdown                    ← no  shut
!
interface Vlan56        ← ip address  192.168.56.13    255.255.255.0 ✓
 no ip route-cache          No shut
!
line con 0
 password cisco
 login
line vty 0 4
 password cisco
 login
line vty 5 15
 password cisco
 login
!
end
```

Task 2: Troubleshoot and Correct the VLAN Configuration

The following is a suggested method for approaching the connectivity problems in the network:

Step 1.   Test connectivity between the switches.

When all errors are corrected, you should be able to freely ping and telnet between S1, S2, and S3.

Do you have connectivity between any of the switches?

_____None_____

If yes, which ones?

_____

_____

Step 2.   Record error messages sent to the console.

Often, misconfigurations will cause error messages to be sent to the console. These messages can offer vital information needed to track down and ultimately solve configuration errors. Are there any error messages appearing on S1, S2, or S3?

_____yes_____

If so, record the content of the message or messages:

_____S1 : Native VLAN Mistmatch on int fas 1 & 2_____

_____

_____

_____

_____

_____

What does this error message or messages tell you about the configuration?

Trunk ports are configured w. different native Vlan

_____

Is there a solution that will stop the error messages? If so, document and then implement the solution:

yes.

None of VLAN exist on S1 and add native. Vlan 56 to fas 1 and 2

_____

Did the error messages stop? Are there new error messages? Did the solutions you implemented solve any connectivity issues? Document your observations:

_____

_____

_____

_____

_____

Step 3. Use verification commands to determine where errors might exist.

Many errors might exist, including some you may have introduced simply by connecting and configuring the topology. However, you know that this lab has configuration errors related to VLANs. To discover errors, use VLAN-related verification commands to investigate the current state of the network. These commands include, but may not be limited to, the following:

- **show vlan brief**

- **show interface trunk**

- **show ip interface brief**

Document the errors you discovered, how you discovered them, and the solutions you implemented:

Command for trouble shoot

1. show vlan

2. show int Trunk

3. show ip int. brief.

4. show int fas 0/1 switch port

_____

_____

_____

S₁   None VLAN exist.

S₂: with show int Trunk but nothing to show.
        need to added command switchport mode trunk on fas 1-5

S₃: show int fas 0/2 switchport → Trunking Native mode
                                    VLAN : 56 (Inactive).
        need to creat a VLAN 56.

Task 3: Document the Switch Configurations

On each switch, capture the running configuration to a text file and save it for future reference. These scripts can be edited to expedite configuring switches in future labs.

Task 4: Clean Up

Unless directed otherwise by your instructor, erase the configurations and reload the switches. Disconnect and store the cabling. For PC hosts that are normally connected to other networks (such as the school LAN or to the Internet), reconnect the appropriate cabling and restore the TCP/IP settings.

Packet Tracer Companion: Troubleshooting VLAN Configurations (3.5.3)

You can now open the file LSG03-Lab353.pka on the CD-ROM that accompanies this book to repeat this hands-on lab using Packet Tracer. Remember, however, that Packet Tracer is not a substitute for a hands-on lab experience with real equipment.

Packet Tracer Skills Integration Challenge

Open the file LSG03-PTSkills3.pka on the CD-ROM that accompanies this book. You will use the topology in Figure 3-7 and the addressing table in Table 3-10 to document your design.

Figure 3-7   Packet Tracer Skills Integration Challenge Topology

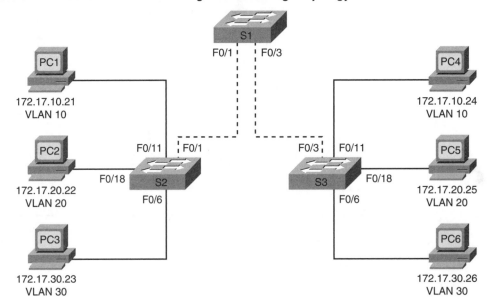

Table 3-10   Addressing Table for the Packet Tracer Skills Integration Challenge Activity

Device	Interface	IP Address	Subnet Mask	Default Gateway
S1	VLAN 99	172.17.99.31	255.255.255.0	172.17.99.1
S2	VLAN 99	172.17.99.32	255.255.255.0	172.17.99.1
S3	VLAN 99	172.17.99.33	255.255.255.0	172.17.99.1
PC1	NIC	172.17.10.21	255.255.255.0	172.17.10.1
PC2	NIC	172.17.20.22	255.255.255.0	172.17.20.1
PC3	NIC	172.17.30.23	255.255.255.0	172.17.30.1
PC4	NIC	172.17.10.24	255.255.255.0	172.17.10.1
PC5	NIC	172.17.20.25	255.255.255.0	172.17.20.1
PC6	NIC	172.17.30.26	255.255.255.0	172.17.30.1

Learning Objectives

Upon completion of this lab, you will be able to

- Add and connect switches

- Add and connect PCs

- Verify basic device configuration and connectivity

- Configure and verify port security

- Configure VLANs on the switches

- Configure trunks on the switches

- Verify end-to-end connectivity

Introduction

In this activity, you will connect and completely configure the Chapter 3 topology, including adding and connecting devices and configuring security and VLANs.

Task 1: Add and Connect the Switches

Step 1.   Add the S2 switch.

S2 must be a 2960 series switch. Change the display name and hostname to **S2**. Names are case sensitive.

Step 2.   Connect S2 to S1.

Connect S2 Fa0/1 to S1 Fa0/1.

Step 3.   Add the S3 switch.

S3 must be a 2960 series switch. Change the display name and hostname to **S3**. Names are case sensitive.

Step 4.   Connect S3 to S1.

Connect S3 Fa0/3 to S1 Fa0/3.

Step 5.   Check results.

Your completion percentage should be 9 percent. If not, click **Check Results** to see which required components are not yet completed.

Task 2: Add and Connect the PCs

Step 1.   Add PC1, PC2, PC3, PC4, PC5, and PC6:

- Add the six PCs according to the chapter topology.

- If necessary, change the display name to match the names in the addressing table. Display names are case sensitive.

Step 2.   Connect PC1, PC2, and PC3 to S2:

- Connect PC1 to Fa0/11 on S2.

- Connect PC2 to Fa0/18 on S2.

- Connect PC3 to Fa0/6 on S2.

Step 3.   Connect PC4, PC5, and PC6 to S3:

- Connect PC4 to Fa0/11 on S3.

- Connect PC5 to Fa0/18 on S3.

- Connect PC6 to Fa0/6 on S3.

Step 4.   Check results.

Your completion percentage should be 29 percent. If not, click **Check Results** to see which required components are not yet completed.

Task 3: Configure Devices and Verify Connectivity

Step 1.   Configure switches with basic commands.

Configure each switch with the following basic settings. Packet Tracer only grades the **hostname** command.

- Hostname on S1

- Banner

- Enable secret password

- Line configurations

- Service encryption

Step 2.   Configure the management VLAN interface on S1, S2, and S3.

Configure VLAN 99 as the management VLAN interface on S1, S2, and S3. This interface is not active until after trunking is configured later in the activity. However, activate the interface at this time with the appropriate command.

Step 3.   Configure PC IP addressing.

Configure the PCs with IP addressing according to the addressing table.

Step 4.   Verify that PCs on the same subnet can ping each other.

Use the Add Simple PDU tool to create pings between PCs on the same VLAN. Verify that the following PCs can ping each other:

- PC1 to PC4

- PC2 to PC5

- PC3 to PC6

Step 5.   In simulation mode, observe the broadcast traffic:

- Clear the learned MAC addresses so that the switches must broadcast ping packets.

- In simulation mode, observe the broadcast traffic that propagates throughout the LAN until the switches learn the ports of each PC.

Step 6.   Check results.

Your completion percentage should be 53 percent. If not, click **Check Results** to see which required components are not yet completed.

Task 4: Configure and Verify Port Security

Step 1.   Configure access links with port security.

Normally, you configure port security on all access ports or shut down the port if it is not in use. Use the following policy to establish port security just on the ports used by the PCs:

- Set the port to access mode.

- Enable port security.

- Allow only one MAC address.

- Configure the first learned MAC address to "stick" to the configuration.

- Set the port to shut down if there is a security violation.

Force the switches to learn the MAC addresses by sending pings across all three switches.

Note: Only enabling port security is graded by Packet Tracer. However, all the port security tasks listed above are required to complete this activity.

Step 2.   Verify port security is active for the interfaces attached to PCs.

What command would you use to verify that port security is active on an interface?

```
Port Security                  : Enabled
Port Status                    : Secure-up
Violation Mode                 : Shutdown
Aging Time                     : 0 mins
Aging Type                     : Absolute
SecureStatic Address Aging     : Disabled
Maximum MAC Addresses          : 1
Total MAC Addresses            : 1
Configured MAC Addresses       : 1
Sticky MAC Addresses           : 0
Last Source Address:Vlan       : 0050.0F00.6668:1
Security Violation Count       : 0
```

Note: The **Last Source Address:Vlan** information should show a MAC address. Your MAC address may be different from the one shown here. If the MAC address in this field is 0000.0000.0000, send traffic to the port by pinging across the switch to the other PC on the same subnet.

Step 3.   Test port security:

- Connect PC2 to the port of PC3, and connect PC3 to the port of PC2.

- Send pings between PCs on the same subnet.

- The ports for PC2 and PC3 should shut down.

Step 4.   Verify that ports are err-disabled and that a security violation has been logged.

What command shows the following output?

```
FastEthernet0/6 is down, line protocol is down (err-disabled)
   Hardware is Lance, address is 000a.41e8.c906 (bia 000a.41e8.c906)
<output omitted>
```

What command shows the following output?

```
Port Security                  : Enabled
Port Status                    : Secure-shutdown
Violation Mode                 : Shutdown
Aging Time                     : 0 mins
Aging Type                     : Absolute
SecureStatic Address Aging     : Disabled
Maximum MAC Addresses          : 1
Total MAC Addresses            : 1
Configured MAC Addresses       : 1
Sticky MAC Addresses           : 0
Last Source Address:Vlan       : 0050.0F00.6668:1
Security Violation Count       : 1
```

Step 5.   Reconnect PCs to the correct port and clear port security violations:

- Connect PC2 and PC3 back to the correct port.

- Clear the port security violation.

- Verify that PC2 and PC3 can send pings across S2.

Step 6.   Check results.

Your completion percentage should be 75 percent. If not, click **Check Results** to see which required components are not yet completed.

Task 5: Configure VLANs on the Switches

Step 1.   Create and name the VLANs.

Create and name the following VLANs on the switches S1, S2, and S3:

- VLAN 10, name = **Faculty/Staff**

- VLAN 20, name = **Students**

- VLAN 30, name = **Guest(Default)**

- VLAN 99, name = **Management&Native**

Step 2.   Assign access ports to the VLANs.

Assign the following PC access ports to the VLANs:

- VLAN 10: PC1 and PC4

- VLAN 20: PC2 and PC5

- VLAN 30: PC3 and PC6

Step 3.   Verify VLAN implementation.

What command verifies the VLAN configuration, including the port assignments?

```
VLAN  Name               Status    Ports
--    ------------------ ------    ------------------------
1     default            active    Fa0/1, Fa0/2, Fa0/3, Fa0/4
                                   Fa0/5, Fa0/7, Fa0/8, Fa0/9
                                   Fa0/10, Fa0/12, Fa0/13, Fa0/14
                                   Fa0/15, Fa0/16, Fa0/17, Fa0/19
                                   Fa0/20, Fa0/21, Fa0/22, Fa0/23
                                   Fa0/24, Gig1/1, Gig1/2
10    Faculty/Staff      active    Fa0/11
20    Students           active    Fa0/18
30    Guest(Default)     active    Fa0/6
99    Management&Native  active
<output omitted>
```

Step 4.   Check results.

Your completion percentage should be 92 percent. If not, click **Check Results** to see which required components are not yet completed.

Task 6: Configure Trunks on the Switches

Step 1.   Configure trunking on the appropriate interfaces:

- Configure trunking on the appropriate interfaces on switch S1.

- Verify that switches S2 and S3 are now in trunking mode.

- Manually configure the appropriate interfaces on S2 and S3 for trunking.

- Configure VLAN 99 as the native VLAN for all trunks.

Step 2.   Test connectivity

After the switch trunk ports transition to the forwarding state (green link lights), you should be able to successfully ping between PCs on the same VLAN.

Step 3.   Check results.

Your completion percentage should be 100 percent. If not, click **Check Results** to see which required components are not yet completed.

As the size of the network for a small or medium-sized business grows, the management involved in maintaining the network grows. The exercises and labs in this chapter explore how you can use the VLAN Trunking Protocol (VTP) to simplify management of the VLAN database across multiple switches.

The Study Guide portion of this chapter uses a combination of matching, fill-in-the-blank, open-ended question, and Packet Tracer exercises to test your knowledge of VLAN concepts and configurations.

The Labs and Activities portion of this chapter includes all the online curriculum labs to ensure that you have mastered the hands-on skills needed to understand VTP management and configuration.

As you work through this chapter, use Chapter 4 in *LAN Switching and Wireless, CCNA Exploration Companion Guide* or use the corresponding Chapter 4 in the Exploration LAN Switching and Wireless online curriculum for assistance.

Study Guide

VTP Concepts

As the number of switches increases on a small or medium-sized business network, the overall administration required to manage VLANs and trunks in a network becomes a challenge. Cisco engineers invented the VLAN Trunking Protocol (VTP), a technology that helps network administrators automate some of the tasks related to VLAN creation, deletion, and synchronization.

Vocabulary Exercise: Matching

Match the definition on the left with a term on the right. All definitions and terms are used exactly one time.

Definitions

a. Switches share VLAN information; boundary is defined by a Layer 3 device.

b. Can only create, delete, and modify local VLANs.

c. Advertises VLAN configuration information; can create, delete, and modify VLANs.

d. Restricts broadcast traffic to those trunks that must be used to reach the destination devices.

e. Stores VLAN information only in RAM.

f. Carries VLAN configuration information.

Terms

___ VTP advertisements

___ VTP client

___ VTP domain

___ VTP pruning

___ VTP server

___ VTP transparent

Vocabulary Exercise: Completion

VTP allows a network manager to configure a switch so that it will propagate _____ configurations to other switches in the network. The switch can be configured in the role of a VTP _____ or a VTP _____ or in the VTP _____ mode. VTP learns about only _____ VLANs (VLAN IDs 1 to 1005). _____ VLANs (IDs greater than 1005) are not supported by VTP.

VTP allows a network manager to make changes on a switch that is configured as a VTP _____. This switch then distributes and synchronizes VLAN information to VTP-enabled switches throughout the switched network. VTP stores VLAN configurations in the _____.

After a trunk is established between VTP-enabled switches, VTP _____ are exchanged between the switches.

In what circumstance would VTP advertisements not be exchanged between a VTP server and client?

_____

List four benefits VTP offers network managers:

- _____

- _____

- _____

- _____

There are number of key components that you need to be familiar with when learning about VTP:

- _____: Consists of one or more interconnected switches. A router or Layer 3 switch defines the boundary.

- _____: Distributed to synchronize the VLAN configuration across a VTP domain.

- _____: Advertises the VTP domain VLAN information to other VTP-enabled switches in the same VTP domain. These switches can create, delete, or modify VLANs for the domain and store the VLAN information for the entire domain in NVRAM.

- _____: Cannot create, change, or delete VLANs. These switches store VLAN information only while the switch is on. A switch reset deletes the VLAN information.

- _____: Forward VTP advertisements to VTP clients and VTP servers, but do not originate or otherwise process VTP advertisements. VLANs that are created, deleted, or modified are local to that switch only.

- _____: Increases available network bandwidth by restricting flooded traffic to trunk links that the traffic must use to reach the destination devices. Enable this VTP feature using the _____ global configuration command only on one VTP _____ switch in the domain.

VTP Concepts and Modes Exercise

Complete the following fill-in-the-blank statements about basic VTP concepts and modes.

1. VTP is an acronym for _____.

2. VTP is a Layer _____ messaging protocol that maintains VLAN configuration consistency by managing the addition, deletion, and renaming of VLANs across multiple Cisco switches in a network.

3. VTP is a _____ protocol available only on Cisco switches.

4. In VTP _____ mode, you can create, modify, and delete VLANs for the entire VTP domain.

5. In VTP _____ mode, the switch does not participate in VTP. However, the switch does forward VTP _____ through _____ interfaces.

6. In VTP _____ mode, you cannot create, modify, or delete VLANs.

7. In VTP _____ mode, VLAN configurations are not saved in NVRAM.

8. VTP _____ mode allows you to create, modify, and delete VLANs on the single switch without affecting the rest of the switches in your network.

9. VTP _____ mode is the default mode for a Cisco switch.

VTP Operation

The exercises in this section delve into the operation of VTP, including the default VTP configuration, VTP domains, VTP messaging, VTP modes, and VTP troubleshooting.

VTP Operations Exercise

Default VTP Configuration

A Catalyst switch comes from the factory with default settings. The default VTP settings are as follows:

- VTP Version: _____

- VTP Domain Name: _____

- VTP Mode: _____

- Configuration Revision: _____

- VLANs: _____

What version of VTP is not currently supported on Catalyst switches?

_____

What version of VTP is configured by default?

_____

What command displays the following output?

```
S1#_____

VTP Version                      : 2

Configuration Revision           : 0

Maximum VLANs supported locally  : 255

Number of existing VLANs         : 5

VTP Operating Mode               : Server

VTP Domain Name                  :

VTP Pruning Mode                 : Disabled

VTP V2 Mode                      : Disabled

VTP Traps Generation             : Disabled
```

```
MD5 digest                        : 0x3F 0x37 0x45 0x9A 0x37 0x53 0xA6 0xDE
Configuration last modified by 0.0.0.0 at 3-1-93 00:14:07
```

VTP Domains

For a VTP server or client switch to participate in a VTP-enabled network, it must be a part of the same VTP _____ or the server and switch will not exchange VTP messages.

VTP Advertising

VTP advertisements (or messages) distribute VTP domain name and VLAN configuration changes to VTP-enabled switches. A VTP frame consists of a _____ field and a _____ field. The VTP information is inserted into the _____ field of an _____ frame. The Ethernet frame is then encapsulated as a _____ frame. Each switch in the domain sends periodic advertisements out of each trunk port to a reserved _____ address. These advertisements are received by neighboring switches, which update their _____ and _____ configurations as necessary.

The following key fields are present when a VTP frame is encapsulated:

- **Destination MAC address:** This address is set to _____, which is the reserved _____ address for all VTP messages.

- **LLC field:** Logical link control (LLC) field contains a destination service access point (DSAP) and a source service access point (SSAP) set to the value of _____.

- **SNAP field:** Subnetwork Access Protocol (SNAP) field has an OUI set to _____ and type set to _____.

- **VTP header field:** The contents vary depending on the VTP message type—_____, _____, or _____—but it always contains these VTP fields:

    - _____

    - _____

    - _____

    - _____

- **VTP message field:** Varies depending on the message type.

The configuration revision number is a _____-bit number that indicates the level of revision for a VTP frame. The default configuration revision number for a switch is _____. Each time a VLAN is added or removed, the configuration revision number _____.

What effect does changing the VTP domain name have on the configuration revision number?

_____

What is the main purpose for having a VTP configuration revision number?

_____

_____

VTP uses advertisements to distribute and synchronize information about domains and VLAN configurations. Each type of VTP advertisement sends information about several parameters used by VTP.

_____ advertisements comprise the majority of VTP advertisement traffic. This type contains the VTP domain name, the current revision number, and some other VTP configuration details. These advertisements are sent:

- Every _____ by a VTP _____ or _____ to inform neighboring VTP-enabled switches of the current VTP _____ for its VTP domain

- Immediately after a _____ has been made

A _____ advertisement contains VLAN information. What will trigger this advertisement type?

_____

- _____
- _____
- _____
- _____

_____ advertisements are sent with a VTP server as the intended recipient of the multicast message. The VTP server responds by sending a _____ advertisement and then a _____ advertisement.

When is this advertisement type sent?

_____

- _____
- _____
  _____
- _____
- _____

VTP Modes

Finish Table 4-1 by first indicating the VTP mode and then answering **Yes** or **No** for each of the features listed.

Table 4-1   VTP Mode Comparisons

Feature	_____ Mode	_____ Mode	_____ Mode
Source VTP messages	___	___	___
Listen to VTP messages	___	___	___
Create VLANs	Yes	No	Yes*
Remember VLANs	___	___	___

*Locally significant only

Internet Research: VTP

At Cisco.com, you will find a very thorough review of VTP, including common configuration errors and troubleshooting techniques. Use the following link to access this VTP lesson online. When you are done, answer the questions that follow.

http://www.cisco.com/warp/public/473/vtp_flash/

Introduction to VTP

VTP is a Layer _____ messaging protocol used to maintain _____ configuration consistency by managing the _____, _____, and _____ of _____ on a network-wide basis.

In a network with six switches and VLANs that are shared across switches, what would you have to do if you did not use VTP?

_____

A VTP frame consists of a VTP _____ and a VTP _____ type. The VTP information is inserted in the _____ portion of an Ethernet frame.

What kind of address do VTP messages use?

_____

How often are summary advertisements sent and what is their purpose?

_____

_____

_____

What does an Advertisement request cause to happen?

_____

VTP Domain and VTP Modes

When a switch has been cleared and rebooted, it has the following VTP configuration:

- VTP Domain Name = _____

- VTP Mode = _____

- Config Revision = _____

- VLANs = _____

The VTP _____ can add, delete, or rename VLANs. It also advertises the _____ name, the _____ configuration, and _____ number to all other switches in the VTP domain. It also maintains a list of all VLANs in _____ so it can retrieve this information if the switch is reset.

A VTP _____ cannot add, delete, or rename VLANs. It does not store VLANs in _____.

Switches in VTP _____ mode must have their VLANs configured manually. They do not participate in VTP or advertise their VLAN configuration. When is it useful to configure a switch in this mode?

_____

_____

Before VLANs will be advertised by the VTP server, you must configure a domain name.

Assume that VLANs 10, 20, and 30 have been added to a VTP server with appropriate names. What is the configuration revision number?

_____

Now assume that the name for VLAN 10 is changed, VLAN 30 is deleted, and VLAN 40 is added. What is the configuration revision number?

_____

List the three types of trunk links that VTP messages will be sent across:

_____

What MAC address are VTP messages sent to?

_____

Assume you configure six VLANs on a VTP transparent switch. What would be the configuration revision number?

_____

In what situations will a VTP transparent switch forward VTP messages to other switches?

_____

Common VTP Issues

Assuming a new switch was configured with the correct domain name, what would happen if you added a VTP client or server switch with a higher configuration revision number to the network?

_____

_____

_____

_____

_____

_____

List three possible ways to reset the configuration revision number on a switch. (Only two methods are discussed in the presentation. Can you think of another way?)

_____

_____

_____

VTP Scenario

In Figure 4-1, S2 failed and is being replaced. The network administrator acquired the S3 switch from another area of the network where it was no longer in use. The administrator erased the configuration of the S3 device and applied the configuration from the old S2 device so that VLAN port assignments would be reapplied. The administrator also added the VTP domain name and set the VTP mode to client. However, when the S3 device was connected to S1 and trunking was restored, all the ports in VLANs 10, 20, and 30 transitioned to the inactive state. Read through all questions before answering.

Figure 4-1   Topology for VTP Scenario

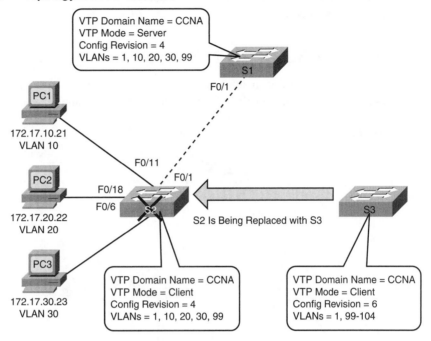

1. After the S2 device is replaced with the S3 device and the trunk links are established, what will be the configuration revision number and VLAN information for switches S1 and S3?

_____

2. Indicate whether each of the following statements is true or false:

    ■ _____: Only subset advertisements contain the configuration revision number.

    ■ _____: Only summary advertisements contain the configuration revision number.

    ■ _____: All VTP messages contain the configuration revision number.

    ■ _____: Higher configuration revision numbers take precedence over lower configuration revision numbers.

    ■ _____: Lower configuration revision numbers take precedence over higher configuration revision numbers.

3. What solution is appropriate to resolve the VLAN configuration discrepancies for the VTP domain and restore connectivity for the PC1, PC2, and PC3 devices?

_____

4. What two methods avoid unintentional VLAN database corruption when adding a new switch?

    ■ _____
    _____

    ■ _____

Configure VTP

Often in computer networking the underlying concepts and processes of a given protocol are complicated, but the configuration is relatively simple. This is the case for VTP, as you will see in the exercises in this section.

VTP Configuration Exercise

VTP configuration is straightforward, so this exercise uses a rather large topology, shown in Figure 4-2, to give you extra practice. Table 4-2 shows the addressing scheme used for this exercise.

Figure 4-2   VTP Configuration Topology

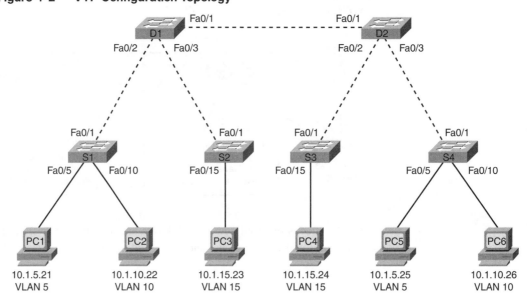

Table 4-2   Addressing Table for VTP Configuration Exercise

Device	Interface	IP Address	Subnet Mask	Default Gateway
D1	VLAN 99	10.1.1.1	255.255.255.0	N/A
D2	VLAN 99	10.1.1.2	255.255.255.0	N/A
S1	VLAN 99	10.1.1.11	255.255.255.0	N/A
S2	VLAN 99	10.1.1.12	255.255.255.0	N/A
S3	VLAN 99	10.1.1.13	255.255.255.0	N/A
S4	VLAN 99	10.1.1.14	255.255.255.0	N/A
PC1	NIC	10.1.5.21	255.255.255.0	10.1.5.1
PC2	NIC	10.1.10.22	255.255.255.0	10.1.10.1
PC3	NIC	10.1.15.23	255.255.255.0	10.1.15.1
PC4	NIC	10.1.15.24	255.255.255.0	10.1.15.1
PC5	NIC	10.1.5.25	255.255.255.0	10.1.5.1
PC6	NIC	10.1.10.26	255.255.255.0	10.1.10.1

Specifications for configuring VLANs and VTP are as follows:

- D1 is responsible for sending VLAN configuration information to all other switches.
- The other switches are clients.
- The domain is **CCNA**.
- The password is **cisco**.
- The VLANs are as follows:
    - VLAN 5: Engineering
    - VLAN 10: Sales
    - VLAN 15: Administration
    - VLAN 99: Management

Enter the commands, including the switch prompt, to configure D1 as the VTP server:

_____
_____
_____
_____
_____
_____
_____
_____
_____
_____
_____

Enter the commands, including the switch prompt, to configure the remaining switches as VTP clients. You need to list the commands only once.

_____
_____
_____

What command displays the following output? Also, indicate which switch this output is from.

```
D1#_____
VTP Version                        : 2
Configuration Revision             : 8
Maximum VLANs supported locally : 64
Number of existing VLANs           : 9
VTP Operating Mode                 : Server
VTP Domain Name                    : CCNA
VTP Pruning Mode                   : Disabled
VTP V2 Mode                        : Disabled
VTP Traps Generation               : Disabled
MD5 digest                         : 0xA0 0xA3 0xB8 0xC9 0x49 0xE2 0x44 0xA6
```

```
Configuration last modified by 0.0.0.0 at 3-1-93 00:12:32
Local updater ID is 10.1.1.1 on interface Vl99 (lowest numbered VLAN interface found)
```

You need to configure another switch for the **CCNA** domain and you forgot the VTP password. How would you find out what the password is?

_____

_____

_____

_____

Packet Tracer Exercise 4-1: VTP Configuration

Now you are ready to use Packet Tracer to apply your answers to the "VTP Configuration Exercise." Open file LSG03-0401.pka on the CD-ROM that accompanies this book to perform this exercise using Packet Tracer.

Note: The following instructions are also contained within the Packet Tracer Exercise.

Learning Objectives

Upon completion of this Packet Tracer Exercise, you will be able to

- Configure VTP

- Configure VLANs

- Configure trunking and verify VTP status

- Assign VLANs to access ports

- Verify connectivity

- Save the Packet Tracer file

Scenario

In this exercise, you will practice configuring VTP and VLANs and establishing trunk links. In addition, you will assign VLANs to access ports and then test connectivity between devices on the same VLAN. The PCs are already configured with IP addressing. The switches have a basic configuration. The passwords are **cisco** for user EXEC mode and **class** for privileged EXEC mode. Use your answers from the "VTP Configuration Exercise" to complete the tasks.

Task 1: Configure VTP

Step 1.   Configure VTP on the switches. Do not configure VLANs yet.

Step 2.   Your completion percentage should be 19 percent. If not, click **Check Results** to see which required components are not yet completed.

Task 2: Configure VLANs

Step 1.   Configure VLANs on the server only.

Step 2.   Your completion percentage should be 24 percent. If not, click **Check Results** to see which required components are not yet completed.

Task 3: Configure Trunking and Verify VTP Status

Step 1. Configure trunking between the switches. Assign VLAN 99 as the native VLAN. The mode must be set for trunking and the links activated.

Step 2. Wait for the link lights between the switches to transition to green, then test connectivity between the switches.

Step 3. Using the **show vtp status** and **show vlan brief** commands, verify the following:

- D1 should show server status.

- The remaining switches should show client status.

- The remaining switches should have VLANs from D1.

Note: VTP advertisements are flooded throughout the management domain every 5 minutes or whenever a change occurs in VLAN configurations. To accelerate this process, you can switch between Realtime mode and Simulation mode until the next round of updates. However, you may have to do this multiple times, because this will only forward Packet Tracer's clock by 10 seconds each time. Alternatively, you can change one of the client switches to transparent mode and then back to client mode.

Step 4. Your completion percentage should be 80 percent. If not, click **Check Results** to see which required components are not yet completed.

Task 4: Assign VLANs to Access Ports

Step 1. Configure access ports and assign VLANs for the PCs. Be sure to activate the links.

Step 2. Your completion percentage should be 100 percent. If not, click **Check Results** to see which required components are not yet completed.

Task 5: Verify Connectivity

All switches should now be able to ping each other. PCs belonging to the same VLAN should be able to ping each other. You can test connectivity using the **ping** command or by creating simple PDUs between devices. Alternatively, you can click **Check Results** and then the **Connectivity Tests** tab. The status of all seven connectivity tests should be listed as Correct.

Task 6: Save the Packet Tracer File

Save your Packet Tracer file as LSG03-00401-end.pka.

Labs and Activities

Command Reference

In Table 4-3, record the command, *including the correct prompt*, that fits the description. Fill in any blanks with the appropriate missing information.

Table 4-3   Commands for VTP Configuration

Command	Description
	Displays the current VTP settings, including the configuration revision number, number of existing VLANs, and VTP operating mode
	Enables VTP pruning
	Configures the switch as the VTP server; other modes include _____ and _____
	Changes the null VTP domain to CCNA
	Configures cisco123 as the VTP password
	Changes to VTP version 2
	Displays the VTP statistics, including the number of VTP advertisements sent and received

Lab 4-1: Basic VTP Configuration (4.4.1)

Figure 4-3 shows the topology diagram for this lab.

Figure 4-3   Topology Diagram for Lab 4-1

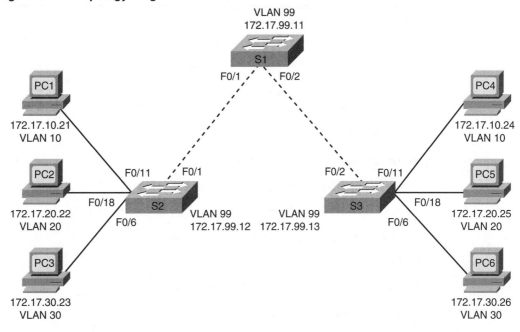

Table 4-4 shows the addressing scheme used in this lab.

Table 4-4   Addressing Table for Lab 4-1

Device	Interface	IP Address	Subnet Mask	Default Gateway
S1	VLAN 99	172.17.99.11	255.255.255.0	N/A
S2	VLAN 99	172.17.99.12	255.255.255.0	N/A
S3	VLAN 99	172.17.99.13	255.255.255.0	N/A
PC1	NIC	172.17.10.21	255.255.255.0	172.17.10.1
PC2	NIC	172.17.20.22	255.255.255.0	172.17.20.1
PC3	NIC	172.17.30.23	255.255.255.0	172.17.30.1
PC4	NIC	172.17.10.24	255.255.255.0	172.17.10.1
PC5	NIC	172.17.20.25	255.255.255.0	172.17.20.1
PC6	NIC	172.17.30.26	255.255.255.0	172.17.30.1

Table 4-5 shows the port assignments used in this lab.

Table 4-5   Initial Port Assignments (Switches 2 and 3)

Ports	Assignment	Network
Fa0/1–0/5	802.1Q Trunks (Native VLAN 99)	172.17.99.0 /24
Fa0/6–0/10	VLAN 30—Guest (Default)	172.17.30.0 /24
Fa0/11–0/17	VLAN 10—Faculty/Staff	172.17.10.0 /24
Fa0/18–0/24	VLAN 20—Students	172.17.20.0 /24

Learning Objectives

Upon completion of this lab, you will be able to

- Cable a network according to the topology diagram
- Erase the startup configuration and reload a switch to the default state
- Perform basic configuration tasks on a switch
- Configure VTP on all switches
- Enable trunking on inter-switch connections
- Verify trunk configuration
- Modify VTP modes and observe the impact
- Create VLANs on the VTP server, and distribute this VLAN information to switches in the network
- Explain the differences in operation between VTP transparent mode, server mode, and client mode
- Assign switch ports to the VLANs
- Save the VLAN configuration
- Enable VTP pruning on the network
- Explain how pruning reduces unnecessary broadcast traffic on the LAN

Task 1: Prepare the Network

Step 1.   Cable a network that is similar to the one shown in Figure 4-3.

You do not need to connect any PCs at this time. You can use any current switch in your lab as long as it has the required interfaces shown in the topology.

Note: If you use 2900 or 2950 switches, the outputs may appear different. Also, certain commands may be different or unavailable.

Step 2.   Clear any existing configurations on the switches.

If necessary, refer to Appendix 1 in "Lab 2-1: Basic Switch Configuration (2.5.1)" for the procedure to clear switch configurations and VLANs. Use the **show vlan** command to confirm that only default VLANs exist and that all ports are assigned to VLAN 1:

```
Switch#show vlan
```

```
VLAN  Name                             Status    Ports
----  -------------------------------  --------  ------------------------------
1     default                          active    Fa0/1, Fa0/2, Fa0/3, Fa0/4
                                                 Fa0/5, Fa0/6, Fa0/7, Fa0/8
                                                 Fa0/9, Fa0/10, Fa0/11, Fa0/12
                                                 Fa0/13, Fa0/14, Fa0/15, Fa0/16
                                                 Fa0/17, Fa0/18, Fa0/19, Fa0/20
                                                 Fa0/21, Fa0/22, Fa0/23, Fa0/24
                                                 Gig1/1, Gig1/2
1002  fddi-default                     active
1003  token-ring-default               active
1004  fddinet-default                  active
1005  trnet-default                    active
```

Step 3.   Disable all ports.

Unlike routers, Cisco switch ports are in the "up" state by default. It is a good practice to disable any unused ports on the switches with the **shutdown** command:

```
Switch#config term
Switch(config)#interface range fa0/1-24
Switch(config-if-range)#shutdown
Switch(config-if-range)#interface range gi0/1-2
Switch(config-if-range)#shutdown
```

Task 2: Perform Basic Switch Configurations

Step 1.   Configure the switches according to the following guidelines:

- Configure the switch hostname.

- Disable DNS lookup.

- Configure an EXEC mode password of **class**.

- Configure a password of **cisco** for console connections.

- Configure a password of **cisco** for vty connections.

Step 2.   Reenable the user ports on S2 and S3:

```
S2(config)#interface range fa0/6, fa0/11, fa0/18
S2(config-if-range)#switchport mode access
S2(config-if-range)#no shutdown
```

```
S3(config)#interface range fa0/6, fa0/11, fa0/18
S3(config-if-range)#switchport mode access
S3(config-if-range)#no shutdown
```

Task 3: Configure and Activate Ethernet Interfaces

Configure the PCs. You can complete this lab using only two PCs by simply changing the IP addressing for the two PCs specific to a test you want to conduct. For example, if you want to test connectivity between PC1 and PC2, then configure the IP addresses for those PCs by referring to Table 4-4 at the beginning of the lab. Alternatively, you can configure all six PCs with the IP addresses and default gateways.

Task 4: Configure VTP on the Switches

VTP allows the network administrator to control the instances of VLANs on the network by creating VTP domains. Within each VTP domain, one or more switches are configured as VTP servers. VLANs are then created on the VTP server and pushed to the other switches in the domain. Common VTP configuration tasks include

- Setting the VTP operating mode

- Changing the domain name from **null**

- Configuring a VTP domain password

In this lab, you will configure S1 as the VTP server. S2 and S3 will be configured in VTP client mode or VTP transparent mode depending on the current task.

Step 1.   Check the current VTP settings on the three switches:

```
S1#show vtp status
VTP Version                        : 2
Configuration Revision             : 0
Maximum VLANs supported locally    : 255
Number of existing VLANs           : 5
VTP Operating Mode                 : Server
VTP Domain Name                    :
VTP Pruning Mode                   : Disabled
VTP V2 Mode                        : Disabled
VTP Traps Generation               : Disabled
MD5 digest                         : 0x57 0xCD 0x40 0x65 0x63 0x59 0x47 0xBD
Configuration last modified by 0.0.0.0 at 0-0-00 00:00:00
Local updater ID is 0.0.0.0 (no valid interface found)

S2#show vtp status
VTP Version                        : 2
Configuration Revision             : 0
Maximum VLANs supported locally    : 255
Number of existing VLANs           : 5
VTP Operating Mode                 : Server
VTP Domain Name                    :
VTP Pruning Mode                   : Disabled
VTP V2 Mode                        : Disabled
VTP Traps Generation               : Disabled
MD5 digest                         : 0x57 0xCD 0x40 0x65 0x63 0x59 0x47 0xBD
Configuration last modified by 0.0.0.0 at 0-0-00 00:00:00
Local updater ID is 0.0.0.0 (no valid interface found)

S3#show vtp status
VTP Version                        : 2
```

```
Configuration Revision            : 0
Maximum VLANs supported locally   : 255
Number of existing VLANs          : 5
VTP Operating Mode                : Server
VTP Domain Name                   :
VTP Pruning Mode                  : Disabled
VTP V2 Mode                       : Disabled
VTP Traps Generation              : Disabled
MD5 digest                        : 0x57 0xCD 0x40 0x65 0x63 0x59 0x47 0xBD
Configuration last modified by 0.0.0.0 at 0-0-00 00:00:00
```

✓ Note that all three switches are in server mode. Server mode is the default VTP mode for most Catalyst switches.

Step 2. Configure the operating mode, domain name, and VTP password on all three switches:

old version IOSI
use Vlan database
mode to configurate
the vtp.
S# vlan database.

- Configure S1 as the VTP server, S2 in client mode, and S3 in transparent mode.

- Set the VTP domain name to **Lab4**.

- Configure **cisco** as the VTP password.

```
S1(config)#vtp mode server
Device mode already VTP SERVER.
S1(config)#vtp domain Lab4
Changing VTP domain name from NULL to Lab4
S1(config)#vtp password cisco
Setting device VLAN database password to cisco
S1(config)#end
```

```
S2(config)#vtp mode client
Setting device to VTP CLIENT mode
S2(config)#vtp domain Lab4
Changing VTP domain name from NULL to Lab4
S2(config)#vtp password cisco
Setting device VLAN database password to cisco
S2(config)#end
```

```
S3(config)#vtp mode transparent
Setting device to VTP TRANSPARENT mode.
S3(config)#vtp domain Lab4
Changing VTP domain name from NULL to Lab4
S3(config)#vtp password cisco
Setting device VLAN database password to cisco
S3(config)#end
```

✓ **Note:** The VTP domain name can be learned by a client switch from a server switch, but only if the client switch domain is in the null state. It does not learn a new name if one has been previously set. For that reason, it is good practice to manually configure the domain name on all switches to ensure that the domain name is configured correctly. Switches in different VTP domains do not exchange VLAN information.

VTP passwords are case sensitive. A common error is to configure the password in a different case. To check the VTP password configured, use the **show vtp password** command:

```
S1#show vtp password
VTP Password: cisco
S1#
```

Step 3.   Configure trunking and the native VLAN for the trunking ports on all three switches.

Use the **interface range** command in global configuration mode to simplify this task:

```
S1(config)#interface range fa0/1-5
S1(config-if-range)#switchport mode trunk
S1(config-if-range)#switchport trunk native vlan 99
S1(config-if-range)#no shutdown
S1(config-if-range)#end
```

```
S2(config)#interface range fa0/1-5
S2(config-if-range)#switchport mode trunk
S2(config-if-range)#switchport trunk native vlan 99
S2(config-if-range)#no shutdown
S2(config-if-range)#end
```

```
S3(config)#interface range fa0/1-5
S3(config-if-range)#switchport mode trunk
S3(config-if-range)#switchport trunk native vlan 99
S3(config-if-range)#no shutdown
S3(config-if-range)#end
```

Step 4.   Configure port security on the S2 and S3 access layer switches.

Configure ports Fa0/6, Fa0/11, and Fa0/18 so that they allow only a single host and learn the MAC address of the host dynamically. Configure the port to shut down if there is a port security violation.

```
S2(config)#interface fa0/6
S2(config-if)#switchport port-security
S2(config-if)#switchport port-security maximum 1
S2(config-if)#switchport port-security mac-address sticky
S2(config-if)#switchport port-security violation shutdown
S2(config-if)#interface fa0/11
S2(config-if)#switchport port-security
S2(config-if)#switchport port-security maximum 1
S2(config-if)#switchport port-security mac-address sticky
S2(config-if)#switchport port-security violation shutdown
S2(config-if)#interface fa0/18
S2(config-if)#switchport port-security
S2(config-if)#switchport port-security maximum 1
S2(config-if)#switchport port-security mac-address sticky
```

```
S2(config-if)#switchport port-security violation shutdown
S2(config-if)#end
```

```
S3(config)#interface fa0/6
S3(config-if)#switchport port-security
S3(config-if)#switchport port-security maximum 1
S3(config-if)#switchport port-security mac-address sticky
S3(config-if)#switchport port-security violation shutdown
S3(config-if)#interface fa0/11
S3(config-if)#switchport port-security
S3(config-if)#switchport port-security maximum 1
S3(config-if)#switchport port-security mac-address sticky
S3(config-if)#switchport port-security violation shutdown
S3(config-if)#interface fa0/18
S3(config-if)#switchport port-security
S3(config-if)#switchport port-security maximum 1
S3(config-if)#switchport port-security mac-address sticky
S3(config-if)#switchport port-security violation shutdown
S3(config-if)#end
```

Step 5. Configure VLANs on the VTP server.

There are four VLANS required in this lab:

- VLAN 99 (Management)

- VLAN 10 (Faculty/Staff)

- VLAN 20 (Students)

- VLAN 30 (Guest)

Configure VLANs only on S1, the VTP server:

```
S1(config)#vlan 99
S1(config-vlan)#name management
S1(config-vlan)#exit
S1(config)#vlan 10
S1(config-vlan)#name faculty/staff
S1(config-vlan)#exit
S1(config)#vlan 20
S1(config-vlan)#name students
S1(config-vlan)#exit
S1(config)#vlan 30
S1(config-vlan)#name guest
S1(config-vlan)#exit
```

Verify that the VLANs have been created on S1 with the **show vlan brief** command.

Step 6.   Check if the VLANs created on S1 have been distributed to S2 and S3.

Use the **show vlan brief** command on S2 and S3 to determine if the VTP server has pushed its VLAN configuration to all the switches:

S2#**show vlan brief**

```
VLAN Name                 Status   Ports
-- ---------------        ----.    --------------
1    default              active   Fa0/1, Fa0/2, Fa0/4, Fa0/5
                                   Fa0/6, Fa0/7, Fa0/8, Fa0/9
                                   Fa0/10, Fa0/11, Fa0/12, Fa0/13
                                   Fa0/14, Fa0/15, Fa0/16, Fa0/17
                                   Fa0/18, Fa0/19, Fa0/20, Fa0/21
                                   Fa0/22, Fa0/23, Fa0/24, Gi0/1
                                   Gi0/2
10   faculty/staff        active
20   students             active
30   guest                active
99   management           active
```

S3#**show vlan brief**

```
VLAN Name                 Status   Ports
-- ---------------        ----.    --------------
1    default              active   Fa0/1, Fa0/2, Fa0/4, Fa0/5
                                   Fa0/6, Fa0/7, Fa0/8, Fa0/9
                                   Fa0/10, Fa0/11, Fa0/12, Fa0/13
                                   Fa0/14, Fa0/15, Fa0/16, Fa0/17
                                   Fa0/18, Fa0/19, Fa0/20, Fa0/21
                                   Fa0/22, Fa0/23, Fa0/24, Gi0/1
                                   Gi0/2
1002 fddi-default         act/unsup
1003 token-ring-default   act/unsup
1004 fddinet-default      act/unsup
1005 trnet-default        act/unsup
```

Are the same VLANs configured on all switches? ___Yes___

Explain why S2 and S3 have different VLAN configurations at this point:

Because S2 serve as a client and S3 as a transparent

Step 7.   Create a new VLAN on S2 and S3:

```
S2(config)#vlan 88
%VTP VLAN configuration not allowed when device is in CLIENT mode.
```

```
S3(config)#vlan 88
S3(config-vlan)#name test
S3(config-vlan)#
```

Why are you prevented from creating a new VLAN on S2 but not on S3?

Because S2 is a client switch and S3 is a transparent switch

Delete VLAN 88 from S3:

```
S3(config)#no vlan 88
```

Step 8.   Manually configure VLANs.

Configure the four VLANs identified in Step 5 on switch S3:

```
S3(config)#vlan 99
S3(config-vlan)#name management
S3(config-vlan)#exit
S3(config)#vlan 10
S3(config-vlan)#name faculty/staff
S3(config-vlan)#exit
S3(config)#vlan 20
S3(config-vlan)#name students
S3(config-vlan)#exit
S3(config)#vlan 30
S3(config-vlan)#name guest
S3(config-vlan)#exit
```

Here you see one of the advantages of VTP. You had to manually configure the VLANs on S3. Manual configuration is tedious and error prone. Any error introduced could prevent intra-VLAN communication. In addition, these types of errors can be difficult to troubleshoot.

Step 9.   Configure the management interface address on all three switches:

```
S1(config)#interface vlan 99
S1(config-if)#ip address 172.17.99.11 255.255.255.0
```

```
S2(config)#interface vlan 99
S2(config-if)#ip address 172.17.99.12 255.255.255.0
```

```
S3(config)#interface vlan 99
S3(config-if)#ip address 172.17.99.13 255.255.255.0
```

Verify that the switches are correctly configured by pinging between them. From S1, ping the management interface on S2 and S3. From S2, ping the management interface on S3.

Were the pings successful?_____yes_____

If not, troubleshoot the switch configurations and try again.

Step 10.   Assign switch ports to VLANs.

Refer to the port assignments in Table 4-5 at the beginning of the lab to assign ports to the VLANs. Use the **interface range** command to simplify this task. Port assignments are not configured through VTP. Port assignments must be configured on each switch manually or dynamically using a VMPS server. The commands are shown for S3 only, but S2 should be similarly configured. Save the configuration when you are done.

```
S3(config)#interface range fa0/6 - 10
S3(config-if-range)#switchport access vlan 30
```

```
S3(config-if-range)#interface range fa0/11 - 17
S3(config-if-range)#switchport access vlan 10
S3(config-if-range)#interface range fa0/18 - 24
S3(config-if-range)#switchport access vlan 20
S3(config-if-range)#end
S3#copy running-config startup-config
Destination filename [startup-config]? [Enter]
Building configuration...
[OK]
S3#
```

Task 5: Configure VTP Pruning on the Switches

VTP pruning allows a VTP server to suppress IP broadcast traffic for specific VLANs to switches that do not have any ports in that VLAN. By default, all unknown unicasts and broadcasts in a VLAN are flooded over the entire VLAN. All switches in the network receive all broadcasts, even in situations in which few users are connected in that VLAN. VTP pruning is used to eliminate or prune this unnecessary traffic. Pruning saves LAN bandwidth because broadcasts do not have to be sent to switches that do not need them.

Pruning is configured on the server switch with the **vtp pruning** command in global configuration mode:

```
S1(config)#vtp pruning
```

The configuration is pushed to client switches. Because S3 is in transparent mode, VTP pruning has no impact.

Confirm VTP pruning configuration on each switch using the **show vtp status** command. VTP pruning mode should be enabled on S1 and S2.

```
S1#show vtp status
VTP Version                     : 2
Configuration Revision          : 5
Maximum VLANs supported locally : 255
Number of existing VLANs        : 9
VTP Operating Mode              : Server
VTP Domain Name                 : Lab4
VTP Pruning Mode                : Enabled
VTP V2 Mode                     : Disabled
VTP Traps Generation            : Disabled
MD5 digest                      : 0x7E 0xE3 0xF6 0x72 0x80 0x6A 0x47 0x1F
Configuration last modified by 172.17.99.11 at 3-1-93 00:39:49
Local updater ID is 172.17.99.11 on interface Vl99 (lowest numbered VLAN interface
    found)
S1#
```

Task 6: Document the Switch Configurations

On each switch, capture the running configuration to a text file and save it for future reference. These scripts can be edited to expedite configuring switches in future labs.

Task 7: Clean Up

Unless directed otherwise by your instructor, erase the configurations and reload the switches. Disconnect and store the cabling. For PC hosts that are normally connected to other networks (such as the school LAN or to the Internet), reconnect the appropriate cabling and restore the TCP/IP settings.

Packet Tracer Companion: Basic VTP Configuration (4.4.1)

You can now open the file LSG03-Lab441.pka on the CD-ROM that accompanies this book to repeat this hands-on lab using Packet Tracer. Remember, however, that Packet Tracer is not a substitute for a hands-on lab experience with real equipment.

Lab 4-2: VTP Configuration Challenge (4.4.2)

Figure 4-4 shows the topology diagram for this lab.

Figure 4-4   Topology Diagram for Lab 4-2

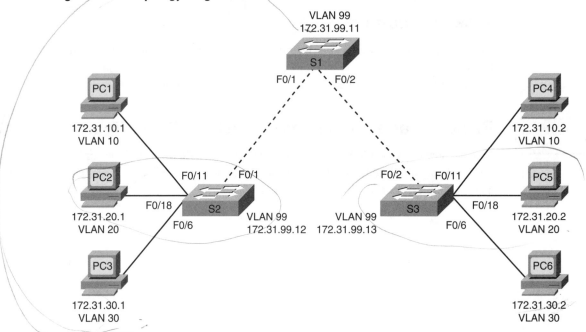

Table 4-6 shows the addressing scheme used in this lab.

Table 4-6   Addressing Table for Lab 4-2

Device	Interface	IP Address	Subnet Mask	Default Gateway
S1	VLAN 99	172.31.99.11	255.255.255.0	N/A
S2	VLAN 99	172.31.99.12	255.255.255.0	N/A
S3	VLAN 99	172.31.99.13	255.255.255.0	N/A
PC1	NIC	172.31.10.1	255.255.255.0	172.31.10.254
PC2	NIC	172.31.20.1	255.255.255.0	172.31.20.254
PC3	NIC	172.31.30.1	255.255.255.0	172.31.30.254
PC4	NIC	172.31.10.2	255.255.255.0	172.31.10.254
PC5	NIC	172.31.20.2	255.255.255.0	172.31.20.254
PC6	NIC	172.31.30.2	255.255.255.0	172.31.30.254

Table 4-7 shows the port assignments used in this lab.

Table 4-7   Initial Port Assignments (Switches 2 and 3)

Ports	Assignment	Network
Fa0/1–0/5	802.1Q Trunks (Native VLAN 99)	172.31.99.0 /24
Fa0/11–0/17	VLAN 10—Engineering	172.31.10.0 /24
Fa0/18–0/24	VLAN 20—Sales	172.31.20.0 /24
Fa0/6–0/10	VLAN 30—Administration	172.31.30.0 /24

Learning Objectives

Upon completion of this lab, you will be able to

- Cable a network according to the topology diagram

- Erase the startup configuration and reload a switch to the default state

- Perform basic configuration tasks on a switch

- Configure VTP on all switches

- Enable trunking on inter-switch connections

- Verify trunk configuration

- Modify VTP modes and observe the impact

- Create VLANs on the VTP server, and distribute this VLAN information to switches in the network

- Explain the differences in operation between VTP transparent mode, server mode, and client mode

- Assign switch ports to the VLANs

- Save the VLAN configuration

Task 1: Prepare the Network

Step 1.   Cable a network that is similar to the one shown in Figure 4-4.

Step 2.   Clear any existing configurations on the switches, and initialize all ports in the shutdown state.

Task 2: Perform Basic Switch Configurations

Step 1.   Configure the switches according to the following guidelines:

- Configure the switch hostname.

- Disable DNS lookup.

- Configure an EXEC mode password of **class**.

- Configure a password of **cisco** for console connections.

- Configure a password of **cisco** for vty connections.

Step 2.   Reenable the user ports on S2 and S3.

Task 3: Configure Host PCs

Configure the PCs. You can complete this lab using only two PCs by simply changing the IP addressing for the two PCs specific to a test you want to conduct. Alternatively, you can configure all six PCs with the IP addresses and default gateways.

Task 4: Configure VTP on the Switches

Step 1.   Check the current VTP settings on the three switches.

What is the current (default) VTP operating mode on the switches? _____*Server*_____

What is the configuration revision on S1 and S2? _*0*__

Step 2.   Configure the operating mode, domain name, and VTP password on all three switches:

- Configure S1 as the VTP server, S2 in client mode, and S3 in transparent mode.

- Set the VTP domain name to **access**.

- Configure **lab4** as the VTP password.

Step 3.   Configure trunking and the native VLAN for the trunking ports on all three switches.

Step 4.   Configure port security on the S2 and S3 access ports.

Configure ports Fa0/6, Fa0/11, and Fa0/18 so that they allow only a single host and learn the MAC address of the host dynamically. Configure the port to shut down if there is a port security violation.

Step 5.   Configure VLANs on the VTP server.

There are four VLANS required in this lab:

- VLAN 99 (Management)  *if more than 2 words, use Colon i.e.*
- VLAN 10 (Engineering) *name "network management"*
- VLAN 20 (Sales)
- VLAN 30 (Administration)

Configure VLANs only on S1, the VTP server. When done, verify that the VLANs have been created on S1.

Step 6.   Check if the VLANs created on S1 have been distributed to S2 and S3.

Are the same VLANs configured on all switches? _____*NO*_____

Explain why S2 and S3 have different VLAN configurations at this point:

_____*Because S2 configured as a client switch and S3*_____
_____*as a transparent switch mode*_____

_____

Step 7.   Manually configure VLANs.

Configure the four VLANs identified in Step 5 on switch S3.

Step 8.   Configure the management interface address on all three switches according to Table 4-6.

Verify that the switches are correctly configured by pinging between them. From S1, ping the management interface on S2 and S3. From S2, ping the management interface on S3.

Were the pings successful? _____

If not, troubleshoot the switch configurations and try again.

Step 9.   Assign switch ports to VLANs.

Refer to the port assignments in Table 4-7 at the beginning of the lab to assign ports to the VLANs. Save the configuration when you are done.

Step 10.   Verify that the trunks are operating correctly.

From PC1, attempt to ping PC4, PC5, and PC6.

Were any of the pings successful?

_____

Why did some of the pings fail?

_____

Which hosts could be reached from PC3?

_____

Task 5: Configure VTP Pruning on the Switches

Configure pruning on the VTP server.

Confirm the VTP pruning configuration was sent to S2.

Task 6: Clean Up

Unless directed otherwise by your instructor, erase the configurations and reload the switches. Disconnect and store the cabling. For PC hosts that are normally connected to other networks (such as the school LAN or to the Internet), reconnect the appropriate cabling and restore the TCP/IP settings.

Packet Tracer Companion: Challenge VTP Configuration (4.4.2)

You can now open the file LSG03-Lab442.pka on the CD-ROM that accompanies this book to repeat this hands-on lab using Packet Tracer. Remember, however, that Packet Tracer is not a substitute for a hands-on lab experience with real equipment.

Lab 4-3: Troubleshooting VTP Configuration (4.4.3)

Learning Objectives

Upon completion of this lab, you will be able to

- Cable a network according to the topology diagram

- Erase the startup configuration and vlan.dat files and reload switches to the default state

- Load the switches with supplied scripts

- Find and correct all configuration errors

- Document the corrected network

Scenario

VTP helps ensure uniform VLAN configurations on your switched network, but it must be configured correctly. In this lab, you will use the supplied scripts to configure S1 as a VTP server, and S2 and S3 as VTP clients. The VTP domain name is **Lab4_3**, and the VTP password is **cisco**. However, there are a number of errors in this configuration that you must troubleshoot and correct before end-to-end connectivity within the VLANs is restored.

You will have successfully resolved all errors when all three switches agree on the VLAN configuration, and you can successfully ping between any two hosts in the same VLAN or between any two switches.

Figure 4-5 shows the topology diagram for this lab.

Figure 4-5   Topology Diagram for Lab 4-3

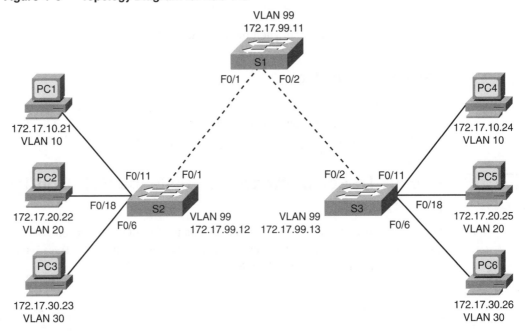

Table 4-8 shows the addressing scheme used in this lab.

Table 4-8   Addressing Table for Lab 4-3

Device	Interface	IP Address	Subnet Mask	Default Gateway
S1	VLAN 99	172.17.99.11	255.255.255.0	N/A
S2	VLAN 99	172.17.99.12	255.255.255.0	N/A
S3	VLAN 99	172.17.99.13	255.255.255.0	N/A
PC1	NIC	172.17.10.21	255.255.255.0	172.17.10.1
PC2	NIC	172.17.20.22	255.255.255.0	172.17.20.1
PC3	NIC	172.17.30.23	255.255.255.0	172.17.30.1
PC4	NIC	172.17.10.24	255.255.255.0	172.17.10.1
PC5	NIC	172.17.20.25	255.255.255.0	172.17.20.1
PC6	NIC	172.17.30.26	255.255.255.0	172.17.30.1

Table 4-9 shows the port assignments used in this lab.

Table 4-9   Initial Port Assignments (Switches 2 and 3)

Ports	Assignment	Network
Fa0/1–0/5	802.1Q Trunks (Native VLAN 99)	172.17.99.0 /24
Fa0/6–0/10	VLAN 30—Guest (Default)	172.17.30.0 /24
Fa0/11–0/17	VLAN 10—Faculty/Staff	172.17.10.0 /24
Fa0/18–0/24	VLAN 20—Students	172.17.20.0 /24

Task 1: Prepare the Network

Step 1.   Cable a network that is similar to the one shown in Figure 4-5.

Step 2.   Clear any existing configurations on the switches.

Step 3.   Configure the Ethernet interfaces on the host PCs.

Step 4.   Apply the following configurations to each switch. Alternatively, you can open the file LSG03-Lab443-Scripts.txt on the CD-ROM that accompanies this book and copy in the scripts for each of the switches.

S1 Beginning Configuration

```
hostname S1
enable secret class
no ip domain-lookup
!
vtp mode server
vtp domain Lab4_3
vtp password Cisco
!
vlan 99
name management
```

[handwritten annotation: wrong password as capital C. ← vtp password cisco]

```
exit
!
vlan 10
name Faculty/Staff
exit
!
vlan 20
name Students
exit
!
vlan 30
name Guest
exit
!
interface FastEthernet0/1
switchport trunk native vlan 99
switchport mode trunk
!
interface FastEthernet0/2
 switchport trunk native vlan 99
 switchport mode access         ←    Switch mode trunk.
!
interface FastEthernet0/3
 switchport trunk native vlan 99
 switchport mode access         ←    Switch mode trunk
interface FastEthernet0/4
 switchport trunk native vlan 99
 switchport mode trunk
!
interface FastEthernet0/5
 switchport trunk native vlan 99
 switchport mode trunk
!
interface range FastEthernet0/6-24    int Range fas 0/6 ← 10
shutdown                                 switchport mode access
!                                          switchport access vlan 30
interface GigabitEthernet0/1                 no shut
shutdown
!                                    . int Range fas 0/11 - 17
interface GigabitEthernet0/2            switchport mode access
shutdown                                  switchport access vlan 10
!                                            no shut.
interface Vlan99        wrong Ip address
```
ip address 172.17.99.11 /24 ip address 179.17.99.11 255.255.255.0
```
 no shutdown                          . int Range fas 0/18 -24
!                                        switchport mode access
line con 0                                switchport access vlan 20
 logging synchronous                        no shut
 password cisco
 login
```

```
line vty 0
 no login                    ← password cisco
line vty 1 4                   login
 password cisco
 login
line vty 5 15
 password cisco
 login
!
end
```

S2 Beginning Configuration

```
hostname S2
!
enable secret class
no ip domain-lookup
!
vtp mode client                          vtp domain Lab4-3
vtp domain Lab4        ← wrong            vtp password cisco
!
interface FastEthernet0/1
 switchport trunk native vlan 99
 switchport mode access     ←    switch mode trunk
!
interface FastEthernet0/2
 switchport trunk native vlan 99
 switchport mode access     ←   switch mode trunk
!
interface FastEthernet0/3
 switchport trunk native vlan 99
 switchport mode trunk
!
interface FastEthernet0/4
 switchport trunk native vlan 99
 switchport mode trunk
!
interface FastEthernet0/5
 switchport trunk native vlan 99
 switchport mode trunk
!
interface range FastEthernet0/6 - 10
 switchport access vlan 10  wrong vlan ← switchport access vlan 30
 switchport mode access
!
interface range FastEthernet0/11 - 17
 switchport access vlan 20  wrong vlan ←   switchport access vlan 10
 switchport mode access
!
interface range FastEthernet0/18 - 24
 switchport access vlan 30  wrong vlan ← switchport access vlan 20
 switchport mode access
!
interface Vlan99
 ip address 172.17.99.12 255.255.255.0
```

```
  no shutdown
  !
  ip http server
  !
  line con 0
    password cisco
   logging synchronous
   login
  line vty 0 4
   password cisco
   login
  line vty 5 15
   password cisco
```

S3 Beginning Configuration

```
hostname S3
!
enable secret class
no ip domain-lookup
!
vtp mode client
vtp domain Lab4          ← wrong          vtp domain Lab4-3
!                                          vtp password cisco
interface FastEthernet0/1
  switchport trunk native vlan 99
  switchport mode trunk
!
interface FastEthernet0/2
  switchport trunk native vlan 99
  switchport mode trunk
!
interface FastEthernet0/3
  switchport trunk native vlan 99
  switchport mode trunk
!
interface FastEthernet0/4
  switchport trunk native vlan 99
  switchport mode trunk
!
interface FastEthernet0/5
  switchport trunk native vlan 99
  switchport mode trunk
!
interface range FastEthernet0/6 - 10
  switchport access vlan 30
  switchport mode access
!
interface range FastEthernet0/11 - 17
  switchport access vlan 10
  switchport mode access
!
interface range FastEthernet0/18 - 24
```

```
 switchport access vlan 20
 switchport mode access
!
interface Vlan99
 ip address 172.17.99.12 255.255.255.0
 no shutdown
!
line con 0
 password cisco
 login
line vty 0 4
 password cisco
 login
line vty 5 15
 password cisco
 login
end
```

(handwritten) ← wrong ip address
ip address 172.17.99.13 255.255.255.0

Task 2: Troubleshoot and Correct VTP and VLAN Configuration

The following is a suggested method for approaching the connectivity problems in the network:

Step 1.   Test connectivity between the switches.

When all errors are corrected, you should be able to freely ping and telnet between S1, S2, and S3.

Do you have connectivity between any of the switches?

_____

If yes, which ones?

Step 2.   Investigate the VLAN and VTP configuration on S1.

What commands can you use to discover errors in the VTP and VLAN configuration?

- *(handwritten)* show vlan brief.   *(handwritten)* show vtp counter
- *(handwritten)* show int trunk
- *(handwritten)* show int fae 0/1 switchport
- *(handwritten)* show vtp status
- _____

Document the errors you discovered, how you discovered them, and solutions you implemented.

(handwritten) For S1.
1. interfaces were not assigned to access mode and into VLAN.
2. interface fas 0/2 need to on trunking mode
3. wrong ip address on the VLAN99 management
4. wrong vtp password as Capital C.

S2:

_____ domain _____ _____

1. wrong Utp domain name as Lab4

2. No Utp password.

3. int fas 0/1 wrong switch port mode as access.
   need change to trunking mode

4. int rang fas 0/6-10 assign to the wrong VLAN
   " 0/11-17 "
   " 0/18-24 "

S3:
1. wrong Utp domain name _____ _____

2. No Utp password

3. wrong management ip address

Task 3: Document the Switch Configurations

On each switch, capture the running configuration to a text file and save it for future reference. These scripts can be edited to expedite configuring switches in future labs.

Task 4: Clean Up

Unless directed otherwise by your instructor, erase the configurations and reload the switches. Disconnect and store the cabling. For PC hosts that are normally connected to other networks (such as the school LAN or to the Internet), reconnect the appropriate cabling and restore the TCP/IP settings.

Packet Tracer Companion: Troubleshooting VTP Configuration (4.4.3)

You can now open the file LSG03-Lab443.pka on the CD-ROM that accompanies this book to repeat this hands-on lab using Packet Tracer. Remember, however, that Packet Tracer is not a substitute for a hands-on lab experience with real equipment.

Packet Tracer Skills Integration Challenge

Open the file LSG03-PTSkills4.pka on the CD-ROM that accompanies this book. You will use the topology in Figure 4-6 and the addressing table in Table 4-10 to document your design.

Figure 4-6   Packet Tracer Skills Integration Challenge Topology

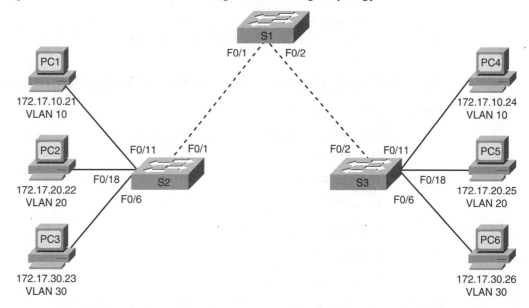

Table 4-10   Addressing Table for the Packet Tracer Skills Integration Challenge Activity

Device	Interface	IP Address	Subnet Mask	Default Gateway
S1	VLAN 99	172.17.99.31	255.255.255.0	172.17.99.1
S2	VLAN 99	172.17.99.32	255.255.255.0	172.17.99.1
S3	VLAN 99	172.17.99.33	255.255.255.0	172.17.99.1
PC1	NIC	172.17.10.21	255.255.255.0	172.17.10.1
PC2	NIC	172.17.20.22	255.255.255.0	172.17.20.1
PC3	NIC	172.17.30.23	255.255.255.0	172.17.30.1
PC4	NIC	172.17.10.24	255.255.255.0	172.17.10.1
PC5	NIC	172.17.20.25	255.255.255.0	172.17.20.1
PC6	NIC	172.17.30.26	255.255.255.0	172.17.30.1

Learning Objectives

Upon completion of this lab, you will be able to

- Configure and verify basic device configurations
- Configure and verify port security
- Configure VTP
- Configure trunking
- Configure VLANs
- Assign VLANs to ports
- Verify end-to-end connectivity

Introduction

In this activity, you will configure switches, including basic configuration, port security, trunking, and VLANs. You will use VTP to advertise the VLAN configurations to other switches.

Task 1: Configure and Verify Basic Device Configurations

Step 1.   Configure basic commands.

Configure each switch with the following basic parameters. Packet Tracer will only grade the **hostname** command.

- Hostname on S1
- Banner
- Enable secret password
- Line configurations
- Service encryption

Step 2.   Configure the management VLAN interface on S1, S2, and S3.

Create and enable interface VLAN 99 on each switch. Use Table 4-10 for address configuration.

Step 3.   Verify that PCs on the same subnet can ping each other.

The PCs are already configured with correct addressing. Create simple PDUs to test connectivity between devices on the same subnet.

Step 4.   Check results.

Your completion percentage should be 15 percent. If not, click **Check Results** to see which required components are not yet completed.

Task 2: Configure and Verify Port Security

Step 1.   Configure all access links with port security.

Normally you configure port security on all access ports or shut down the port if it is not in use. Use the following policy to establish port security just on the ports used by the PCs:

- Set the port to access mode.

- Enable port security.

- Allow only one MAC address.

- Configure the first learned MAC address to "stick" to the configuration.

- Set the port to shut down if there is a security violation.

- Force the switches to learn the MAC addresses by sending pings across all three switches.

Note: Only enabling port security is graded by Packet Tracer. However, all the port security tasks listed above are required to complete this activity.

Step 2.   Test port security:

- Connect PC2 to PC3's port and connect PC3 to PC2's port.

- Send pings between PCs on the same subnet.

- The ports for PC2 and PC3 should shut down.

Step 3.   Verify that ports are "err-disabled" and that a security violation has been logged.

Step 4.   Reconnect PCs to the correct port and clear port security violations:

- Connect PC2 and PC3 back to the correct port.

- Clear the port security violation.

- Verify that PC2 and PC3 can now send pings across S2.

Step 5.   Check results.

Your completion percentage should be 55 percent. If not, click **Check Results** to see which required components are not yet completed.

Task 3: Configure VTP

Step 1.   Configure the VTP mode on all three switches.

Configure S1 as the server. Configure S2 and S3 as clients.

Step 2.   Configure the VTP domain name on all three switches.

Use **CCNA** as the VTP domain name.

Step 3.   Configure the VTP domain password on all three switches.

Use **cisco** as the VTP domain password.

Step 4.   Check results.

Your completion percentage should be 70 percent. If not, click **Check Results** to see which required components are not yet completed.

Task 4: Configure Trunking

Step 1.   Configure trunking on S1, S2, and S3.

Configure the appropriate interfaces in trunking mode and assign VLAN 99 as the native VLAN.

Step 2.   Check results.

Your completion percentage should be 83 percent. If not, click **Check Results** to see which required components are not yet completed.

Task 5: Configure VLANs

Step 1.   Create the VLANs on S1.

Create and name the following VLANs on S1 only. VTP will advertise the new VLANs to S1 and S2.

- VLAN 10 Faculty/Staff
- VLAN 20 Students
- VLAN 30 Guest (Default)
- VLAN 99 Management&Native

Step 2.   Verify that VLANs have been sent to S2 and S3.

Use appropriate commands to verify that S2 and S3 now have the VLANs you created on S1. It may take a few minutes for Packet Tracer to simulate the VTP advertisements.

Step 3.   Check results.

Your completion percentage should be 90 percent. If not, click **Check Results** to see which required components are not yet completed.

Task 6: Assign VLANs to Ports

Step 1.   Assign VLANs to access ports on S2 and S3.

Assign the PC access ports to VLANs:

- VLAN 10: PC1 and PC4
- VLAN 20: PC2 and PC5
- VLAN 30: PC3 and PC6

Step 2.   Verify the VLAN implementation.

Use the appropriate command to verify your VLAN implementation.

Step 3.   Check results.

Your completion percentage should be 100 percent. If not, click **Check Results** to see which required components are not yet completed.

Task 7: Verify End-to-End Connectivity

Step 1.   Verify that PC1 and PC4 can ping each other.

Step 2.   Verify that PC2 and PC5 can ping each other.

Step 3.   Verify that PC3 and PC6 can ping each other.

Step 4.   PCs on different VLANs should not be able to ping each other.

Computer networks are inextricably linked to productivity in today's small and medium-sized businesses. Consequently, IT administrators have to implement redundancy in their hierarchical networks. When a switch connection is lost, another link needs to quickly take its place without introducing any traffic loops. The exercises and labs in this chapter explore how Spanning Tree Protocol (STP) logically blocks physical loops in the network and how STP has evolved into a robust protocol that rapidly calculates which ports should be blocked in a VLAN-based network.

The Study Guide portion of this chapter uses a combination of matching, fill-in-the-blank, and open-ended question exercises to test your knowledge of STP concepts and configurations.

The Labs and Activities portion of this chapter includes all the online curriculum labs to ensure that you have mastered the hands-on skills needed to understand STP management and configuration.

As you work through this chapter, use Chapter 5 in *LAN Switching and Wireless, CCNA Exploration Companion Guide* or use the corresponding Chapter 5 in the Exploration LAN Switching and Wireless online curriculum for assistance.

Study Guide

Redundant Layer 2 Topologies

The hierarchical design model addresses issues found in "flat" Layer 2 network topologies. One of the issues is redundancy. Layer 2 redundancy improves the availability of the network by implementing alternate network paths using equipment and cabling. In this section, you will answer some reflection questions and draw a redundant topology.

Redundancy Reflection Questions

Why is redundancy an important aspect of a hierarchical network infrastructure?

_____

_____

_____

In which layers of the hierarchical model should redundancy be implemented?

_____

_____

As described and illustrated in Chapter 5 of *LAN Switching and Wireless, CCNA Exploration Companion Guide*, name the four types of failures in the hierarchical network that STP can recover from and prevent disruption of traffic:

_____

_____

_____

_____

If a routing loop develops at Layer 3, an IP packet will eventually be dropped. Explain why, in a Layer 2 loop, an Ethernet frame will continue to be forwarded endlessly through a switched network:

_____

_____

What is the definition of a broadcast storm?

_____

_____

Redundant Topologies Exercise

In Figure 5-1, draw the redundant links between the access, distribution, and core switches.

Figure 5-1   Redundant Topology

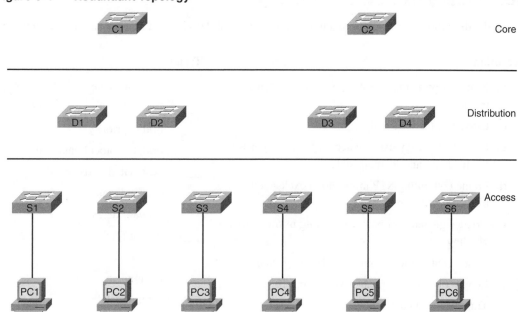

Introduction to STP

Redundancy increases the availability of a network topology by protecting the network from a single point of failure, such as a failed network cable or switch. STP was developed to address the issue of loops in a redundant Layer 2 design.

Vocabulary Exercise: Matching

Match the definition on the left with a term on the right. All definitions and terms are used exactly one time.

Definitions

a. Non-root ports that are still permitted to forward traffic.

b. Closest to the root bridge.

c. Cisco technology used on access ports to bypass the listening and learning states.

d. Frame containing STP information exchanged between switches.

e. Nondesignated port not participating in frame forwarding.

f. Time spent in the listening and learning states.

g. Length of time a port saves BPDU information.

h. Time between each BPDU sent on a port.

i. The switch with the lowest BID.

j. Port is administratively shut down.

k. Ports in a blocking state.

l. Sending and receiving data frames.

m. Number of switches a frame has to traverse to travel between the two farthest points within a broadcast domain.

n. Building the MAC address table, but does forward user data frames.

o. Customizable value used to influence which switch becomes root.

p. Sending and receiving BPDUs, but does not learn addresses or forward frames.

q. Used to determine which switch ports on a network need to be blocking in order to prevent loops from occurring.

r. Published as IEEE 802.1D in 1990.

s. Contains a priority value and the MAC address.

Terms

____ blocking state

____ bridge ID

____ bridge priority

____ bridge protocol data unit

____ designated ports

____ disabled state

____ forward delay

____ forwarding state

____ hello time

____ learning state

____ listening state

____ maximum age

____ nondesignated ports

____ PortFast

____ root bridge

____ root ports

____ Spanning Tree Protocol

____ spanning-tree algorithm

____ switch diameter

STP Concepts Exercise

The _____ (STP) was developed by _____ and published as IEEE
Standard _____ in 1990 to address the issue of loops in a redundant switched network.

Spanning-Tree Algorithm

STP ensures that there is only one logical path between all destinations on the network by intentionally blocking redundant paths that could cause a _____. A switch port is considered _____ when network traffic is prevented from entering or leaving that port.

STP uses the _____ (STA) to determine which switch ports on a network need to be _____ in order to prevent loops from occurring. The STA designates a single switch as the _____ and uses it as the reference point for all subsequent calculations. Switches participating in STP determine which switch has the _____ ID (BID) on the network. This switch automatically becomes the _____.

A _____ (BPDU) is a frame containing STP information exchanged by switches running STP. Each BPDU contains a BID that identifies the switch that sent the BPDU. The _____ BID value determines which switch is root.

After the root bridge has been determined, the STA calculates the shortest path to the root bridge. If there is more than one path to choose from, STA chooses the path with the lowest _____.

When the STA has determined the "best" paths emanating from the root bridge, it configures the switch ports into distinct port roles. The port roles describe their relation in the network to the root bridge and whether they are allowed to forward traffic:

- _____ **ports:** Switch ports closest to the root bridge

- _____ **ports:** Non-root ports that are still permitted to forward traffic on the network

- _____ **ports:** Ports in a blocking state to prevent loops

- _____ **port:** Ports that are administratively shut down

After a switch boots, it sends BPDU frames containing the switch BID and the root ID every __ seconds. Initially, each switch identifies itself as the _____ after bootup.

How would a switch determine that another switch is now the root bridge?

_____

_____

How does the STA determine path cost?

_____

_____

Port Costs

Record the default port costs for various link speeds in Table 5-1.

Table 5-1   Port Costs

Link Speed	Cost (Revised IEEE Specification)	Cost (Previous IEEE Specification)
10 Gbps		
1 Gbps		
100 Mbps		
10 Mbps		

Although switch ports have a default port cost associated with them, the port cost is configurable.

To configure the port cost of an interface, enter the _____ command in interface configuration mode. The range value can be between ____ and _____.

Enter the commands, including switch prompt, to configure the port cost for Fa0/1 as 25:

_____

_____

To verify the port and path cost to the root bridge, enter the _____ privileged EXEC mode command, as shown here:

S2#_____

```
VLAN0001
  Spanning tree enabled protocol ieee
  Root ID    Priority 27589
             Address      000A.0033.3333
             Cost         19
             Port         1
             Hello Time   2 sec  Max Age 20 sec  Forward Delay 15 sec

  Bridge ID  Priority     32769  (priority 32768 sys-id-ext 1)
             Address      000A.0011.1111
             Hello Time   2 sec  Max Age 20 sec  Forward Delay 15 sec
             Aging Time 300

Interface        Role Sts Cost      Prio.Nbr Type
---------------- ---- --- --------- -------- --------------------------
F0/1             Root FWD 19        128.1    Edge P2p
F0/2             Desg FWD 19        128.2    Edge P2p
```

Bridge ID

The BID field of a BPDU frame contains three separate fields: _____, _____, and _____.

Of these three fields, the _____ is a customizable value that you can use to influence which switch becomes the root bridge. The default value for this filed is _____.

Cisco enhanced its implementation of STP to include support for the extended system ID field, which contains the ID of the _____ with which the BPDU is associated.

Because using the extended system ID changes the number of bits available for the bridge priority, the customizable values can only be multiples of _____.

When two switches are configured with the same priority and have the same extended system ID, the switch with the lowest _____ has the lower BID.

Enter the two different configuration commands that you can use to configure the bridge priority value so that the switch is root for VLAN 1. Use the value 4096 when necessary.

_____

_____

_____

Enter the command to verify that the local switch is now root:

```
S1#_____

VLAN0001
  Spanning tree enabled protocol ieee
  Root ID    Priority    24577
             Address     000A.0033.3333
             This bridge is the root
             Hello Time   2 sec  Max Age 20 sec  Forward Delay 15 sec

  Bridge ID  Priority    24577  (priority 24576 sys-id-ext 1)
             Address     0019.aa9e.b000
             Hello Time   2 sec  Max Age 20 sec  Forward Delay 15 sec
             Aging Time 300

Interface        Role Sts Cost      Prio.Nbr Type
---------------- ---- --- --------- -------- ----------------------

Fa0/1            Desg FWD 4         128.1    Shr
Fa0/2            Desg FWD 4         128.2    Shr
```

Port Roles

When there are two switch ports that have the same path cost to the root bridge, the switch needs to determine which switch port is the root port. The switch uses the configurable port priority value, or the lowest port number if both port priority values are the same. The port number is appended to the port priority to form the port ID.

You can configure the port priority value using the _____ interface configuration mode command. The port priority values range from ____ to ____, in increments of ___. The default port priority value is _____.

Enter the commands, including switch prompt, to configure Fa0/1 with a port priority of 96:

_____

_____

The root bridge automatically configures all of its switch ports in the _____ role. Other switches in the topology configure their non-root ports as _____ or _____ ports.

_____ ports are configured for all LAN segments. When two switches are connected to the same LAN segment, the two switches have to decide which port is to be configured as a _____ port and which one is left as the _____ port. Generally, the switch with the lower _____ is selected as the _____ port, while the switch with the higher _____ is selected as the _____ port.

STP Port States and BPDU Timers

To facilitate the learning of the logical spanning tree and avoid loops, each switch port transitions through five possible port states and uses three BPDU timers.

The five STP port states are as follows:

- _____: The port is a nondesignated port and does not participate in frame forwarding. The port continues to process received BPDU frames to determine the location and root ID of the root bridge and what port role the switch port should assume in the final active STP topology.

- _____: STP has determined that the port can be selected as a root port or designated port based upon the information in the BPDU frames it has received so far. At this point, the switch port is not only receiving BPDU frames, it is also transmitting its own BPDU frames and informing adjacent switches that the switch port is preparing to participate in the active topology. The port returns to blocking state if it is determined that the port does not provide the lowest cost path to the root bridge.

- _____: The port prepares to participate in frame forwarding and begins to populate the MAC address table.

- _____: The port is considered part of the active topology and forwards frames and also sends and receives BPDU frames.

- _____: The Layer 2 port does not participate in spanning tree and does not forward or process frames. The switch port is administratively disabled.

Once stable, every active port in the switched network is either in the _____ state or the _____ state.

The amount of time that a port stays in the various port states depends on the BPDU timers. The following timers determine STP performance and state changes:

- _____: The time between each BPDU frame sent on a port. The default is ___ seconds, but can be tuned between ___ and ___ seconds.

- _____: The time spent in the listening and learning states. The default is ___ seconds, but can be tuned between ___ and ___ seconds.

- _____: Controls the maximum length of time a switch port saves configuration BPDU information. The default is ___ seconds, but can be tuned between ___ and ___ seconds.

The _____ (also known as network diameter) is the number of switches a frame has to traverse to travel between the two farthest points within the broadcast domain. It is not recommended that the BPDU timers be adjusted directly because the values have been optimized for the seven-switch diameter, which functions well for a broadcast domain in a modern switched LAN.

However, if after research a network administrator determines that the convergence time of the network could be optimized, the administrator would do so by reconfiguring the network diameter, not the BPDU timers.

To configure a different network diameter for STP, use the _____
_____ global configuration mode command on the root bridge. The _____ parameter can take any value between ___ and ___.

Enter the command, including switch prompt, to configure the network diameter to 5:

_____

To speed up convergence on access ports that are attached to end devices not participating in STP, you can use a Cisco technology called PortFast.

Describe the benefit of using PortFast on access ports:

_____

_____

Enter the commands, including switch prompt, to configure the Fa0/11 port on S2 with PortFast:

_____

_____

STP Convergence

Convergence is an important aspect of the spanning-tree process. Convergence is the time it takes for the network to determine which switch is going to assume the role of the root bridge, go through all the different port states, and set all switch ports to their final spanning-tree port roles, thus eliminating all potential loops. The exercises in this section cover determining the root bridge and port roles, STP recalculation, and STP topology changes.

Determine the Root Bridge and Port Role Exercise

The root bridge is chosen based on the _____ BID. After the root bridge is selected, a non-root bridge looks at the following components in sequence to determine which ports will process user data and which ports will discard user data:

1. On each non-root bridge, the port with the lowest path cost to root is the root port.

2. If two or more bridges are members of the same segment and have the same cost to reach the root bridge, then the bridge with the lowest BID is the designated port for that segment.

3. If a bridge has two or more equal cost paths to root, then the port with the lowest ID is the designated port. The other port(s) is blocking.

In the topologies shown in Figures 5-2, 5-3, and 5-4, circle the root bridge. On non-root bridges, label root ports with an **R**, designated ports with a **D**, and ports that are in the blocking state with a **B**. Use the revised IEEE costs to make your determinations. In the space provided after each topology, draw the logical loop-free spanning-tree topology with the root bridge at the top.

Figure 5-2   Determine the Root Bridge and Port Roles: Topology 1

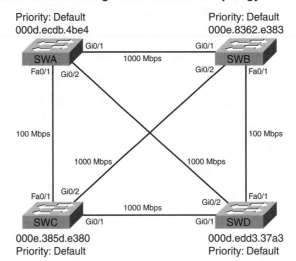

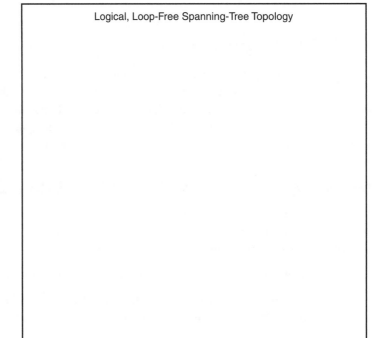

Logical, Loop-Free Spanning-Tree Topology

Figure 5-3   Determine the Root Bridge and Port Roles: Topology 2

Figure 5-4   Determine the Root Bridge and Port Roles: Topology 3

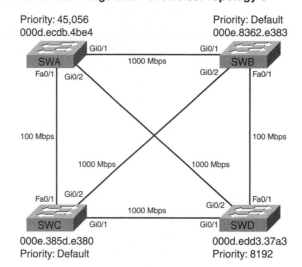

Logical, Loop-Free Spanning-Tree Topology

Spanning-Tree Recalculation Exercise

Figure 5-5 is the same as Figure 5-3 in the preceding section. However, now the Gigabit Ethernet link between SWC and SWB has gone down, as indicated by the X. As you did before, circle the root bridge. On non-root bridges, label root ports with an **R**, designated ports with a **D**, and ports that are in the blocking state with a **B**. Use the revised IEEE costs to make your determinations. In the space provided after the topology, draw the logical loop-free spanning-tree topology with the root bridge at the top.

Figure 5-5   Spanning-Tree Recalculation Exercise

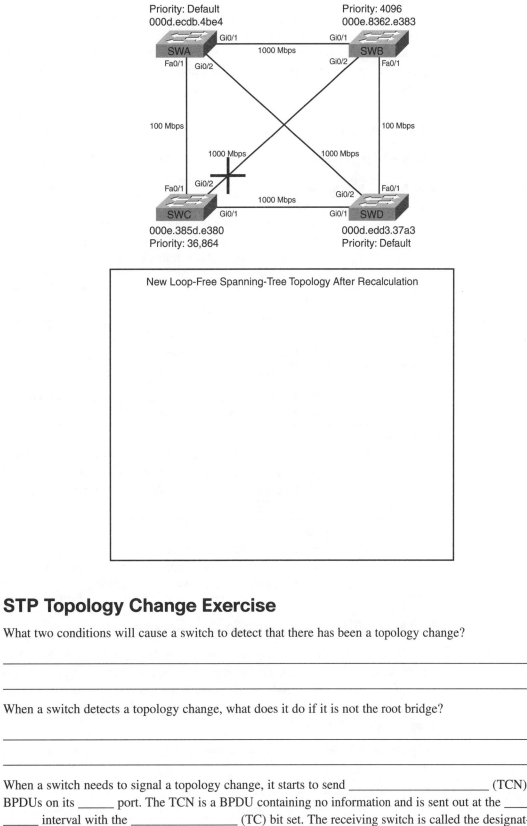

STP Topology Change Exercise

What two conditions will cause a switch to detect that there has been a topology change?

_____

_____

When a switch detects a topology change, what does it do if it is not the root bridge?

_____

_____

When a switch needs to signal a topology change, it starts to send _____ (TCN) BPDUs on its _____ port. The TCN is a BPDU containing no information and is sent out at the _____ _____ interval with the _____ (TC) bit set. The receiving switch is called the designated bridge and it acknowledges the TCN by immediately sending back a _____ BPDU with the _____ (TCA) bit set.

PVST+, RSTP, and Rapid PVST+

Like many networking standards, the evolution of STP has been driven by the need to create industry-wide specifications when proprietary protocols become de facto standards. When a proprietary protocol becomes so prevalent that all competitors in the market need to support it, agencies like the IEEE step in and create a public specification. The exercises in this section cover the STP variants and configurations.

STP Variants Exercise

Complete Table 5-2, which summarizes the evolution of STP and its variants.

Table 5-2   STP Variants

Cisco Proprietary	PVST
	■ Uses the Cisco proprietary _____ trunking protocol.
	■ Each VLAN has an instance of spanning tree.
	■ Ability to load balance traffic at Layer 2.
	■ Includes extensions _____Fast, _____Fast, and _____Fast.
	PVST+
	■ Supports _____ and _____ trunking.
	■ Supports Cisco proprietary STP extensions.
	■ Adds _____ guard and _____ guard enhancements.
	Rapid PVST+
	■ Based on _____ standard.
	■ Has faster convergence than 802.1D.
IEEE Standard	RSTP
	■ Introduced in 1982 and provides faster convergence than 802.1D.
	■ Implements generic versions of the Cisco-proprietary STP extensions.
	■ IEEE has incorporated RSTP into 802.1D, identifying the specification as _____.
	MSTP
	■ Multiple VLANs can be mapped to the same spanning-tree instance.
	■ Inspired by the Cisco Multiple Instances Spanning Tree Protocol (MISTP).
	■ IEEE 802.1Q (2003) now includes MSTP.

Default STP Configuration Exercise

Cisco developed PVST+ so that a network can run an STP instance for each VLAN in the network. With PVST+, trunks can selectively block traffic on a per-VLAN basis, depending on the spanning tree built for each VLAN. Therefore, you can tune the spanning-tree parameters so that half of the VLANs forward on each uplink trunk, thus efficiently utilizing bandwidth on all trunk links by providing Layer 2 load sharing

Complete Table 5-3 to show the default spanning-tree configuration for a Cisco Catalyst 2960 series switch.

Table 5-3   Default Switch Configuration

Feature	Default Setting
Enable state	Enabled on VLAN 1
Spanning-tree mode	
Switch priority	
Spanning-tree port priority (configurable on a per-interface basis)	
Spanning-tree port cost (configurable on a per-interface basis)	1000 Mbps: ____, 100 Mbps: ____, 10 Mbps: ____
Spanning-tree VLAN port priority (configurable on a per-VLAN basis)	
Spanning-tree VLAN port cost (configurable on a per-VLAN basis)	1000 Mbps: ____, 100 Mbps: ____, 10 Mbps: ____
Spanning-tree timers	Hello time: _____ seconds Forward-delay time: _____ seconds Maximum-aging time: _____ seconds Transmit hold count: _____ BPDUs

PVST+ Configuration Exercise

Without explicitly configuring priority for the switches in Figure 5-6, you would have no control over which switch becomes root. In this hierarchical design, the network administrator has determined that C1 should be root and C2 should be the backup root. In addition, the network administrator wants to ensure that an access layer switch never becomes root.

Figure 5-6   Configuring Root in PVST+

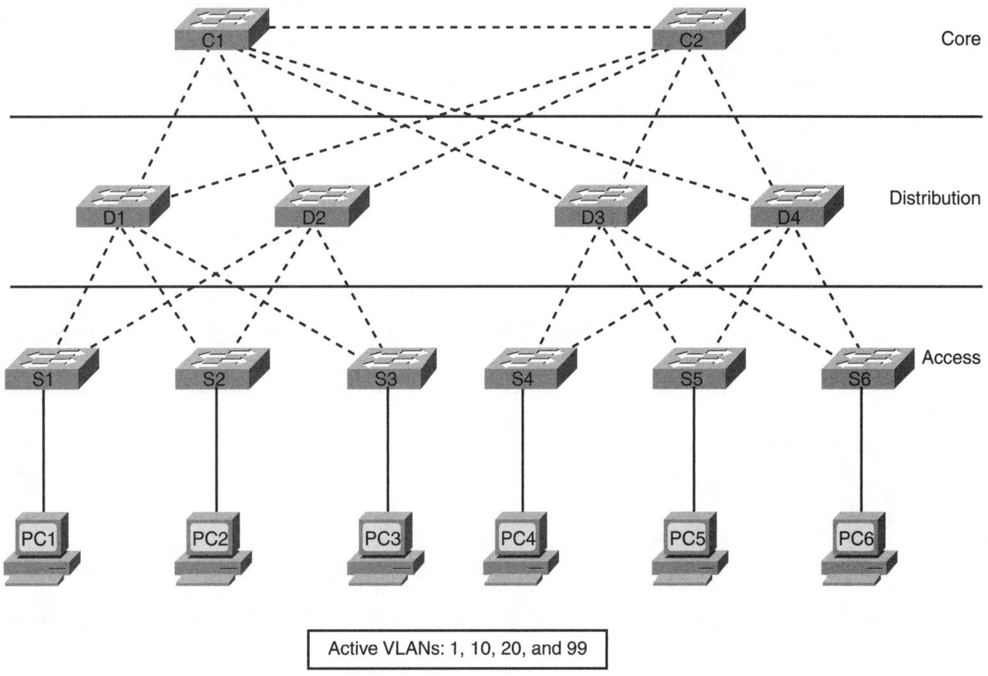

Active VLANs: 1, 10, 20, and 99

Enter the commands, including the switch prompt, to implement the following:

- C1 is the primary root for VLANs 1 and 10.

- C1 is the secondary root for VLANs 20 and 99.

- C2 is the primary root for VLANs 20 and 99.

- C2 is the secondary root for VLANs 1 and 10.

- All distribution switches have a priority of 4096 (you need to record this command only once, because it is the same for all distribution switches).

_____

_____

_____

_____

_____

_____

_____

RSTP Concepts Exercise

RSTP

RSTP is specified in IEEE 802.1____ and is an evolution of the 802.1____ standard. Most parameters have been left unchanged.

RSTP supports a new port type called an _____ port, which is in discarding state. RSTP does not have a _____ port state. RSTP defines port states as _____, _____, or _____.

Why does RSTP have a faster convergence time than standard STP?

_____

_____

802.1____ supersedes 802.1____ while retaining backward compatibility. RSTP keeps the same BPDU format as IEEE 802.1___, except that the version field is set to ___ to indicate RSTP.

Edge Ports

What is the definition of an edge port?

_____

_____

How do edge ports in RSTP differ from ports configured with PortFast in STP?

_____

_____

Link Types

Non-edge ports are categorized into two link types, _____ and _____. The link type is automatically determined, but can be overwritten with an explicit port configuration.

_____ ports and _____ links are candidates for rapid transition to forwarding state.

RSTP Port States and Port Roles Exercise

Complete Table 5-4, which compares 802.1D and RSTP port states.

Table 5-4   Comparing 802.1D and RSTP Port States

Operational Port State	802.1D Port State	RSTP Port State
Enabled		
Enabled		
Enabled		
Enabled		
Disabled		

In Figure 5-7, S1 is the root bridge. Assume that S3 has a higher priority than S2. Using the abbreviations shown, label each port with the correct RSTP port role.

Figure 5-7   RSTP Port Roles

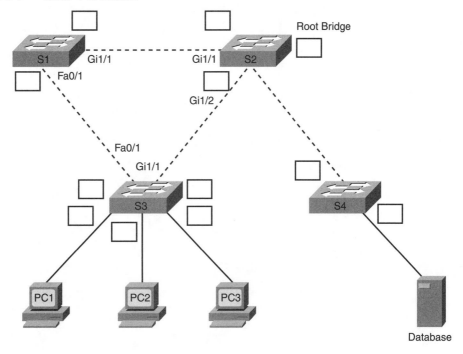

Rapid PVST+ Configuration Exercise

Rapid PVST+ is a Cisco implementation of RSTP. It supports one instance of RSTP for each VLAN. This is the desired choice of STP for a modern switched LAN in a small to medium-sized business.

Refer to the simple, nonredundant topology shown in Figure 5-8. Enter the commands to configure Rapid PVST+ and set the trunk links to point-to-point. Also, include the command that restarts the protocol migration process on the entire switch.

Figure 5-8   Rapid PVST+ Configuration

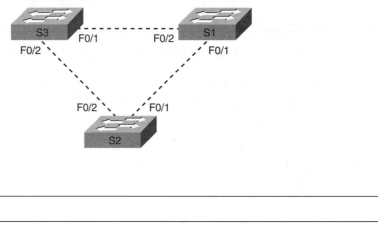

_____

_____

_____

_____

_____

Labs and Activities

Command Reference

In Table 5-5, record the command, *including the correct prompt*, that fits the description. Fill in any blanks with the appropriate missing information.

Table 5-5   Commands for STP Configuration

Command	Description
	Changes the STP port cost to 110
	Displays the STP port and path cost to the root bridge
	Configures the local switch as the primary root bridge for VLAN 1
	Configures the local switch as the backup root bridge for VLAN 1
	Configures the local switch with 24576 as the STP priority for VLAN 1
	Configures the STP port priority to 100, changing it from the default value of _____
	Adjusts the spanning-tree diameter for VLAN 1 on the primary root bridge to 4
	Configures an access port to bypass the typical STP listening and learning states, immediately transitioning to the forwarding state
	Displays STP configuration details for the active interfaces only
	Configures the switch to use rapid PVST+
	Configures an interface as a point-to-point link for RSTP

Lab 5-1: Basic Spanning Tree Protocol (5.5.1)

Learning Objectives

Upon completion of this lab, you will be able to

- Cable a network according to the topology diagram

- Erase the startup configuration and reload the default configuration, setting a switch to the default state

- Perform basic configuration tasks on a switch

- Observe and explain the default behavior of Spanning Tree Protocol (STP, 802.1D)

- Observe the response to a change in the spanning-tree topology

Figure 5-9 shows the topology diagram for this lab.

Figure 5-9   Topology Diagram for Lab 5-1

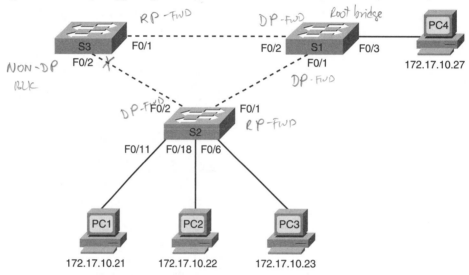

Table 5-6 shows the addressing scheme used in this lab.

Table 5-6   Addressing Table for Lab 5-1

Device	Interface	IP Address	Subnet Mask	Default Gateway
S1	VLAN 1	172.17.10.1	255.255.255.0	N/A
S2	VLAN 1	172.17.10.2	255.255.255.0	N/A
S3	VLAN 1	172.17.10.3	255.255.255.0	N/A
PC1	NIC	172.17.10.21	255.255.255.0	172.17.10.254
PC2	NIC	172.17.10.22	255.255.255.0	172.17.10.254
PC3	NIC	172.17.10.23	255.255.255.0	172.17.10.254
PC4	NIC	172.17.10.27	255.255.255.0	172.17.10.254

Task 1: Perform Basic Switch Configurations

Step 1.   Cable a network that is similar to the one shown in Figure 5-9.

You can use any current switch in your lab as long as it has the required interfaces shown in Figure 5-9. The output shown in this lab is based on Cisco 2960 switches. Other switch models may produce different output.

Set up console connections to all three switches.

Step 2.   Clear any existing configurations on the switches.

delete flash: vlan.data Clear NVRAM, delete the vlan.dat file, and reload the switches. Refer to Lab 2.5.1 for the procedure. After the reload is complete, use the **show vlan** privileged EXEC command to confirm that only default VLANs exist and that all ports are assigned to VLAN 1.

```
S1#show vlan

VLAN Name                             Status    Ports
---- -------------------------------- --------- -------------------------------
1    default                          active    Fa0/1, Fa0/2, Fa0/3, Fa0/4
                                                Fa0/5, Fa0/6, Fa0/7, Fa0/8
                                                Fa0/9, Fa0/10, Fa0/11, Fa0/12
                                                Fa0/13, Fa0/14, Fa0/15,Fa0/16
                                                Fa0/17, Fa0/18, Fa0/19,Fa0/20
                                                Fa0/21, Fa0/22, Fa0/23,Fa0/24
                                                Gig0/1, Gig0/2
1002 fddi-default                     active
1003 token-ring-default               active
1004 fddinet-default                  active
1005 trnet-default                    active
```

Step 3.   Configure basic switch parameters.

Configure the S1, S2, and S3 switches according to the following guidelines:

- Configure the switch hostname.

- Disable DNS lookup.

- Configure an EXEC mode password of **class**.

- Configure a password of **cisco** for console connections.

- Configure a password of **cisco** for vty connections.

Only the commands for S1 are shown here:

```
Switch>enable
Switch#configure terminal
Enter configuration commands, one per line.  End with CNTL/Z.
Switch(config)#hostname S1
S1(config)#enable secret class
S1(config)#no ip domain-lookup
S1(config)#line console 0
S1(config-line)#password cisco
S1(config-line)#login
S1(config-line)#line vty 0 15
```

```
S1(config-line)#password cisco
S1(config-line)#login
S1(config-line)#end
%SYS-5-11ONFIG_I: Configured from console by console
S1#copy running-config startup-config
Destination filename [startup-config]?
Building configuration...
[OK]
```

Task 2: Prepare the Network

Step 1.   Disable all ports by using the **shutdown** command.

Ensure that the initial switch port states are inactive with the **shutdown** command. Use the **interface range** command to simplify this task.

Only the commands for S1 are shown here:

```
S1(config)#interface range fa0/1-24
S1(config-if-range)#shutdown
S1(config-if-range)#interface range gi0/1-2
S1(config-if-range)#shutdown
```

Step 2.   Reenable the user ports on S1 and S2 in access mode.

Figure 5-9 shows which switch ports on S1 and S2 need to be activated for end-user device access. These ports will be configured for access mode and enabled with the **no shutdown** command.

```
S1(config)#interface fa0/3
S1(config-if)#switchport mode access
S1(config-if)#no shutdown
```
_____
```
S2(config)#interface range fa0/6, fa0/11, fa0/18
S2(config-if-range)#switchport mode access
S2(config-if-range)#no shutdown
```

Step 3.   Enable trunk ports on S1, S2, and S3.

Although only a single VLAN is being used in this lab, enable trunking on all links between switches to allow for additional VLANs to be added in the future.

if only one vlan is used, trunking is optional (handwritten)

Only the commands for S1 are shown here:

```
S1(config-if-range)#interface range fa0/1, fa0/2
S1(config-if-range)#switchport mode trunk
S1(config-if-range)#no shutdown
```

Step 4.   Configure the management interface address on all three switches:

```
S1(config)#interface vlan1
S1(config-if)#ip address 172.17.10.1 255.255.255.0
S1(config-if)#no shutdown
```
_____
```
S2(config)#interface vlan1
S2(config-if)#ip address 172.17.10.2 255.255.255.0
```

```
S2(config-if)#no shutdown
```

```
S3(config)#interface vlan1
S3(config-if)#ip address 172.17.10.3 255.255.255.0
S3(config-if)#no shutdown
```

Verify that the switches are correctly configured by pinging between them. From S1, ping the management interface on S2 and S3. From S2, ping the management interface on S3.

Were the pings successful? _yes_

If not, troubleshoot the switch configurations and try again.

Task 3: Configure Host PCs (Optional)

It is not necessary to configure the PCs for this lab. If you wish to generate command output similar to what is shown in this lab, then configure the PCs according to the addressing in Table 5-6 at the beginning of the lab.

Task 4: Examine Spanning Tree Protocol Default Operation

Step 1.   Examine the default configuration of 802.1D STP.

On each switch, display the spanning-tree table with the **show spanning-tree** command. Root selection varies depending on the BID of each switch. Your output and the selection of which switch is the root bridge will likely be different from the following:

```
S1#show spanning-tree

VLAN0001
  Spanning tree enabled protocol ieee
  Root ID    Priority    32769
             Address        0019.068d.6980
             This bridge is the root
             Hello Time   2 sec  Max Age 20 sec  Forward Delay 15 sec

  Bridge ID  Priority    32769  (priority 32768 sys-id-ext 1)
             Address     0019.068d.6980
             Hello Time   2 sec  Max Age 20 sec  Forward Delay 15 sec
             Aging Time 300

Interface        Role Sts Cost      Prio.Nbr Type
---------------- ---- --- --------- -------- --------------------------------
Fa0/1            Desg FWD 19        128.3    P2p
Fa0/2            Desg FWD 19        128.4    P2p
Fa0/3            Desg FWD 19        128.5    P2p

S2#show spanning-tree

VLAN0001
  Spanning tree enabled protocol ieee
  Root ID    Priority    32769
```

```
                Address      0019.068d.6980
                Cost         19
                Port         1 (FastEthernet0/1)
                Hello Time   2 sec  Max Age 20 sec  Forward Delay 15 sec

     Bridge ID  Priority     32769  (priority 32768 sys-id-ext 1)
                Address      001b.0c68.2080
                Hello Time   2 sec  Max Age 20 sec  Forward Delay 15 sec
                Aging Time 300


  Interface        Role Sts Cost      Prio.Nbr Type
  ---------------  ---- --- ---------  -------- --------------------

  Fa0/1            Root FWD 19          128.1    P2p
  Fa0/2            Desg FWD 19          128.2    P2p
  Fa0/6            Desg FWD 19          128.6    P2p
  Fa0/11           Desg FWD 19          128.11   P2p
  Fa0/18           Desg FWD 19          128.18   P2p
```

S3#show spanning-tree

```
  VLAN0001
    Spanning tree enabled protocol ieee
    Root ID    Priority     32769
               Address      0019.068d.6980
               Cost         19
               Port         1 (FastEthernet0/1)
               Hello Time   2 sec  Max Age 20 sec  Forward Delay 15 sec

     Bridge ID  Priority     32769  (priority 32768 sys-id-ext 1)
                Address      001b.5303.1700
                Hello Time   2 sec  Max Age 20 sec  Forward Delay 15 sec
                Aging Time 300


  Interface        Role Sts Cost      Prio.Nbr Type
  ---------------  ---- --- ---------  -------- --------------------

  Fa0/1            Root FWD 19          128.1    P2p
  Fa0/2            Altn BLK 19          128.2    P2p
```

√ **Step 2.**   Interpret the output of the **show spanning-tree** command.

The bridge identifier (bridge ID), stored in the spanning-tree BPDU, consists of the bridge priority, the system ID extension, and the MAC address. The combination or addition of the bridge priority and the system ID extension is known as the *bridge ID priority*. The system ID extension is always the number of the VLAN. For example, the system ID extension for VLAN 100 is 100. Using the default bridge priority value of 32768, the *bridge ID priority* for VLAN 100 would be 32868 (32768 + 100).

The **show spanning-tree** command displays the value of *bridge ID priority*.

Note: The "priority" value within the parentheses represents the bridge priority value, which is followed by the value of the system ID extension.

---

note: the answer is according to this manual, not the actual lab.

Answer the following questions based on the preceding output—not the output from your switches:

1. What is the bridge ID priority for switches S1, S2, and S3 on VLAN 1?

   a. S1: _____ 32768 + 1 = 32769 _____

   b. S2: _____ 32769 _____

   c. S3: _____ 32769 _____

2. Which switch is the root for the VLAN 1 spanning tree? _____ S1 _____

3. On S1, which spanning-tree ports are in the blocking state on the root switch? _____ Fa 0/2 _____

4. On S3, which spanning-tree port is in the blocking state? _____ Fa 0/2 _____

5. How does STP elect the root switch? _____ The root bridge is the bridge w. the best bridge ID priority. _____

6. Because the bridge priorities are all the same, what else does the switch use to determine the root? _____ MAC address of the interface _____

Task 5: Observe the Response to the Topology Change in 802.1D STP

Now observe what happens when you intentionally simulate a broken link:

Step 1. Place the switches in spanning-tree debug mode using the command **debug spanning-tree** events:

PT does not support

```
S1#debug spanning-tree events
Spanning Tree event debugging is on
```

```
S2#debug spanning-tree events
Spanning Tree event debugging is on
```

```
S3#debug spanning-tree events
Spanning Tree event debugging is on
```

Step 2. Intentionally shut down port Fa0/1 on S1:

```
S1(config)#interface fa0/1
S1(config-if)#shutdown
```

Step 3. Record the debug output from S2 and S3:

```
S2#
STP: VLAN0001 we are the spanning tree root
%LINEPROTO-5-UPDOWN: Line protocol on Interface FastEthernet0/1, changed
state to down
%LINK-3-UPDOWN: Interface FastEthernet0/1, changed state to down
S2#
STP: VLAN0001 heard root 32769-0019.068d.6980 on Fa0/2
     supersedes 32769-001b.0c68.2080
```

S1 *Replace* *32*

S2

```
STP: VLAN0001 new root is 32769, 0019.068d.6980 on port Fa0/2, cost 38
STP: VLAN0001 sent Topology Change Notice on Fa0/2
```

```
S3#                                          S2
STP: VLAN0001 heard root 32769-001b.0c68.2080 on Fa0/2
STP: VLAN0001 Fa0/2 -> listening
STP: VLAN0001 Topology Change rcvd on Fa0/2
STP: VLAN0001 sent Topology Change Notice on Fa0/1
STP: VLAN0001 Fa0/2 -> learning
STP: VLAN0001 sent Topology Change Notice on Fa0/1
STP: VLAN0001 Fa0/2 -> forwarding
```

Using the preceding debug output, answer the following questions:

When the link from S2 that is connected to the root switch goes down, what is its initial conclusion about the spanning-tree root?

We are the spanning tree root

When S2 receives new information on Fa0/2, what new conclusion does it draw?

_____

Port Fa0/2 on S3 was previously in a blocking state before the link between S2 and S1 went down. What states does it go through as a result of the topology change?

Forwarding

Step 4.   Examine what has changed in the spanning-tree topology using the **show spanning-tree** command:

`S2#show spanning-tree`

```
VLAN0001
  Spanning tree enabled protocol ieee
  Root ID    Priority    32769
             Address     0019.068d.6980   S1
             Cost        38
             Port        2 (FastEthernet0/2)
             Hello Time   2 sec  Max Age 20 sec  Forward Delay 15 sec

  Bridge ID  Priority    32769   (priority 32768 sys-id-ext 1)
             Address     001b.0c68.2080
             Hello Time   2 sec  Max Age 20 sec  Forward Delay 15 sec
             Aging Time 300

Interface          Role Sts Cost       Prio.Nbr Type
---------------    --  --  ---------.   ----  ---------------
Fa0/2              Root FWD  19          128.2    P2p
Fa0/6              Desg FWD  19          128.6    P2p
Fa0/11             Desg FWD  19          128.11   P2p
Fa0/18             Desg FWD  19          128.18   P2p
```

`S3#show spanning-tree`

S1 is still the root bridge.

```
VLAN0001
  Spanning tree enabled protocol ieee
  Root ID    Priority    32769
             Address       0019.068d.6980   S₁
             Cost          19
             Port          1 (FastEthernet0/1)
             Hello Time    2 sec  Max Age 20 sec  Forward Delay 15 sec

  Bridge ID  Priority    32769   (priority 32768 sys-id-ext 1)
             Address       001b.5303.1700
             Hello Time    2 sec  Max Age 20 sec  Forward Delay 15 sec
             Aging Time 300

Interface        Role Sts Cost      Prio.Nbr Type
---------------- ---- --- --------- -------- --------------------------------

Fa0/1            Root FWD 19        128.1    P2p
Fa0/2            Desg FWD 19        128.2    P2p
```

Answer the following questions based on the preceding output:

What has changed about the way that S2 forwards traffic?

Fa0/2 on S2 change to Root Port from Destinated. port

What has changed about the way that S3 forwards traffic?

Fa 0/2 on S3 change to Designated Port from non Dest port.

Task 6: Document the Switch Configurations

On each switch, capture the running configuration to a text file and save it for future reference. These scripts can be edited to expedite configuring switches in future labs.

Task 7: Clean Up

Unless directed otherwise by your instructor, erase the configurations and reload the switches. Disconnect and store the cabling. For PC hosts that are normally connected to other networks (such as the school LAN or to the Internet), reconnect the appropriate cabling and restore the TCP/IP settings.

Lab 5-2: Challenge Spanning Tree Protocol (5.5.2)

Learning Objectives

Upon completion of this lab, you will be able to

- Cable a network according to the topology diagram

- Erase the startup configuration and reload the default configuration, setting a switch to the default state

- Perform basic configuration tasks on a switch

- Configure VTP on all switches

- Observe and explain the default behavior of STP (802.1D)

- Modify the placement of the spanning-tree root

- Observe the response to a change in the spanning-tree topology

- Explain the limitations of 802.1D STP in supporting continuity of service

- Configure Rapid STP (802.1w)

- Observe and explain the improvements offered by Rapid STP

Figure 5-10 shows the topology diagram for this lab.

Figure 5-10   Topology Diagram for Lab 5-2

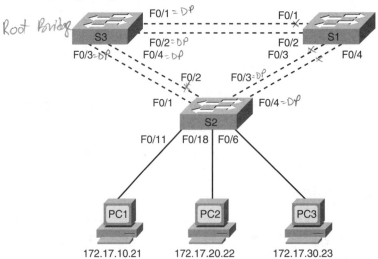

Table 5-7 shows the addressing scheme used in this lab.

Table 5-7   Addressing Table for Lab 5-2

Device	Interface	IP Address	Subnet Mask	Default Gateway
S1	VLAN 99	172.17.99.11	255.255.255.0	N/A
S2	VLAN 99	172.17.99.12	255.255.255.0	N/A
S3	VLAN 99	172.17.99.13	255.255.255.0	N/A
PC1	NIC	172.17.10.21	255.255.255.0	172.17.10.1
PC2	NIC	172.17.20.22	255.255.255.0	172.17.20.1
PC3	NIC	172.17.30.23	255.255.255.0	172.17.30.1

Table 5-8 shows the port assignments used in this lab.

Table 5-8   Port Assignments

Ports	Assignment	Network
Fa0/1–0/4	802.1Q Trunks (Native VLAN 99)	172.17.99.0 /24
Fa0/5–0/10	VLAN 30—Guest (Default)	172.17.30.0 /24
Fa0/11–0/17	VLAN 10—Faculty/Staff	172.17.10.0 /24
Fa0/18–0/24	VLAN 20—Students	172.17.20.0 /24

Task 1: Prepare the Network

Step 1. Cable a network that is similar to the one shown in Figure 5-10.

Set up console connections to all three switches.

Step 2. Clear any existing configurations on the switches.

Step 3. Disable all ports by using the **shutdown** command.

Step 4. Enable and activate access ports.

Refer to Figure 5-10 to determine which switch ports should be set to access mode and activated.

Task 2: Perform Basic Switch Configurations

Configure the switches according to the following guidelines:

■ Configure the switch hostname.

■ Disable DNS lookup.

■ Configure an EXEC mode password of **class**.

■ Configure a password of **cisco** for console connections.

■ Configure a password of **cisco** for vty connections.

Task 3: Configure Host PCs (Optional)

It is not necessary to configure the PCs for this lab. You will need PC3 for a task later in the lab, but it will use different IP addressing from what is shown in Table 5-7. However, if you wish to generate command output similar to what is shown in this lab, then configure all the PCs according to the addressing in Table 5-7 at the beginning of the lab.

Task 4: Configure VTP and VLANs

Step 1.   Configure VTP.

Configure VTP on the three switches using the following guidelines:

- S1 is the VTP server; S2 and S3 are VTP clients.

- The VTP domain name is **Lab5**.

- The VTP password is **cisco**.

Remember that VTP domain names and passwords are case sensitive. The default operating mode is server.

Step 2.   Configure trunk links and native VLAN.

For each switch, configure ports Fa0/1 through Fa0/4 as trunking ports. Designate VLAN 99 as the native VLAN for these trunks. Remember to activate the ports.

Step 3.   Configure the VTP server with VLANs.

Configure the following VLANs on the VTP server only:

- VLAN 10: Faculty/Staff

- VLAN 20: Students

- VLAN 30: Guest

- VLAN 99: Management

Step 4.   Verify the VLANs.

Verify that all four VLANs have been distributed to the client switches. You should have output similar to the following:

S2#**show vlan brief**

```
VLAN  Name              Status    Ports
——  ——————————————  ————.  —————————————————.
1     default           active    Fa0/1, Fa0/2, Fa0/4, Fa0/5
                                  Fa0/6, Fa0/7, Fa0/8, Fa0/9
                                  Fa0/10, Fa0/11, Fa0/12, Fa0/13
                                  Fa0/14, Fa0/15, Fa0/16, Fa0/17
                                  Fa0/18, Fa0/19, Fa0/20, Fa0/21
                                  Fa0/22, Fa0/23, Fa0/24, Gi0/1
                                  Gi0/2
```

```
10    faculty/staff        active
20    students             active
30    guest                active
99    management           active
```

S3#**show vlan brief**

```
VLAN  Name             Status    Ports
--    --------------   -----.    --------------.
1     default          active    Fa0/1, Fa0/2, Fa0/4, Fa0/5
                                 Fa0/6, Fa0/7, Fa0/8, Fa0/9
                                 Fa0/10, Fa0/11, Fa0/12, Fa0/13
                                 Fa0/14, Fa0/15, Fa0/16, Fa0/17
                                 Fa0/18, Fa0/19, Fa0/20, Fa0/21
                                 Fa0/22, Fa0/23, Fa0/24, Gi0/1
                                 Gi0/2
10    faculty/staff    active
20    students         active
30    guest            active
99    management       active
```

Step 5.   Configure the management interface address on all three switches.

Verify that the switches are correctly configured by pinging between them. From S1, ping the management interface on S2 and S3. From S2, ping the management interface on S3.

Were the pings successful? _Yes_

If not, troubleshoot the switch configurations and try again.

Step 6.   Assign switch ports to the VLANs.

Assign ports to VLANs on S2 according to Table 5-8 at the beginning of the lab. Activate the ports connected to the PCs.

int vlan 99 - to creat vlan 99 and place vlan 99 up & upstate

Task 5: Examine Spanning Tree Protocol Default Operation

Step 1.   Examine the default operation of STP on S1.

The output shown is for S1 only. Root selection varies depending on the BID of each switch in your lab. In this output, S1 is not root. S1 is using Fa0/2 to reach the root bridge.

S1#**show spanning-tree**

```
VLAN0001
  Spanning tree enabled protocol ieee
  Root ID    Priority    32769
             Address     000a.b769.f6c0
             Cost        19
             Port        2 (FastEthernet0/2)
             Hello Time   2 sec  Max Age 20 sec  Forward Delay 15 sec

  Bridge ID  Priority    32769  (priority 32768 sys-id-ext 1)
             Address     001b.5302.4e80
             Hello Time   2 sec  Max Age 20 sec  Forward Delay 15 sec
             Aging Time 300

Interface         Role Sts Cost      Prio.Nbr Type
---------------- ---- --- --------- -------- --------------------
Fa0/1             Altn BLK 19        128.1    P2p
Fa0/2             Root FWD 19        128.2    P2p
Fa0/3             Altn BLK 19        128.3    P2p
Fa0/4             Altn BLK 19        128.4    P2p


VLAN0010
  Spanning tree enabled protocol ieee
  Root ID    Priority    32778
             Address     000a.b769.f6c0
             Cost        19
             Port        2 (FastEthernet0/2)
             Hello Time   2 sec  Max Age 20 sec  Forward Delay 15 sec

  Bridge ID  Priority    32778  (priority 32768 sys-id-ext 10)
             Address     001b.5302.4e80
             Hello Time   2 sec  Max Age 20 sec  Forward Delay 15 sec
             Aging Time 300

Interface         Role Sts Cost      Prio.Nbr Type
---------------- ---- --- --------- -------- --------------------
Fa0/1             Altn BLK 19        128.1    P2p
Fa0/2             Root FWD 19        128.2    P2p
Fa0/3             Altn BLK 19        128.3    P2p
Fa0/4             Altn BLK 19        128.4    P2p
```

```
VLAN0020
   Spanning tree enabled protocol ieee
   Root ID    Priority    32788
              Address     000a.b769.f6c0
              Cost        19
              Port        2 (FastEthernet0/2)
              Hello Time   2 sec  Max Age 20 sec  Forward Delay 15 sec


   Bridge ID  Priority    32788  (priority 32768 sys-id-ext 20)
              Address     001b.5302.4e80
              Hello Time   2 sec  Max Age 20 sec  Forward Delay 15 sec
              Aging Time 300


Interface        Role Sts Cost      Prio.Nbr Type
---------------- ---- --- --------- -------- --------------------

Fa0/1            Altn BLK 19        128.1    P2p
Fa0/2            Root FWD 19        128.2    P2p
Fa0/3            Altn BLK 19        128.3    P2p
Fa0/4            Altn BLK 19        128.4    P2p



VLAN0030
   Spanning tree enabled protocol ieee
   Root ID    Priority    32798
              Address     000a.b769.f6c0
              Cost        19
              Port        2 (FastEthernet0/2)
              Hello Time   2 sec  Max Age 20 sec  Forward Delay 15 sec


   Bridge ID  Priority    32798  (priority 32768 sys-id-ext 30)
              Address     001b.5302.4e80
              Hello Time   2 sec  Max Age 20 sec  Forward Delay 15 sec
              Aging Time 300


Interface        Role Sts Cost      Prio.Nbr Type
---------------- ---- --- --------- -------- --------------------

Fa0/1            Altn BLK 19        128.1    P2p
Fa0/2            Root FWD 19        128.2    P2p
Fa0/3            Altn BLK 19        128.3    P2p
Fa0/4            Altn BLK 19        128.4    P2p



VLAN0099
   Spanning tree enabled protocol ieee
   Root ID    Priority    32867
              Address     000a.b769.f6c0
              Cost        19
              Port        2 (FastEthernet0/2)
              Hello Time   2 sec  Max Age 20 sec  Forward Delay 15 sec
```

```
 Bridge ID  Priority    32867  (priority 32768 sys-id-ext 99)
            Address     001b.5302.4e80
            Hello Time   2 sec  Max Age 20 sec  Forward Delay 15 sec
            Aging Time 300


Interface          Role Sts Cost      Prio.Nbr Type
———————————— —— —. ————. ———— ————————————————
Fa0/1              Altn BLK 19        128.1    P2p
Fa0/2              Root FWD 19        128.2    P2p
Fa0/3              Altn BLK 19        128.3    P2p
Fa0/4              Altn BLK 19        128.4    P2p
```

Note that there are five instances of the spanning tree on each switch. The default STP configuration on Cisco switches is Per-VLAN Spanning Tree (PVST+), which creates a separate spanning tree for each VLAN (VLAN 1 and any user-configured VLANs). You can verify the current spanning-tree mode with the **show running-config** command:

```
S1#show run
Building configuration...
<output omitted>
!
hostname S1
!
<output omitted>
no file verify auto
spanning-tree mode pvst
spanning-tree extend system-id
!
interface FastEthernet0/1
 switchport trunk native vlan 99
 switchport mode trunk
!
<output omitted>
```

Step 2.   Examine the VLAN 99 spanning tree for all three switches:

```
S1#show spanning-tree vlan 99


VLAN0099
  Spanning tree enabled protocol ieee
  Root ID    Priority    32867
             Address     000a.b769.f6c0
             Cost        19
             Port        2 (FastEthernet0/2)
             Hello Time   2 sec  Max Age 20 sec  Forward Delay 15 sec


  Bridge ID  Priority    32867  (priority 32768 sys-id-ext 99)
             Address     001b.5302.4e80
             Hello Time   2 sec  Max Age 20 sec  Forward Delay 15 sec
             Aging Time 300
```

```
Interface           Role Sts Cost       Prio.Nbr Type
--------         -- --  -----  ----  ----------------

Fa0/1               Altn BLK 19         128.1    P2p
Fa0/2               Root FWD 19         128.2    P2p
Fa0/3               Altn BLK 19         128.3    P2p
Fa0/4               Altn BLK 19         128.4    P2p
```

S2#show spanning-tree vlan 99

```
VLAN0099
  Spanning tree enabled protocol ieee
  Root ID    Priority    32867
             Address     000a.b769.f6c0
             Cost        19
             Port        3 (FastEthernet0/1)
             Hello Time  2 sec  Max Age 20 sec  Forward Delay 15 sec

  Bridge ID  Priority    32867  (priority 32768 sys-id-ext 99)
             Address     0017.59a7.5180
             Hello Time  2 sec  Max Age 20 sec  Forward Delay 15 sec
             Aging Time 300

Interface           Role Sts Cost       Prio.Nbr Type
--------         -- --  -----  ----  ----------------

Fa0/1               Root FWD 19         128.3    P2p
Fa0/2               Altn BLK 19         128.4    P2p
Fa0/3               Desg FWD 19         128.5    P2p
Fa0/4               Desg FWD 19         128.6    P2p
```

S3#show spanning-tree vlan 99

```
VLAN0099
  Spanning tree enabled protocol ieee
  Root ID    Priority    32867
             Address     000a.b769.f6c0
        -- This bridge is the root
             Hello Time  2 sec  Max Age 20 sec  Forward Delay 15 sec

  Bridge ID  Priority    32867  (priority 32768 sys-id-ext 99)
             Address     000a.b769.f6c0
             Hello Time  2 sec  Max Age 20 sec  Forward Delay 15 sec
             Aging Time 300

Interface           Role Sts Cost       Prio.Nbr Type
--------         -- --  -----  ----  ----------------

Fa0/1               Root FWD 19         128.1    P2p
Fa0/2               Root FWD 19         128.2    P2p
Fa0/3               Root FWD 19         128.3    P2p
Fa0/4               Root FWD 19         128.4    P2p
```

Note:

Answer according to manual Data

Step 3. Interpret the output of the **show spanning-tree** command.

Answer the following questions based on the output:

Bridge ID priority =
Default Bridge priority +
Sys ID Extention (Vlan ID)
32768 + 99 = 32867.

1. What is the bridge ID priority for switches S1, S2, and S3 on VLAN 99?

   a. S1: _____ *32867* _____

   b. S2: _____ *32 867* _____

   c. S3: _____ *32867* _____

2. What is the bridge ID priority for S1 on VLANs 10, 20, 30, and 99?

   a. VLAN 10: _____ *32768+10 = 32778* _____

   b. VLAN 20: _____ *32768+20 = 32788* _____

   c. VLAN 30: _____ *32768+30 = 32798* _____

   d. VLAN 99: _____ *32768+99 = 32867* _____

3. Which switch is the root for the VLAN 99 spanning tree?

   _____ *S3* _____

4. On VLAN 99, which spanning-tree ports are in the blocking state on the root switch? *none*

5. On VLAN 99, which spanning-tree ports are in the blocking state on the non-root switches?

   on S1 of fast ethernets 1, 3 & 4

   on S2 of fasten ethernet 2.

6. How does STP elect the root switch? *With the best bridge ID priority*

7. Because the bridge priorities are all the same, what else does the switch use to determine the root?

   MAC address

Task 6: Optimize STP

Because there is a separate instance of the spanning tree for every active VLAN, a separate root election is conducted for each instance. If the default switch priorities are used in root selection, the same root is elected for every spanning tree, as we have seen. This could lead to an inferior design. Some reasons to control the selection of the root switch include:

- The root switch is responsible for generating BPDUs in STP 802.1D and is the focal point for spanning-tree control traffic. The root switch must be capable of handling this additional processing load.

- The placement of the root defines the active switched paths in the network. Random placement is likely to lead to suboptimal paths. Ideally, the root is in the distribution layer.

- Consider the topology used in this lab. Of the six trunks configured, only two are carrying traffic. While this prevents loops, it is a waste of resources. Because the root can be defined on the basis of the VLAN, you can have some ports blocking for one VLAN and forwarding for another. This is demonstrated next.

In this example, it has been determined that the root selection using default values has led to underutilization of the available switch trunks. Therefore, it is necessary to force another switch to become the root switch for VLAN 99 to impose some load-sharing on the trunks.

Selection of the root switch is accomplished by changing the spanning-tree priority for the VLAN. Because the default root switch may vary in your lab environment, we will configure S1 and S3 to be the root switches for specific VLANs. The default priority, as you have observed, is 32768 plus the VLAN ID. The lower number indicates a higher priority for root selection.

Set the priority for VLAN 99 on S3 to 4096. This configuration will force an STP election for VLAN 99.

The following command sequences show the options available for the global configuration **spanning-tree** command:

```
S3(config)#spanning-tree vlan 99 ?
  forward-time  Set the forward delay for the spanning tree
  hello-time    Set the hello interval for the spanning tree
  max-age       Set the max age interval for the spanning tree
  priority      Set the bridge priority for the spanning tree
  root          Configure switch as root
  <cr>


S3(config)#spanning-tree vlan 99 priority ?
  <0-61440>  bridge priority in increments of 4096


S3(config)#spanning-tree vlan 99 priority 4096
S3(config)#exit
```

Set the priority for VLANs 1, 10, 20, and 30 on S1 to 4096. You can enter the **spanning-tree vlan** command individually for each VLAN or enter separate VLAN numbers with a comma as shown here:

```
S1(config)#spanning-tree vlan 1,10,20,30 priority 4096
S1(config)#exit
```

Give the switches a little time to recalculate the spanning tree and then check the tree for VLAN 99 on switch S1 and switch S3:

```
S1#show spanning-tree vlan 99


VLAN0099
  Spanning tree enabled protocol ieee
  Root ID    Priority    4195
             Address     001b.5303.1700
             Cost        19
             Port        3 (FastEthernet0/1)
             Hello Time   2 sec  Max Age 20 sec  Forward Delay 15 sec


  Bridge ID  Priority    32867  (priority 32768 sys-id-ext 99)
```

```
              Address       0019.068d.6980
              Hello Time    2 sec   Max Age 20 sec   Forward Delay 15 sec
              Aging Time 300


Interface          Role Sts Cost       Prio.Nbr Type
--------------- ---- --- --------- -------- --------------------------------
Fa0/1              Root FWD 19         128.3    P2p
Fa0/2              Altn BLK 19         128.4    P2p
Fa0/3              Desg FWD 19         128.5    P2p
Fa0/4              Desg FWD 19         128.6    P2p
```

S3#**show spanning-tree vlan 99**

```
VLAN0099

VLAN0099
  Spanning tree enabled protocol ieee
  Root ID    Priority    4195
             Address     000a.b769.f6c0
             This bridge is the root
             Hello Time    2 sec   Max Age 20 sec   Forward Delay 15 sec


  Bridge ID  Priority    4195    (priority 4096 sys-id-ext 99)
             Address     000a.b769.f6c0
             Hello Time    2 sec   Max Age 20 sec   Forward Delay 15 sec
             Aging Time 300


Interface          Role Sts Cost       Prio.Nbr Type
--------------- ---- --- --------- -------- --------------------------------
Fa0/1              Desg FWD 19         128.1    P2p
Fa0/2              Desg FWD 19         128.2    P2p
Fa0/3              Desg FWD 19         128.3    P2p
Fa0/4              Desg FWD 19         128.4    P2p
```

Which switch is the root for VLAN 99? _S3_

On VLAN 99, which spanning-tree ports are in the blocking state on the new root switch? _None_

On VLAN 99, which spanning-tree ports are in the blocking state on the old root switch? _Fa 0/2_
_____

Compare the S3 VLAN 99 spanning tree above with the S3 VLAN 10 spanning tree:

S3#**show spanning-tree vlan 10**

```
VLAN0010
  Spanning tree enabled protocol ieee
  Root ID    Priority    4106
             Address     0019.068d.6980
             Cost        19
```

```
          Port        1 (FastEthernet0/1)
          Hello Time   2 sec  Max Age 20 sec  Forward Delay 15 sec


 Bridge ID  Priority    32778  (priority 32768 sys-id-ext 10)
            Address     001b.5303.1700
            Hello Time   2 sec  Max Age 20 sec  Forward Delay 15 sec
            Aging Time 300


Interface        Role Sts Cost      Prio.Nbr Type
---------------- ---- --- --------- -------- --------------------------

Fa0/1            Root FWD 19        128.1    P2p
Fa0/2            Altn BLK 19        128.2    P2p
Fa0/3            Altn BLK 19        128.3    P2p
Fa0/4            Altn BLK 19        128.4    P2p
```

Note that S3 can now use all four ports for VLAN 99 traffic as long as they are not blocked at the other end of the trunk. However, the original spanning-tree topology, with three of four S3 ports in blocking mode, is still in place for the four other active VLANs. By configuring groups of VLANs to use different trunks as their primary forwarding path, we retain the redundancy of failover trunks, without having to leave trunks totally unused.

Task 7: Observe the Response to the Topology Change in 802.1D STP

To observe continuity across the LAN during a topology change, follow these steps:

Step 1.   Reconfigure PC3, which is connected to port S2 Fa0/6, with IP address 172.17.99.23/24. You do not need a default gateway.

Step 2.   Reassign S2 port Fa0/6 to VLAN 99. This allows you to continuously ping across the LAN from the host.

Step 3.   Verify that the switches can ping the host.

Step 4.   On S1, turn on debugging to monitor changes during the topology change.

debug spanning-tree events

Step 5.   Open a command window on PC3 and begin a continuous ping to the S1 management interface with the command **ping –t 172.17.99.11**. Currently, the spanning tree on S2 is sending data through S3 for VLAN 99, so pings to the VLAN 99 interface on S1 will go through S3.

Step 6.   Disconnect the trunk links on S1 Fa0/1 and Fa0/2. Monitor the pings. They will begin to time out as connectivity across the LAN is interrupted. As soon as connectivity has been reestablished, terminate the pings by pressing **Ctrl-C**.

The following is the debug output you will see on S1:

```
S1#debug spanning-tree events
```

```
Spanning Tree event debugging is on
S1#
%LINEPROTO-5-UPDOWN: Line protocol on Interface FastEthernet0/2, changed
    state to down
%LINK-3-UPDOWN: Interface FastEthernet0/2, changed state to down
%LINEPROTO-5-UPDOWN: Line protocol on Interface FastEthernet0/1, changed
    state to down
%LINK-3-UPDOWN: Interface FastEthernet0/1, changed state to down
%LINEPROTO-5-UPDOWN: Line protocol on Interface Vlan99, changed state to
    down
06:07:45: STP: VLAN0099 new root port Fa0/3, cost 38
06:07:45: STP: VLAN0099 Fa0/3 -> listening
06:07:47: STP: VLAN0099 sent Topology Change Notice on Fa0/3
06:08:00: STP: VLAN0099 Fa0/3 -> learning
06:08:04: STP: VLAN0001 Topology Change rcvd on Fa0/3
06:08:04: STP: VLAN0010 Topology Change rcvd on Fa0/3
06:08:04: STP: VLAN0020 Topology Change rcvd on Fa0/3
06:08:04: STP: VLAN0030 Topology Change rcvd on Fa0/3
06:08:15: STP: VLAN0099 Fa0/3 -> forwarding
%LINEPROTO-5-UPDOWN: Line protocol on Interface Vlan99, changed state to up
S1#
```

Recall that when the ports are in listening and learning mode, they are not forwarding
frames, and the LAN is essentially down. The spanning-tree recalculation can take up to 50
seconds to complete—a significant interruption in network services. The output of the continuous pings in Figure 5-11 shows the actual interruption of traffic while STP reconverges.
In this case, it was about 30 seconds, as can be seen from the timestamp highlighted in the
output for S1. Although 802.1D STP effectively prevents switching loops, this long restoration time is considered a serious drawback in the high-availability LANs of today.

Figure 5-11   Pings from PC3 Fail While STP Converges

Step 7.   On S1, turn off debugging with the **no debug spanning-tree events** command and reconnect the Fa0/1 and Fa0/2 links.

Task 8: Configure PVST Rapid Spanning Tree Protocol

Cisco has developed several features to address the slow convergence times associated with standard
STP. PortFast, UplinkFast, and BackboneFast are features that, when properly configured, can dramatically reduce the time required to restore connectivity. Incorporating these features requires manual
configuration, and care must be taken to do it correctly. The longer-term solution is Rapid STP
(RSTP), 802.1w, which incorporates these features, among others. RSTP-PVST is configured as follows:

```
S1(config)#spanning-tree mode rapid-pvst
```

Configure all three switches in this manner.

Use the command **show spanning-tree summary** to verify that RSTP is enabled:

```
S1#show spanning-tree summary
Switch is in rapid-pvst mode
Root bridge for: VLAN0001, VLAN0010, VLAN0020, VLAN0030
Extended system ID             is enabled
Portfast Default               is disabled
PortFast BPDU Guard Default    is disabled
Portfast BPDU Filter Default   is disabled
Loopguard Default              is disabled
EtherChannel misconfig guard   is enabled
UplinkFast                     is disabled
BackboneFast                   is disabled
Configured Pathcost method used is short
```

Name	Blocking	Listening	Learning	Forwarding	STP Active
VLAN0001	0	0	1	3	4
VLAN0010	0	0	1	3	4
VLAN0020	0	0	1	3	4
VLAN0030	0	0	1	3	4
VLAN0099	3	0	0	1	4
5 vlans	3	0	4	13	20

Task 9: Observe the Convergence Time of RSTP

Repeat the following steps from Task 7 to observe the convergence time of RSTP:

- Enable spanning-tree event debugging on S1.
- Start a continuous ping on PC3 to the management interface on S1.
- Disconnect the cables connected to ports Fa0/1 and Fa0/2.
- Observe the time required to reestablish a stable spanning tree.

The following is the partial debug output:

```
S1#debug spanning-tree events
Spanning Tree event debugging is on
S1#
06:20:00: RSTP(99): updt roles, root port Fa0/1 going down
06:20:00: RSTP(99): Fa0/2 is now root port
06:20:00: RSTP(99): Fa0/2 received a tc ack
06:20:00: RSTP(99): updt roles, root port Fa0/2 going down
06:20:00: RSTP(99): Fa0/3 is now root port
S1#
%LINEPROTO-5-UPDOWN: Line protocol on Interface FastEthernet0/1, changed state to down
%LINEPROTO-5-UPDOWN: Line protocol on Interface FastEthernet0/2, changed state to down
S1#
%LINK-3-UPDOWN: Interface FastEthernet0/1, changed state to down
%LINK-3-UPDOWN: Interface FastEthernet0/2, changed state to down
```

Refer to the timestamp in the preceding output. RSTP converged on a new spanning tree for VLAN 99 in less than a second. On PC3, not a single ping was dropped, as can be seen in Figure 5-12.

Figure 5-12   No Pings from PC3 Are Lost Because RSTP Converges in Less than a Second

Task 10: Document the Switch Configurations

On each switch, capture the running configuration to a text file and save it for future reference. These scripts can be edited to expedite configuring switches in future labs.

Task 11: Clean Up

Unless directed otherwise by your instructor, erase the configurations and reload the switches. Disconnect and store the cabling. For PC hosts that are normally connected to other networks (such as the school LAN or to the Internet), reconnect the appropriate cabling and restore the TCP/IP settings.

Packet Tracer Companion: Challenge Spanning Tree Protocol (5.5.2)

You can now open the file LSG03-Lab552.pka on the CD-ROM that accompanies this book to repeat this hands-on lab using Packet Tracer. Remember, however, that Packet Tracer is not a substitute for a hands-on lab experience with real equipment.

Lab 5-3: Troubleshooting Spanning Tree Protocol (5.5.3)

Learning Objectives

Upon completion of this lab, you will be able to

- Analyze a congestion problem in a redundant, switched LAN network

- Recognize the capabilities for per-VLAN load balancing with PVST

- Modify the default STP configuration to optimize available bandwidth

- Verify that modifications have had the intended effect

Scenario

You are responsible for the operation of the redundant switched LAN shown in the topology diagram in Figure 5-13. You and your users have been observing increased latency during peak usage times, and your analysis points to congested trunks. You recognize that of the six trunks configured, only two are forwarding packets in the default STP configuration currently running. The solution to this problem requires more effective use of the available trunks. The PVST+ feature of Cisco switches provides the required flexibility to distribute the inter-switch traffic using all six trunks.

This lab is complete when all wired trunks are carrying traffic, and all three switches are participating in per-VLAN load balancing for the three user VLANs.

Figure 5-13   Topology Diagram for Lab 5-3

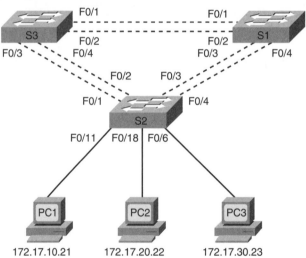

Table 5-9 shows the addressing scheme used in this lab.

Table 5-9   Addressing Table for Lab 5-3

Device Gateway	Interface	IP Address	Subnet Mask	Default
S1	VLAN 99	172.17.99.11	255.255.255.0	N/A
S2	VLAN 99	172.17.99.12	255.255.255.0	N/A
S3	VLAN 99	172.17.99.13	255.255.255.0	N/A
PC1	NIC	172.17.10.21	255.255.255.0	172.17.10.1
PC2	NIC	172.17.20.22	255.255.255.0	172.17.20.1
PC3	NIC	172.17.30.23	255.255.255.0	172.17.30.1

Table 5-10 shows the port assignments used in this lab.

Table 5-10   Port Assignments

Ports	Assignment	Network
Fa0/1–0/4	802.1Q Trunks (Native VLAN 99)	172.17.99.0 /24
Fa0/5–0/10	VLAN 30—Guest (Default)	172.17.30.0 /24
Fa0/11–0/17	VLAN 10—Faculty/Staff	172.17.10.0 /24
Fa0/18–0/24	VLAN 20—Students	172.17.20.0 /24

Task 1: Prepare the Network

Step 1.   Cable a network that is similar to the one shown in Figure 5-13.

Step 2.   Clear any existing configurations on the switches.

Step 3.   Apply the following configurations to each switch. Alternatively, you can open the file LSG03-Lab553-Scripts.txt on the CD-ROM that accompanies this book and copy in the scripts for each of the switches.

S1 Configuration

```
hostname S1
enable secret class
no ip domain-lookup
!
vtp mode server
vtp domain Lab5
vtp password cisco
!
vlan 99
name Management
exit
!
```

Note: All switches Running Config is correct

```
vlan 10
name Faculty/Staff
exit
!
vlan 20
name Students
exit
!
vlan 30
name Guest
exit
!
interface range FastEthernet0/1 - 4
 switchport trunk native vlan 99
 switchport mode trunk
 no shutdown
!
interface range FastEthernet0/5-24
shutdown
!
interface GigabitEthernet0/1 - 2
 shutdown
!
interface Vlan99
 ip address 172.17.99.11 255.255.255.0
 no shutdown
!
line con 0
 logging synchronous
 password cisco
 login
line vty 0 15
 password cisco
 login
!
end
```

S2 Configuration

```
hostname S2
!
enable secret class
no ip domain-lookup
!
vtp mode client
```

```
vtp domain Lab5
vtp password cisco
!
interface range FastEthernet0/5 - 24
 shutdown
interface range GigabitEthernet0/1 - 2
 shutdown
!
interface range FastEthernet0/1 - 4
 switchport trunk native vlan 99
 switchport mode trunk
 no shutdown
!
interface range FastEthernet0/5 - 10
 switchport access vlan 30
 switchport mode access
!
interface range FastEthernet0/11 - 17
 switchport access vlan 10
 switchport mode access
!
interface range FastEthernet0/18 - 24
 switchport access vlan 20
 switchport mode access
!
interface fa0/6
 no shutdown
interface fa0/11
 no shutdown
interface fa0/18
 no shutdown
!
interface Vlan99
 ip address 172.17.99.12 255.255.255.0
 no shutdown
!
line con 0
 password cisco
 logging synchronous
 login
line vty 0 15
 password cisco          ← login
!
end
```

S3 Configuration

```
hostname S3
!
enable secret class
no ip domain-lookup
!
vtp mode client
vtp domain Lab5
vtp password cisco
!
interface range FastEthernet0/5 - 24
 shutdown
interface range GigabitEthernet0/1 - 2
 shutdown
!
interface range FastEthernet0/1 - 4
 switchport trunk native vlan 99
 switchport mode trunk
 no shutdown
!
interface Vlan99
 ip address 172.17.99.13 255.255.255.0
 no shutdown
!
line con 0
 password cisco
 login
line vty 0 15
 password cisco
 login
!
end
```

Task 2: Configure Host PCs (Optional)

It is not necessary to configure the host PCs for this lab. They are shown in Figure 5-13 for consistency. If you wish to configure the PCs anyway, use the addressing in Table 5-9.

Task 3: Identify the Initial State of All Trunks

On each of the switches, display the spanning-tree table with the **show spanning-tree** command. Note which ports are forwarding on each switch, and identify which trunks are not being used in the default configuration. You can use Figure 5-13 to document the initial state of all trunk ports.

Task 4: Modify Spanning Tree to Achieve Load Balancing

Modify the spanning-tree configuration so that all six trunks are in use. Assume that the three user LANs (10, 20, and 30) carry an equal amount of traffic. Aim for a solution that will have a different set of ports forwarding for each of the three user VLANs. At a minimum, each of the three user VLANs should have a different switch as the root of the spanning tree.

Task 5: Document the Switch Configurations

On each switch, capture the running configuration to a text file and save it for future reference. These scripts can be edited to expedite configuring switches in future labs.

Task 6: Clean Up

Unless directed otherwise by your instructor, erase the configurations and reload the switches. Disconnect and store the cabling. For PC hosts that are normally connected to other networks (such as the school LAN or to the Internet), reconnect the appropriate cabling and restore the TCP/IP settings.

Packet Tracer Companion: Troubleshooting Spanning Tree Protocol (5.5.3)

You can now open the file LSG03-Lab553.pka on the CD-ROM that accompanies this book to repeat this hands-on lab using Packet Tracer. Remember, however, that Packet Tracer is not a substitute for a hands-on lab experience with real equipment.

Packet Tracer Skills Integration Challenge

Open the file LSG03-PTSkills5.pka on the CD-ROM that accompanies this book. You will use the topology in Figure 5-14 and the addressing table in Table 5-11 to document your design.

Figure 5-14   Packet Tracer Skills Integration Challenge Topology

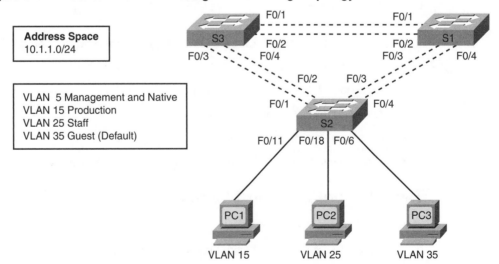

Table 5-11 Addressing Table for the Packet Tracer Skills Integration Challenge Activity

Device	Interface	IP Address	Subnet Mask	Default Gateway
S1	VLAN 5	10.1.1.226	255.255.255.240	10.1.1.225
S2	VLAN 5	10.1.1.227	255.255.255.240	10.1.1.225
S3	VLAN 5	10.1.1.228	255.255.255.240	10.1.1.225
PC1 *(VLAN 15)*	NIC	10.1.1.2	255.255.255.128	10.1.1.1
PC2 *(VLAN 25)*	NIC	10.1.1.130	255.255.255.192	10.1.1.129
PC3 *(VLAN 35)*	NIC	10.1.1.194	255.255.255.224	10.1.1.193

Handwritten notes:

Address space - 10.1.1.0/24

# Host	power	Prefix	NT	Broadcast
prod 100	$2^7 = 128$	/25	1.0	- .127
Staff 50	$2^6 = 64$	/26	1.128	- .191
Guest 20	$2^5 = 32$	/27	1.192	- 223
mang 10	$2^4 = 16$	/28	1.224	- 239.

Learning Objectives

Upon completion of this lab, you will be able to

- Design and document an addressing scheme
- Configure and verify basic device configurations
- Configure VTP
- Configure trunking
- Configure VLANs
- Assign VLANs to ports
- Configure STP
- Configure host PCs

Introduction

In this activity, you will configure a redundant network with VTP, VLANs, and STP. In addition, you will design an addressing scheme based on user requirements. The VLANs in this activity are different from what you have seen in previous chapters. It is important for you to know that the management and native VLAN does not have to be 99. It can be any number you choose. Therefore, we use VLAN 5 in this activity.

Task 1: Design and Document an Addressing Scheme

Your addressing scheme needs to satisfy the following requirements:

- Production VLAN needs 100 host addresses. *- VLAN 15*
- Staff VLAN needs 50 host addresses. *- VLAN - 25*
- Guest VLAN needs 20 host addresses. *- VLAN 35*
- Management&Native VLAN needs 10 host address. *- VLAN 5*

Task 2: Configure and Verify Basic Device Configurations

Step 1. Configure basic commands.

Configure each switch with the following basic parameters. Packet Tracer only grades the hostnames and default gateways.

- Hostnames
- Banner

- Enable secret password
- Line configurations
- Service encryption
- Default gateways *on all switches. @ config mode. ip default-gateway 10.1.1.225*

Step 2. Configure the management VLAN interface on S1, S2, and S3.

Create and enable interface VLAN 5 on each switch. Use your addressing scheme for the address configuration.

Step 3. Check results.

Your completion percentage should be 18 percent. If not, click **Check Results** to see which required components are not yet completed.

Task 3: Configure VTP

Step 1. Configure the VTP mode on all three switches.

Configure S1 as the server. Configure S2 and S3 as clients.

Step 2. Configure the VTP domain name on all three switches.

Use **XYZCORP** as the VTP domain name.

Step 3. Configure the VTP domain password on all three switches.

Use **westbranch** as the VTP domain password.

Step 4. Check results.

Your completion percentage should be 30 percent. If not, click **Check Results** to see which required components are not yet completed.

Task 4: Configure Trunking

Step 1. Configure trunking on S1, S2, and S3.

Configure the appropriate interfaces in trunking mode and assign VLAN 5 as the native VLAN.

Step 2. Check results.

Your completion percentage should be 66 percent. If not, click **Check Results** to see which required components are not yet completed.

Task 5: Configure VLANs

Step 1. Create the VLANs on S1.

Create and name the following VLANs on S1 only. VTP will advertise the new VLANs to S1 and S2.

- VLAN 15: Production
- VLAN 25: Staff
- VLAN 35: Guest(Default)
- VLAN 5: Management&Native

Step 2.   Verify that VLANs have been sent to S2 and S3.

Use appropriate commands to verify that S2 and S3 now have the VLANs you created on S1. It may take a few minutes for Packet Tracer to simulate the VTP advertisements.

Step 3.   Check results.

Your completion percentage should be 72 percent. If not, click **Check Results** to see which required components are not yet completed.

Task 6: Assign VLANs to Ports

Step 1.   Assign VLANs to access ports on S2.

Assign the PC access ports to VLANs:

- VLAN 15: PC1 connected to Fa0/11

- VLAN 25: PC2 connected to Fa0/18

- VLAN 35: PC3 connected to Fa0/6

Step 2.   Verify VLAN implementation.

Use the appropriate command to verify your VLAN implementation.

Step 3.   Check results.

Your completion percentage should be 81 percent. If not, click **Check Results** to see which required components are not yet completed.

Task 7: Configure STP

Step 1.   Ensure that S1 is the root bridge.

Set the priority level on S1 so that it is always the root bridge for all VLANs.

Step 2.   Verify that S1 is the root bridge.

Step 3.   Check results.

Your completion percentage should be 87 percent. If not, click **Check Results** to see which required components are not yet completed.

Task 8: Configure Host PCs

Step 1.   Configure the host PCs.

Use your addressing scheme to configure the PCs' Fast Ethernet interface and default gateway.

Step 2.   Check results.

Your completion percentage should be 100 percent. If not, click **Check Results** to see which required components are not yet completed.

CHAPTER 6

Inter-VLAN Routing

Now that you have a network with many different VLANs, the next question is, "How do you permit devices on separate VLANs to communicate?" The exercises in this chapter review the concepts of inter-VLAN routing and how it is used to permit devices on separate VLANs to communicate.

The Study Guide portion of this chapter uses a combination of fill-in-the-blank, open-ended question, and Packet Tracer exercises to test your knowledge of inter-VLAN routing concepts and configurations.

The Labs and Activities portion of this chapter includes all the online curriculum labs to ensure that you have mastered the hands-on skills needed to understand inter-VLAN routing concepts and configuration.

As you work through this chapter, use Chapter 6 in *LAN Switching and Wireless, CCNA Exploration Companion Guide* or use the corresponding Chapter 6 in the Exploration LAN Switching and Wireless online curriculum for assistance.

Study Guide

Inter-VLAN Routing

The exercise in this section covers what inter-VLAN routing is and some of the different ways to accomplish inter-VLAN routing on a network.

Inter-VLAN Routing Concepts Exercise

Introducing Inter-VLAN Routing

Define inter-VLAN routing:

_____

_____

Briefly explain traditional inter-VLAN routing:

_____

_____

_____

_____

Briefly explain "router-on-a-stick" inter-VLAN routing:

_____

_____

_____

_____

What are subinterfaces?

_____

_____

Interfaces and Subinterfaces

In Figure 6-1, PC1 and PC3 need connectivity between each other. However, each is on a different VLAN. Assume S1 is already configured for traditional inter-VLAN routing. In Figure 6-1, connect S1 and R1 and label the interfaces. Then record the commands to configure R1 with traditional inter-VLAN routing. Use the first available IP addresses in each VLAN for the router interfaces.

Figure 6-1   Traditional Inter-VLAN Routing Configuration

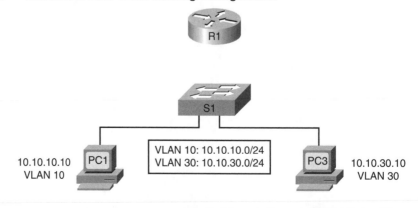

VLAN 10: 10.10.10.0/24
VLAN 30: 10.10.30.0/24

10.10.10.10   PC1
VLAN 10

PC3   10.10.30.10
VLAN 30

In the following lines, record the commands to configure R1 with traditional inter-VLAN routing:

_____

_____

_____

_____

_____

_____

In Figure 6-2, PC1 and PC3 need connectivity between each other. However, each is on a different VLAN. Assume S1 is already configured for router-on-a-stick inter-VLAN routing. In Figure 6-2, connect S1 and R1 and label the interfaces. Then record the commands to configure R1 with router-on-a-stick inter-VLAN routing. Use the first available IP addresses in each VLAN for the router interfaces.

Figure 6-2   Router-on-a-Stick Inter-VLAN Routing Configuration

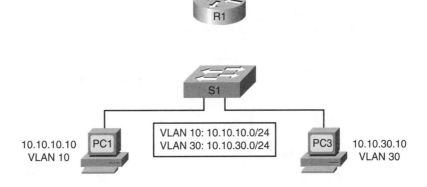

In the following lines, record the commands to configure R1 with router-on-a-stick inter-VLAN routing:

_____

_____

_____

_____

_____

_____

_____

_____

Complete Table 6-1, which compares the characteristics of configuring traditional inter-VLAN routing with router-on-a-stick inter-VLAN routing.

Table 6-1   Comparing Traditional and Router-on-a-Stick Inter-VLAN Routing Characteristics

Characteristic	Traditional	Router-on-a-Stick
Physical interfaces		
Bandwidth		
Switch port configuration		

Table 6-1   Comparing Traditional and Router-on-a-Stick Inter-VLAN Routing Characteristics   *continued*

Characteristic	Traditional	Router-on-a-Stick
Expense		
Physical complexity		

Configuring Inter-VLAN Routing

The exercises in this section cover how to configure inter-VLAN routing and review the commands to configure a switch to support inter-VLAN routing.

Inter-VLAN Routing Configuration Exercise

Figure 6-3 shows two topologies. One topology is using traditional inter-VLAN routing and the other topology is using router-on-a-stick inter-VLAN routing. The addressing for both topologies is shown in Table 6-2. For this exercise, you will not configure a separate management or native VLAN.

Figure 6-3   Inter-VLAN Routing Configuration Topology

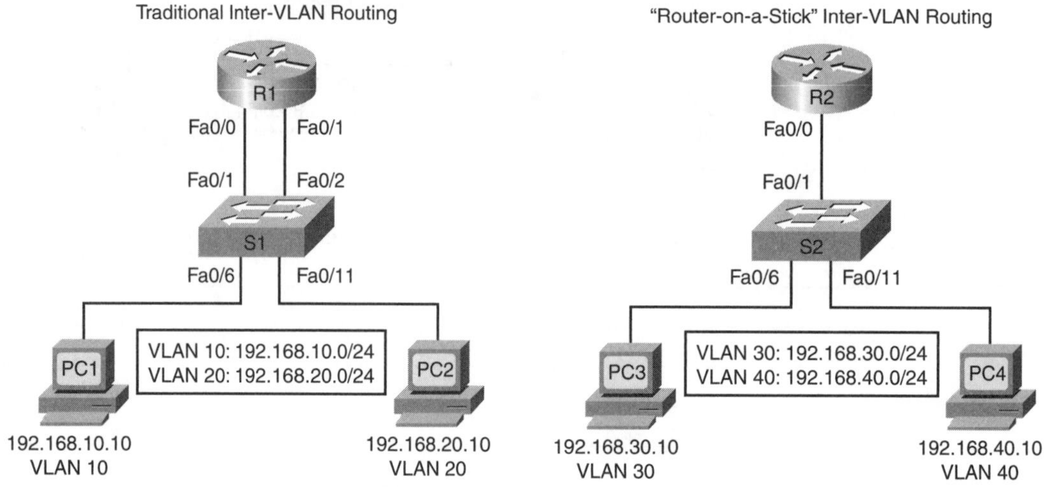

Table 6-2   Addressing Table for Inter-VLAN Routing Configuration Exercise

Device	Interface	IP Address	Subnet Mask	Default Gateway
R1	Fa0/0	192.168.10.1	255.255.255.0	—
	Fa0/1	192.168.20.1	255.255.255.0	—
PC1	NIC	192.168.10.10	255.255.255.0	192.168.10.1
PC2	NIC	192.168.20.10	255.255.255.0	192.168.20.10
R2	Fa0/0.30	192.168.30.1	255.255.255.0	—
	Fa0/0.40	192.168.40.1	255.255.255.0	—
PC3	NIC	192.168.30.10	255.255.255.0	192.168.30.1
PC4	NIC	192.168.40.10	255.255.255.0	192.168.40.1

Enter the commands, including the router prompt, to configure R1 for traditional inter-VLAN routing:

_____

_____

_____

_____

_____

_____

Enter the commands, including the switch prompt, to configure S1 to forward VLAN traffic. Assume the VLANs are already created in the VLAN database. However, VLANs have not yet been assigned to any ports.

_____

_____

_____

_____

_____

_____

Enter the commands, including the router prompt, to configure R2 for router-on-a-stick inter-VLAN routing:

_____

_____

_____

_____

_____

_____

_____

Enter the commands, including the switch prompt, to configure S2 to forward VLAN traffic. Assume the VLANs are already created in the VLAN database. However, VLANs have not yet been assigned to any ports.

_____

_____

_____

_____

_____

_____

_____

Packet Tracer Exercise 6-1: Inter-VLAN Configuration

Now you are ready to use Packet Tracer to apply your answers to the "Inter-VLAN Routing Configuration Exercise." Open file LSG03-0601.pka on the CD-ROM that accompanies this book to perform this exercise using Packet Tracer.

Note: The following instructions are also contained within the Packet Tracer Exercise.

Learning Objectives

Upon completion of this Packet Tracer Exercise, you will be able to

- Configure traditional inter-VLAN routing
- Configure router-on-a-stick inter-VLAN routing
- Verify connectivity
- Save the Packet Tracer file

Scenario

In this exercise, you will practice configuring both traditional and router-on-a-stick inter-VLAN routing. The routers and switches have a basic configuration. The passwords are **cisco** for user EXEC mode and **class** for privileged EXEC mode. Use your answers from the "Inter-VLAN Routing Configuration Exercise" to complete the tasks.

Task 1: Configure Traditional Inter-VLAN Routing

Step 1.   Configure R1 for traditional inter-VLAN routing.

Step 2.   Configure S1 to forward VLAN traffic.

Step 3.   Your completion percentage should be 53 percent. If not, click **Check Results** to see which required components are not yet completed.

Task 2: Configure Router-on-a-Stick Inter-VLAN Routing

Step 1.   Configure R2 for router-on-a-stick inter-VLAN routing.

Step 2.   Configure S2 to forward VLAN traffic.

Step 3.   Your completion percentage should be 100 percent. If not, click **Check Results** to see which required components are not yet completed.

Task 3: Verify Connectivity

PC1 should be able to ping PC2. PC3 should be able to ping PC4. Alternatively, you can click **Check Results** and then the **Connectivity Tests** tab. The status of both connectivity tests should be listed as "Correct."

Task 4: Save the Packet Tracer File

Save your Packet Tracer file as LSG03-0601-end.pka.

Troubleshooting Inter-VLAN Routing

The exercises in this section explore common issues and troubleshooting methods to identify and correct problems in inter-VLAN routing implementations.

Common Errors and Troubleshooting Tools Exercise

Using the examples shown in the chapter, list at least six common errors in the inter-VLAN routing implementations.

Switch Configuration Issues:

- _____
- _____
- _____

Router Configuration Issues:

- _____
- _____

IP Addressing Issues:

- _____
- _____
- _____

What are some useful commands you can use to isolate problems in an inter-VLAN routing network?

Switch IOS Commands:

- _____
- _____

Router IOS Commands:

- _____
- _____

PC Commands:

- _____

Packet Tracer Exercise 6-2: Troubleshooting Inter-VLAN Routing

Now you are ready to use Packet Tracer to apply your knowledge of troubleshooting techniques. Open file LSG03-0602.pka on the CD-ROM that accompanies this book to perform this exercise using Packet Tracer.

Note: The following instructions are also contained within the Packet Tracer Exercise.

Learning Objectives

Upon completion of this Packet Tracer Exercise, you will be able to

- Test connectivity between the PCs and the router

- Gather data on the problems

- Implement solutions and test connectivity

Scenario

In this exercise, you will practice troubleshooting both traditional and router-on-a-stick inter-VLAN routing. The routers, switches, and PCs are already configured and are using the IP addresses listed in Table 6-2. You cannot access the routers or switches directly. Instead, you must use the available console connections through the PCs. The passwords are **cisco** for user EXEC mode and **class** for privileged EXEC mode. Use connectivity tests and **show** commands to discover problems and troubleshoot the networks. The exercise is complete when you achieve 100 percent and the two PCs on each network can ping each other.

Task 1: Configure Traditional Inter-VLAN Routing

The following tests should be successful at the conclusion of this activity:

- PC1 can ping R1.

- PC2 can ping R1.

- PC1 can ping PC2.

- PC3 can ping R2.

- PC4 can ping R2.

- PC3 can ping PC4.

Each of these tests should fail on the first attempt.

Task 2: Gather Data on the Problems

Step 1.   Verify the configuration on the PCs.

Are the following configurations for each PC correct?

- IP address

- Subnet mask

- Default gateway

_____

Step 2.   Verify the configuration on the switches.

Are the configurations on the switches correct? Be sure to verify the following:

- Ports assigned to the correct VLANs

- Ports configured for the correct mode

- Ports connected to the correct device

_____

_____

Step 3.   Verify the configuration on the routers.

Are the configurations on the routers correct? Be sure to verify the following:

- IP addresses

- Interface status

- Encapsulation and VLAN assignment

_____

_____

Step 4.   Document the problems and suggest solutions.

What are the reasons connectivity failed between the PCs? What are the solutions? There could be more than one problem and more than one solution. All solutions must conform to the topology diagram in Figure 6-3 and the addressing in Table 6-2.

List the problems, if any, and the solutions for the PCs:

_____

List the problems, if any, and the solutions for the switches:

_____

_____

_____

_____

_____

_____

List the problems, if any, and the solutions for routers:

_____

_____

_____

_____

Task 3: Implement the Solution and Test Connectivity

Step 1.   Make changes according to the suggested solutions in Task 2.

Note: If you make changes to the switch configuration, you should make the changes in Realtime mode rather than Simulation mode. This is necessary so that the switch port will proceed to the forwarding state.

Step 2.   Test connectivity between PCs and R1.

If you change any IP configurations, you should create new pings because the prior pings use the old IP address:

- PC1 should be able to ping R1.

- PC2 should be able to ping R1.

- PC1 should be able to ping PC2.

- PC3 should be able to ping R2.

- PC4 should be able to ping R2.

- PC3 should be able to ping PC4.

If any pings fail, return to Task 2 to continue troubleshooting.

Step 3.   Check results.

Your completion percentage should be 100 percent. If not, return to Step 1 and continue to implement your suggested solutions. You will not be able to click **Check Results** and see which required components are not yet completed. However, you can click **Check Results** and then the **Connectivity Tests** tab. The status of all six connectivity tests should be listed as "Correct."

Task 4: Save the Packet Tracer File

Save your Packet Tracer file as LSG03-0602-end.pka.

Labs and Activities

Command Reference

In Table 6-3, record the command, *including the correct prompt*, that fits the description. Fill in any blanks with the appropriate missing information.

Table 6-3   Commands for Inter-VLAN Routing Configuration

Command	Description
	Creates a subinterface numbered 10 on the router for Fa0/0
	Specifies IEEE 801.1Q as the VLAN tagging method for VLAN 10 on this subinterface

Lab 6-1: Basic Inter-VLAN Routing (6.4.1)

Learning Objectives

Upon completion of this lab, you will be able to

- Cable a network according to the topology diagram in Figure 6-4

- Clear configurations and reload a switch and a router to the default state

- Perform basic configuration tasks on a switched LAN and router

- Configure VLANs and VLAN Trunking Protocol (VTP) on all switches

- Demonstrate and explain the impact of Layer 3 boundaries imposed by creating VLANs

- Configure a router to support 802.1Q trunking on a Fast Ethernet interface

- Configure a router with subinterfaces corresponding to the configured VLANs

- Demonstrate and explain inter-VLAN routing

Figure 6-4 shows the topology diagram for this lab.

Figure 6-4   Topology Diagram for Lab 6-1

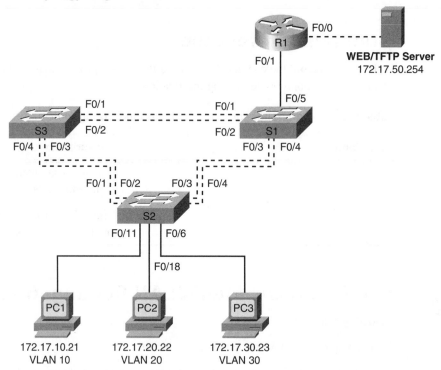

Table 6-4 shows the addressing scheme used in this lab.

Table 6-4   Addressing Table for Lab 6-1

Device	Interface	IP Address	Subnet Mask	Default Gateway
R1	Fa0/0	172.17.50.1	255.255.255.0	—
	Fa0/1.1	172.17.1.1	255.255.255.0	—
	Fa0/1.10	172.17.10.1	255.255.255.0	—
	Fa0/1.20	172.17.20.1	255.255.255.0	—
	Fa0/1.30	172.17.30.1	255.255.255.0	—
	Fa0/1.99	172.17.99.1	255.255.255.0	—
S1	VLAN 99	172.17.99.11	255.255.255.0	172.17.99.1
S2	VLAN 99	172.17.99.12	255.255.255.0	172.17.99.1
S3	VLAN 99	172.17.99.13	255.255.255.0	172.17.99.1
PC1	NIC	172.17.10.21	255.255.255.0	172.17.10.1
PC2	NIC	172.17.20.22	255.255.255.0	172.17.20.1
PC3	NIC	172.17.30.23	255.255.255.0	172.17.30.1
Web server	NIC	172.17.50.254	255.255.255.0	172.17.50.1

Table 6-5 shows the port assignments used in this lab.

Table 6-5   Port Assignments for S2

Ports	Assignment	Network
Fa0/1–0/4	802.1Q Trunks (Native VLAN 99)	172.17.99.0 /24
Fa0/5–0/10	VLAN 30—Guest (Default)	172.17.30.0 /24
Fa0/11–0/17	VLAN 10—Faculty/Staff	172.17.10.0 /24
Fa0/18–0/24	VLAN 20—Students	172.17.20.0 /24

Task 1: Prepare the Network

Step 1.   Cable a network that is similar to the one shown in Figure 6-4.

You can use any current switch in your lab as long as it has the required interfaces shown in Figure 6-4 and supports 802.1Q encapsulation. The router you choose must support inter-VLAN routing. The output shown in this lab is based on Cisco 2960 switches and an 1841 router. Other switch or router models may produce different output.

Set up console connections to all three switches.

Step 2.   Clear any existing configurations on the switches.

Clear NVRAM, delete the vlan.dat file, and reload the switches. Refer to "Lab 2-1: Basic Switch Configuration (2.5.1)" if necessary for the procedure. After the reload is complete, use the **show vlan** command to confirm that only default VLANs exist and that all ports are assigned to VLAN 1.

```
S1#show vlan

VLAN Name                             Status    Ports
---- -------------------------------- --------- -------------------------------
1    default                          active    Fa0/1, Fa0/2, Fa0/3, Fa0/4
                                                 Fa0/5, Fa0/6, Fa0/7, Fa0/8
                                                 Fa0/9, Fa0/10, Fa0/11, Fa0/12
                                                 Fa0/13, Fa0/14, Fa0/15,Fa0/16
                                                 Fa0/17, Fa0/18, Fa0/19,Fa0/20
                                                 Fa0/21, Fa0/22, Fa0/23,Fa0/24
                                                 Gig1/1, Gig1/2
1002 fddi-default                     active
1003 token-ring-default               active
1004 fddinet-default                  active
1005 trnet-default                    active
```

Step 3. Disable all ports on the switches using the **shutdown** command.

Ensure that the initial switch port states are inactive by disabling all ports. Use the **interface range** command to simplify this task. Commands for S1 are shown here:

```
S1(config)#interface range fa0/1-24
S1(config-if-range)#shutdown
S1(config-if-range)#interface range gi0/1-2
S1(config-if-range)#shutdown
```

Step 4. Reenable the active user ports on S2 in access mode:

```
S2(config)#interface fa0/6
S2(config-if)#switchport mode access
S2(config-if)#no shutdown
S2(config-if)#interface fa0/11
S2(config-if)#switchport mode access
S2(config-if)#no shutdown
S2(config-if)#interface fa0/18
S2(config-if)#switchport mode access
S2(config-if)#no shutdown
```

Task 2: Perform Basic Switch Configurations

Configure the S1, S2, and S3 switches according to the addressing table and the following guidelines:

- Configure the switch hostname.
- Disable DNS lookup.
- Configure an enable secret password of **class**.
- Configure a password of **cisco** for the console connections.
- Configure a password of **cisco** for vty connections.
- Configure the default gateway on each switch.

Only the commands for S1 are shown here:

```
Switch>enable
Switch#configure terminal
Enter configuration commands, one per line.  End with CNTL/Z.
Switch(config)#hostname S1
S1(config)#enable secret class
S1(config)#no ip domain-lookup
S1(config)#ip default-gateway 172.17.99.1
S1(config)#line console 0
S1(config-line)#password cisco
S1(config-line)#login
S1(config-line)#line vty 0 15
S1(config-line)#password cisco
S1(config-line)#login
S1(config-line)#end
%SYS-5-CONFIG_I: Configured from console by console
```

```
S1#copy running-config startup-config
Destination filename [startup-config]?
Building configuration...
[OK]
```

Task 3: Configure Host PCs

Configure the Ethernet interfaces of PC1, PC2, PC3, and the remote web/TFTP server with the IP addresses in Table 6-4.

Task 4: Configure VTP on the Switches

Step 1.   Configure VTP.

Configure VTP on the three switches using the following guidelines:

- S1 is the VTP server; S2 and S3 are VTP clients.

- The VTP domain name is **Lab6**.

- The VTP password is **cisco**.

Remember that VTP domain names and passwords are case sensitive. The default operating mode is server.

```
S1(config)#vtp mode server
Device mode already VTP SERVER.
S1(config)#vtp domain Lab6
Changing VTP domain name from NULL to Lab6
S1(config)#vtp password cisco
Setting device VLAN database password to cisco
```

```
S2(config)#vtp mode client
Setting device to VTP CLIENT mode
S2(config)#vtp domain Lab6
Changing VTP domain name from NULL to Lab6
S2(config)#vtp password cisco
Setting device VLAN database password to cisco
```

```
S3(config)#vtp mode client
Setting device to VTP CLIENT mode
S3(config)#vtp domain Lab6
Changing VTP domain name from NULL to Lab6
S3(config)#vtp password cisco
Setting device VLAN database password to cisco
S3(config)#end
```

√   **Step 2.**   Configure trunk links and the native VLAN.

For each switch, configure ports Fa0/1 through Fa0/4 as trunking ports. The Fa0/5 port on S1 also needs to be configured as a trunking port because it will trunk to the router, R1. Designate VLAN 99 as the native VLAN for these trunks. Remember to activate the ports.

Only the commands for S1 are shown here:

```
S1(config)#interface range fa0/1-5
S1(config-if-range)#switchport mode trunk
S1(config-if-range)#switchport trunk native vlan 99
S1(config-if-range)#no shutdown
```

Step 3. Configure the VTP server with VLANs.

Configure the following VLANs on the VTP server only:

- VLAN 10: Faculty/Staff
- VLAN 20: Students
- VLAN 30: Guest
- VLAN 99: Management

```
S1(config)#vlan 10
S1(config-vlan)#name faculty/staff
S1(config-vlan)#vlan 20
S1(config-vlan)#name students
S1(config-vlan)#vlan 30
S1(config-vlan)#name guest
S1(config-vlan)#vlan 99
S1(config-vlan)#name management
S1(config-vlan)#end
S1#
```

Step 4. Verify the VLANs.

Verify that all four VLANs have been distributed to the client switches. You should have output similar to the following:

```
S2#show vlan brief
```

VLAN	Name	Status	Ports
1	default	active	Fa0/1, Fa0/2, Fa0/4, Fa0/5
			Fa0/6, Fa0/7, Fa0/8, Fa0/9
			Fa0/10, Fa0/11, Fa0/12,Fa0/13
			Fa0/14, Fa0/15, Fa0/16,Fa0/17
			Fa0/18, Fa0/19, Fa0/20,Fa0/21
			Fa0/22, Fa0/23, Fa0/24, Gi0/1
			Gi0/2
10	faculty/staff	active	
20	students	active	
30	guest	active	
99	management	active	

```
S3#show vlan brief
```

```
VLAN  Name              Status   Ports
----  ----------------  ------.  ------------------.
1     default           active   Fa0/1, Fa0/2, Fa0/4, Fa0/5
                                 Fa0/6, Fa0/7, Fa0/8, Fa0/9
                                 Fa0/10, Fa0/11, Fa0/12,Fa0/13
                                 Fa0/14, Fa0/15, Fa0/16,Fa0/17
                                 Fa0/18, Fa0/19, Fa0/20,Fa0/21
                                 Fa0/22, Fa0/23, Fa0/24, Gi0/1
                                 Gi0/2
10    faculty/staff     active
20    students          active
30    guest             active
99    management        active
```

Step 5.   Configure the management interface address on all three switches:

```
S1(config)#interface vlan99
S1(config-if)#ip address 172.17.99.11 255.255.255.0
S1(config-if)#no shutdown
```

```
S2(config)#interface vlan99
S2(config-if)#ip address 172.17.99.12 255.255.255.0
S2(config-if)#no shutdown
```

```
S3(config)#interface vlan99
S3(config-if)#ip address 172.17.99.13 255.255.255.0
S3(config-if)#no shutdown
```

Verify that the switches are correctly configured by pinging between them. From S1, ping the management interface on S2 and S3. From S2, ping the management interface on S3.

Were the pings successful?

_____ yes _____

If not, troubleshoot the switch configurations and try again.

Step 6.   Assign switch ports to the VLANs.

Assign ports to VLANs on S2 according to Table 6-5 at the beginning of the lab. Activate the ports connected to the PCs.

```
S2(config)#interface range fa0/5-10
S2(config-if-range)#switchport access vlan 30
S2(config-if-range)#interface range fa0/11-17
S2(config-if-range)#switchport access vlan 10
S2(config-if-range)#interface range fa0/18-24
S2(config-if-range)#switchport access vlan 20
S2(config-if-range)#end
S2#
```

fa 0/5 to be mode trunk on PT to receive credit

Step 7.   Check connectivity between VLANs.

Open command windows on the three hosts connected to S2. Ping from PC1
(172.17.10.21) to PC2 (172.17.20.22). Ping from PC2 to PC3 (172.17.30.23).

Are the pings successful?

_____ *NO* _____

If not, why do these pings fail?

because when ping from vlan to another vlan, it
require a layer 3 involve

_____

Task 5: Configure the Router and the Remote Server LAN

Step 1.   Clear the configuration on the router and reload.

Step 2.   Create a basic configuration on the router:

- Configure the router with hostname R1.

- Disable DNS lookup.

- Configure an EXEC mode password of **cisco**.

- Configure a password of **cisco** for the console connection.

- Configure a password of **cisco** for the vty connections.

Step 3.   Configure the trunking interface on R1.

You have demonstrated that connectivity between VLANs requires routing at the network
layer, exactly like connectivity between any two remote networks. There are a couple of
options for configuring routing between VLANs.

The first is something of a brute-force approach. A Layer 3 device, either a router or a
Layer 3–capable switch, is connected to a LAN switch with multiple physical connections—a separate connection for each VLAN that requires inter-VLAN connectivity. Each
of the switch ports used by the Layer 3 device is configured in a different VLAN on the
switch. After IP addresses are assigned to the interfaces on the Layer 3 device, the routing
table has directly connected routes for all VLANs, and inter-VLAN routing is enabled.
The limitations to this approach are the lack of sufficient Fast Ethernet ports on routers,
underutilization of ports on Layer 3 switches and routers, and excessive wiring and manual
configuration. The topology used in this lab does not use this approach.

A better approach is to use one physical Fast Ethernet connection between the Layer 3
device (the router) and the distribution layer switch. This connection is configured as an
IEEE 802.1Q trunk to allow all inter-VLAN traffic to be carried to and from the routing
device on a single trunk. However, it requires that the Layer 3 interface be configured with
multiple IP addresses. This is done by creating "virtual" interfaces, called subinterfaces, on
one of the router Fast Ethernet ports. Each subinterface is then configured for 802.1Q
encapsulation.

Using the subinterface configuration approach requires these steps:

1. Enter subinterface configuration mode.

2. Establish trunking encapsulation.

3. Associate a VLAN with the subinterface.

4. Assign an IP address from the VLAN to the subinterface.

The commands are as follows:

```
R1(config)#interface fastethernet 0/1
R1(config-if)#no shutdown
R1(config-if)#interface fastethernet 0/1.1
R1(config-subif)#encapsulation dot1q 1
R1(config-subif)#ip address 172.17.1.1 255.255.255.0
R1(config-subif)#interface fastethernet 0/1.10
R1(config-subif)#encapsulation dot1q 10
R1(config-subif)#ip address 172.17.10.1 255.255.255.0
R1(config-subif)#interface fastethernet 0/1.20
R1(config-subif)#encapsulation dot1q 20
R1(config-subif)#ip address 172.17.20.1 255.255.255.0
R1(config-subif)#interface fastethernet 0/1.30
R1(config-subif)#encapsulation dot1q 30
R1(config-subif)#ip address 172.17.30.1 255.255.255.0
R1(config-subif)#interface fastethernet 0/1.99
R1(config-subif)#encapsulation dot1q 99 native
R1(config-subif)#ip address 172.17.99.1 255.255.255.0
```

To set encapsulation type to 802.1Q and assign VLAN 1 to the virtual interface

Note the following points highlighted in the preceding configuration:

■ The physical interface is enabled using the **no shutdown** command, because router interfaces are down by default. The virtual interfaces are up by default.

■ The subinterface can use any number that can be described with 32 bits, but it is good practice to assign the number of the VLAN as the interface number, as has been done here.

■ The native VLAN is specified on the Layer 3 device so that it is consistent with the switches. Otherwise, VLAN 1 would be the native VLAN by default, and there would be no communication between the router and the management VLAN on the switches.

Step 4. Configure the server LAN interface on R1:

```
R1(config)#interface FastEthernet0/0
R1(config-if)#ip address 172.17.50.1 255.255.255.0
R1(config-if)#description server interface
R1(config-if)#no shutdown
R1(config-if)#end
```

There are now six networks configured. Verify that you can route packets to all six by checking the routing table on R1:

```
R1#show ip route
<output omitted>

Gateway of last resort is not set
```

```
          172.17.0.0/24 is subnetted, 6 subnets
C          172.17.50.0 is directly connected, FastEthernet0/0
C          172.17.30.0 is directly connected, FastEthernet0/1.30
C          172.17.20.0 is directly connected, FastEthernet0/1.20
C          172.17.10.0 is directly connected, FastEthernet0/1.10
C          172.17.1.0 is directly connected, FastEthernet0/1.1
C          172.17.99.0 is directly connected, FastEthernet0/1.99
```

If your routing table does not show all six networks, troubleshoot your configuration and resolve the problem before proceeding.

Step 5.   Verify inter-VLAN routing.

From PC1, verify that you can ping the remote server (172.17.50.254) and the other two hosts (172.17.20.22 and 172.17.30.23). It may take a couple of pings before the end-to-end path is established.

Are the pings successful?

 yes.
_____

If not, troubleshoot your configuration. Check to make sure that the default gateways have been set on all PCs and all switches. If any of the hosts have gone into hibernation, the connected interface may go down.

Task 6: Reflection

In Task 5, it was recommended that you configure VLAN 99 as the native VLAN in the router Fa0/0.99 interface configuration. Why would packets from the router or hosts fail when trying to reach the switch management interfaces if the native VLAN were left in default?

_____
_____
_____
_____

Task 7: Document the Switch Configurations

On the router and each switch, capture the running configuration to a text file and save it for future reference. These scripts can be edited to expedite configuring switches in future labs.

Task 8: Clean Up

Unless directed otherwise by your instructor, erase the configurations and reload the router and switches. Disconnect and store the cabling. For PC hosts that are normally connected to other networks (such as the school LAN or to the Internet), reconnect the appropriate cabling and restore the TCP/IP settings.

Packet Tracer Companion: Basic Inter-VLAN Routing (6.4.1)

You can now open the file LSG03-Lab641.pka on the CD-ROM that accompanies this book to repeat this hands-on lab using Packet Tracer. Remember, however, that Packet Tracer is not a substitute for a hands-on lab experience with real equipment.

Lab 6-2: Challenge Inter-VLAN Routing (6.4.2)

Learning Objectives

Upon completion of this lab, you will be able to

- Cable a network according to the topology diagram in Figure 6-5

- Clear configurations and reload a switch and a router to the default state

- Perform basic configuration tasks on a switched LAN and a router

- Configure VLANs and VLAN Trunking Protocol (VTP) on all switches

- Configure a router to support 802.1Q trunking on a Fast Ethernet interface

- Configure a router with subinterfaces corresponding to the configured VLANs

- Demonstrate inter-VLAN routing

Figure 6-5 shows the topology diagram for this lab.

Figure 6-5   Topology Diagram for Lab 6-2

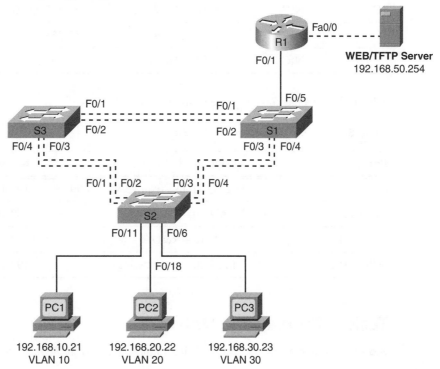

Table 6-6 shows the addressing scheme used in this lab.

Table 6-6   Addressing Table for Lab 6-2

Device	Interface	IP Address	Subnet Mask	Default Gateway
R1	Fa0/0	192.168.50.1	255.255.255.0	—
	Fa0/1.1	192.168.1.1	255.255.255.0	—
	Fa0/1.10	192.168.10.1	255.255.255.0	—
	Fa0/1.20	192.168.20.1	255.255.255.0	—
	Fa0/1.30	192.168.30.1	255.255.255.0	—
	Fa0/1.99	192.168.99.1	255.255.255.0	—
S1	VLAN 99	192.168.99.11	255.255.255.0	192.168.99.1
S2	VLAN 99	192.168.99.12	255.255.255.0	192.168.99.1
S3	VLAN 99	192.168.99.13	255.255.255.0	192.168.99.1
PC1	NIC	192.168.10.21	255.255.255.0	192.168.10.1
PC2	NIC	192.168.20.22	255.255.255.0	192.168.20.1
PC3	NIC	192.168.30.23	255.255.255.0	192.168.30.1
Server	NIC	192.168.50.254	255.255.255.0	192.168.50.1

Table 6-7 shows the port assignments used in this lab.

Table 6-7   Port Assignments for S2

Ports	Assignment	Network
Fa0/1–0/4	802.1Q Trunks (Native VLAN 99)	192.168.99.0 /24
Fa0/5–0/10	VLAN 30—Sales	192.168.30.0 /24
Fa0/11–0/17	VLAN 10—R&D	192.168.10.0 /24
Fa0/18–0/24	VLAN 20—Engineering	192.168.20.0 /24

Task 1: Prepare the Network

Step 1.   Cable a network that is similar to the one shown in Figure 6-5.

Step 2.   Clear any existing configurations on the switches, and initialize all ports in the shutdown state.

Task 2: Perform Basic Switch Configurations

Step 1.   Configure the switches according to the following guidelines:

- Configure the switch hostname.

- Disable DNS lookup.

- Configure an EXEC mode password of **class**.

- Configure a password of **cisco** for console connections.

- Configure a password of **cisco** for vty connections.

Step 2. Reenable the user ports on S2.

Task 3: Configure Host PCs

Configure the PCs. You can complete this lab using only two PCs by simply changing the IP addressing for the two PCs specific to a test you want to conduct. Alternatively, you can configure all three PCs with the IP addresses and default gateways.

Task 4: Configure VTP and VLANs

Step 1. Configure VTP.

Configure VTP on the three switches using the following guidelines:

- S1 is the VTP server; S2 and S3 are VTP clients.

- The VTP domain name is **Lab6**.

- The VTP password is **cisco**.

Remember that VTP domain names and passwords are case sensitive. The default operating mode is server.

Step 2. Configure trunk links and the native VLAN.

For each switch, configure ports Fa0/1 through Fa0/4 as trunking ports. The Fa0/5 port on S1 also needs to be configured as a trunking port because it will trunk to the router, R1. Designate VLAN 99 as the native VLAN for these trunks. Remember to activate the ports.

Step 3. Configure the VTP server with VLANs.

Configure the following VLANs on the VTP server only:

- VLAN 10: R&D

- VLAN 20: Engineering

- VLAN 30: Sales

- VLAN 99: Management

Step 4. Verify the VLANs.

Verify that all four VLANs have been distributed to the client switches. At this point in the lab, all ports should be in VLAN 1. You should have output similar to the following:

```
S2#show vlan brief

VLAN Name                             Status    Ports
---- -------------------------------- --------- -------------------------------
1    default                          active    Fa0/1, Fa0/2, Fa0/4, Fa0/5
                                                Fa0/6, Fa0/7, Fa0/8, Fa0/9
                                                Fa0/10, Fa0/11, Fa0/12,Fa0/13
                                                Fa0/14, Fa0/15, Fa0/16,Fa0/17
                                                Fa0/18, Fa0/19, Fa0/20,Fa0/21
                                                Fa0/22, Fa0/23, Fa0/24, Gi0/1
                                                Gi0/2
```

```
10    R&D                      active
20    Engineering              active
30    Sales                    active
99    Management               active


S3#show vlan brief

VLAN Name                     Status   Ports
--   -----------------        -----    -----------------

1    default                  active   Fa0/1, Fa0/2, Fa0/4, Fa0/5
                                       Fa0/6, Fa0/7, Fa0/8, Fa0/9
                                       Fa0/10, Fa0/11, Fa0/12,Fa0/13
                                       Fa0/14, Fa0/15, Fa0/16,Fa0/17
                                       Fa0/18, Fa0/19, Fa0/20,Fa0/21
                                       Fa0/22, Fa0/23, Fa0/24, Gi0/1
                                       Gi0/2
10    R&D                      active
20    Engineering              active
30    Sales                    active
99    Management               active
```

Step 5. Configure the management interface address on all three switches.

Verify that the switches are correctly configured by pinging between them. From S1, ping the management interface on S2 and S3. From S2, ping the management interface on S3.

Were the pings successful?

_____ yes _____

If not, troubleshoot the switch configurations and try again.

Step 6. Assign switch ports to the VLANs.

Assign ports to VLANs on S2 according to Table 6-7 at the beginning of the lab. Activate the ports connected to the PCs.

Step 7. Check connectivity between VLANs.

Open command prompt windows on the three hosts connected to S2. Ping from PC1 (192.168.10.21) to PC2 (192.168.20.22). Ping from PC2 to PC3 (192.168.30.23).

Are the pings successful?

_____ NO _____

If not, why do these pings fail?

Because PCs are on seperate NTs and the vouter is
is not configurated.

Task 5: Configure the Router

Step 1.   Clear the configuration on the router and reload.

Step 2.   Create a basic configuration on the router:

- Configure the router with hostname R1.
- Disable DNS lookup.
- Configure an EXEC mode password of **class**.
- Configure a password of **cisco** for console connections.
- Configure a password of **cisco** for vty connections.

Step 3.   Configure the trunking interface on R1.

Configure the Fa0/1 interface on R1 with five subinterfaces as designated in Table 6-6. Configure these subinterfaces with dot1q encapsulation and assign the correct address. Specify VLAN 99 as the native VLAN on its subinterface. Do not assign an IP address to the physical interface, but be sure to enable it.

Step 4.   Configure the server LAN interface on R1.

Refer to Table 6-6 to configure Fa0/0 with the correct IP address and mask.

Step 5.   Verify the routing configuration.

At this point, there should be six networks configured on R1. Verify that you can route packets to all six by checking the routing table on R1.

If your routing table does not show all six networks, troubleshoot your configuration and resolve the problem before proceeding.

Step 6.   Verify inter-VLAN routing.

From PC1, verify that you can ping the remote server (192.168.50.254) and the other two hosts (192.168.20.22 and 192.168.30.23). It may take a couple of pings before the end-to-end path is established.

Are the pings successful?

yes.

If not, troubleshoot your configuration. Check to make sure the default gateways have been set on all PCs and all switches. If any of the hosts have gone into hibernation, the connected interface may go down.

At this point, you should be able to ping any node on any of the six networks configured on your LAN, including the switch management interfaces.

Task 6: Document the Switch Configurations

On the router and each switch, capture the running configuration to a text file and save it for future reference. These scripts can be edited to expedite configuring switches in future labs.

Task 7: Clean Up

Unless directed otherwise by your instructor, erase the configurations and reload the router and switches. Disconnect and store the cabling. For PC hosts that are normally connected to other networks (such as the school LAN or to the Internet), reconnect the appropriate cabling and restore the TCP/IP settings.

Packet Tracer Companion: Challenge Inter-VLAN Routing (6.4.2)

You can now open the file LSG03-Lab642.pka on the CD-ROM that accompanies this book to repeat this hands-on lab using Packet Tracer. Remember, however, that Packet Tracer is not a substitute for a hands-on lab experience with real equipment.

Lab 6-3: Troubleshooting Inter-VLAN Routing (6.4.3)

Learning Objectives

Upon completion of this lab, you will be able to

- Cable a network according to the topology diagram in Figure 6-6

- Erase any existing configurations and reload switches and the router to the default state

- Load the switches and the router with supplied scripts

- Find and correct all configuration errors

- Document the corrected network

Scenario

The network is designed and configured to support five VLANs and a separate server network. Inter-VLAN routing is provided by an external router in a router-on-a-stick configuration. However, the network is not working as designed and complaints from your users do not provide much insight into the source of the problems. You must first define what is not working as expected, and then analyze the existing configurations to determine and correct the source of the problems.

This lab is complete when you can demonstrate IP connectivity between each of the user VLANs and the external server network, and between the switch management VLAN and the server network.

Figure 6-6 shows the topology diagram for this lab.

Figure 6-6   Topology Diagram for Lab 6-3

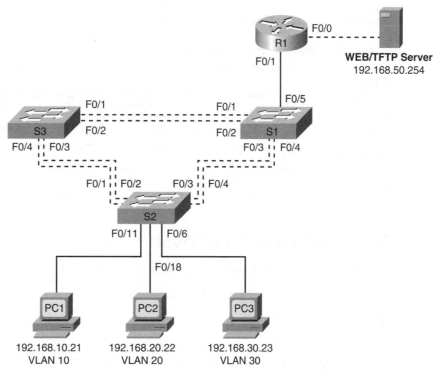

Table 6-8 shows the addressing scheme used in this lab.

Table 6-8   Addressing Table for Lab 6-3

Device	Interface	IP Address	Subnet Mask	Default Gateway
R1	Fa0/0	192.168.50.1	255.255.255.0	—
	Fa0/1.1	192.168.1.1	255.255.255.0	—
	Fa0/1.10	192.168.10.1	255.255.255.0	—
	Fa0/1.20	192.168.20.1	255.255.255.0	—
	Fa0/1.30	192.168.30.1	255.255.255.0	—
	Fa0/1.99	192.168.99.1	255.255.255.0	—
S1	VLAN 99	192.168.99.11	255.255.255.0	192.168.99.1
S2	VLAN 99	192.168.99.12	255.255.255.0	192.168.99.1
S3	VLAN 99	192.168.99.13	255.255.255.0	192.168.99.1
PC1	NIC	192.168.10.21	255.255.255.0	192.168.10.1
PC2	NIC	192.168.20.22	255.255.255.0	192.168.20.1
PC3	NIC	192.168.30.23	255.255.255.0	192.168.30.1
Server	NIC	192.168.50.254	255.255.255.0	192.168.50.1

Table 6-9 shows the port assignments used in this lab.

Table 6-9   Port Assignments for S2

Ports	Assignment	Network
Fa0/1–0/4	802.1Q Trunks (Native VLAN 99)	192.168.99.0 /24
Fa0/5–0/10	VLAN 30—Sales	192.168.30.0 /24
Fa0/11–0/17	VLAN 10—R&D	192.168.10.0 /24
Fa0/18–0/24	VLAN 20—Engineering	192.168.20.0 /24

Task 1: Prepare the Network

Step 1.   Cable a network that is similar to the one shown in Figure 6-6.

Step 2.   Clear any existing configurations on the router and switches.

Step 3.   Configure the Ethernet interfaces on the host PCs and the server.

Step 4.   Apply the following configurations to the router and each switch. Alternatively, you can open the file LSG03-Lab643-Scripts.txt on the CD-ROM that accompanies this book and copy in the scripts for each of the switches.

note: it is little difference than PT

R1 Configuration

```
hostname R1
!
no ip domain lookup
!
interface FastEthernet0/0
 ip address 192.168.50.1 255.255.255.192
!
interface FastEthernet0/1
 no ip address
!
interface FastEthernet0/1.1
 encapsulation dot1Q 1
 ip address 192.168.1.1 255.255.255.0
!
interface FastEthernet0/1.10
 encapsulation dot1Q 11
 ip address 192.168.10.1 255.255.255.0
!
interface FastEthernet0/1.20
 encapsulation dot1Q 20
 ip address 192.168.20.1 255.255.255.0
!
interface FastEthernet0/1.30
 ip address 192.168.30.1 255.255.255.0
!
interface FastEthernet0/1.99
 encapsulation dot1Q 99 native
 ip address 192.168.99.1 255.255.255.0
!
line con 0
 password cisco
 login
!
line vty 0 4
password cisco
 login
!
end
```

← wrong mask - 255.255.255.0
. no shut

← no shut

Assign wrong VLAN for the virtual interface
. encapsulation dot1Q 10

S1 Configuration

← . no ip domain lookup
. enable secret class

```
hostname S1
!
```

```
vtp mode server
vtp domain lab6_3
vtp password cisco
!
vlan 99
name Management
vlan 10
name R&D
vlan 30
name Sales
exit
!
interface FastEthernet0/1
 switchport trunk native vlan 99
 switchport mode trunk
 no shutdown
!
interface FastEthernet0/2
 switchport trunk native vlan 99
 switchport mode trunk
 no shutdown
!
interface FastEthernet0/3
 switchport trunk native vlan 99
 switchport mode trunk
 no shutdown
!
interface FastEthernet0/4
 switchport trunk native vlan 99
 switchport mode trunk
 no shutdown
!
!
interface range FastEthernet0/5 - 24
 shutdown
!
interface Vlan99
 ip address 192.168.99.11 255.255.255.0
 no shutdown
!
exit
!
ip default-gateway 192.168.99.1
!
```

Missing VLAN 20
· name Engineering

```
line con 0
 logging synchronous
 password cisco
 login
!
line vty 0 4
password cisco
 login
!
line vty 5 15
 password cisco
 login
!
end
```

S2 Configuration

```
!
hostname S2
no ip domain-lookup
enable secret class
!
vtp mode client
vtp domain lab6_3
vtp password cisco
!
interface FastEthernet0/1
 switchport trunk native vlan 99
 switchport mode trunk            ← no shut
!
interface FastEthernet0/2
 switchport trunk native vlan 99
 switchport mode trunk
!                                 ← no shut
interface FastEthernet0/3
 switchport trunk native vlan 99
 switchport mode trunk            ← no shut
!
interface FastEthernet0/4
 switchport trunk native vlan 99
 switchport mode trunk            ← no shut
!
 interface range FastEthernet0/5 - 11
 switchport access vlan 30
 switchport mode access           ← no shut
```

```
!
interface range FastEthernet0/12 - 17  ←  switchport mode access
 switchport access vlan 10                    no shut
!
interface range FastEthernet0/18 -24
 switchport mode access
 switchport access vlan 20                  ← no shut
!
interface Vlan99
 ip address 192.168.99.12 255.255.255.0
 no shutdown
!
ip default-gateway 192.168.99.1
!
line con 0
 password cisco
 logging synchronous
 login
line vty 0 4
 password cisco
 login
line vty 5 15
 password cisco
 login
!
end
```

S3 Configuration

```
!
hostname S3
!                       ←  no ip domain-lookup
enable secret class
!
vtp mode client
vtp domain lab6_3
vtp password cisco
!
interface FastEthernet0/1
 switchport trunk native vlan 99
 switchport mode trunk
 no shutdown
!
```

```
interface FastEthernet0/2
 switchport trunk native vlan 99
 switchport mode trunk
 no shutdown
!
interface FastEthernet0/3
 switchport trunk native vlan 99
 switchport mode trunk
 no shutdown
!
interface FastEthernet0/4
 switchport trunk native vlan 99
 switchport mode trunk
 no shutdown
!
interface range FastEthernet0/5 - 24
 shutdown
 exit
!
!
ip default-gateway 192.168.99.1
!
line con 0
 logging synchronous
 password cisco
 login
!
line vty 0 4
password cisco
 login
!
line vty 5 15
 password cisco
 login
!
end
```

← Int VLAN 99
· ip address 192.168.99.13 255.255.255.0
  no shut·

PT. S2: Fas 0/11 on wrong VLAN

Task 2: Troubleshoot and Correct the Inter-VLAN Configuration

The following is a suggested method for approaching the connectivity problems in the network:

Step 1.   Evaluate any console messages.

When pasting or typing in the scripts, did you get any console messages from the system? If so, what were they and what is the solution?

_____

_____

_____

_____

_____

_____

_____

_____

_____

Step 2.   Test and establish connectivity between devices.

When all errors are corrected, you should be able to freely ping and telnet between R1, S1, S2, and S3. PCs should be able to ping each other and the server.

Do you have connectivity between any of the devices?

_____

If yes, which ones?

_____

_____

_____

Step 3.   Investigate connectivity issues between the devices and implement solutions. Document the results of your investigation and the solutions you implemented.

_____

_____

_____

_____

_____

_____

_____

_____

_____

_____

_____

_____

_____

_____

_____

_____

_____

_____

_____

_____

_____

_____

_____

_____

_____

_____

_____

_____

_____

_____

_____

_____

_____

_____

_____

_____

Task 3: Document the Switch Configurations

On each switch, capture the running configuration to a text file and save it for future reference. These scripts can be edited to expedite configuring switches in future labs.

Task 4: Clean Up

Unless directed otherwise by your instructor, erase the configurations and reload the router and switches. Disconnect and store the cabling. For PC hosts that are normally connected to other networks (such as the school LAN or to the Internet), reconnect the appropriate cabling and restore the TCP/IP settings.

Packet Tracer Companion: Troubleshooting Inter-VLAN Routing (6.4.3)

You can now open the file LSG03-Lab643.pka on the CD-ROM that accompanies this book to repeat this hands-on lab using Packet Tracer. Remember, however, that Packet Tracer is not a substitute for a hands-on lab experience with real equipment.

Packet Tracer Skills Integration Challenge

Open the file LSG03-PTSkills6.pka on the CD-ROM that accompanies this book. You will use the topology in Figure 6-7 and the addressing table in Table 6-10 to document your design.

Figure 6-7   Packet Tracer Skills Integration Challenge Topology

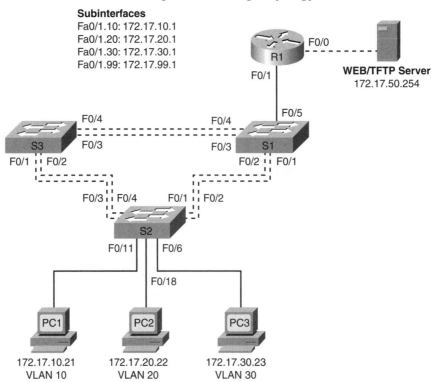

Table 6-10   Addressing Table for the Packet Tracer Skills Integration Challenge Activity

Device	Interface	IP Address	Subnet Mask	Default Gateway
R1	Fa0/0	172.17.50.1	255.255.255.0	—
	Fa0/1.10	172.17.10.1	255.255.255.0	—
	Fa0/1.20	172.17.20.1	255.255.255.0	—
	Fa0/1.30	172.17.30.1	255.255.255.0	—
	Fa0/1.99	172.17.99.1	255.255.255.0	—
S1	VLAN 99	172.17.99.31	255.255.255.0	172.17.99.1

Table 6-10   Addressing Table for the Packet Tracer Skills Integration Challenge Activity *continued*

Device	Interface	IP Address	Subnet Mask	Default Gateway
S2	VLAN 99	172.17.99.32	255.255.255.0	172.17.99.1
S3	VLAN 99	172.17.99.33	255.255.255.0	172.17.99.1
PC1	NIC	172.17.10.21	255.255.255.0	172.17.10.1
PC2	NIC	172.17.20.22	255.255.255.0	172.17.20.1
PC3	NIC	172.17.30.23	255.255.255.0	172.17.30.1

Learning Objectives

Upon completion of this lab, you will be able to

- Configure and verify basic device configurations
- Configure VTP
- Configure trunking
- Configure VLANs
- Assign VLANs to ports
- Configure STP
- Configure router-on-a-stick Inter-VLAN routing
- Verify end-to-end connectivity

Introduction

In this activity, you will demonstrate and reinforce your ability to configure switches and routers for inter-VLAN communication. Among the skills you will demonstrate are configuring VLANs, VTP, and trunking on switches. You will also administer STP on switches and configure a router-on-a-stick using subinterfaces.

Task 1: Configure and Verify Basic Device Configurations

Step 1.   Configure basic commands.

Configure the router and each switch with the following basic commands. Packet Tracer grades only the hostnames and default gateways.

- Hostnames
- Banner
- Enable secret password
- Line configurations
- Service password encryption
- Switch default gateways

Step 2.   Configure the management VLAN interface on S1, S2, and S3.

Create and enable interface VLAN 99 on each switch. Use the addressing table for address configuration.

Step 3.   Check results.

Your completion percentage should be 17 percent. If not, click **Check Results** to see which required components are not yet completed.

Task 2: Configure VTP

Step 1.   Configure the VTP mode on all three switches.

Configure S1 as the server. Configure S2 and S3 as clients.

Step 2.   Configure the VTP domain name on all three switches.

Use **CCNA** as the VTP domain name.

Step 3.   Configure the VTP domain password on all three switches.

Use **cisco** as the VTP domain password.

Step 4.   Check results.

Your completion percentage should be 28 percent. If not, click **Check Results** to see which required components are not yet completed.

Task 3: Configure Trunking

Step 1.   Configure trunking on S1, S2, and S3.

Configure the appropriate interfaces in trunking mode and assign VLAN 99 as the native VLAN.

Step 2.   Check results.

Your completion percentage should be 62 percent. If not, click **Check Results** to see which required components are not yet completed.

Task 4: Configure VLANs

Step 1.   Create the VLANs on S1.

Create and name the following VLANs on S1 only. VTP advertises the new VLANs to S1 and S2.

- VLAN 10, name = **Faculty/Staff**

- VLAN 20, name = **Students**

- VLAN 30, name = **Guest(Default)**

- VLAN 99, name = **Management&Native**

Step 2.   Verify that VLANs have been sent to S2 and S3.

Use the appropriate commands to verify that S2 and S3 now have the VLANs you created on S1. It may take a few minutes for Packet Tracer to simulate the VTP advertisements.

Step 3.   Check results.

Your completion percentage should be 67 percent. If not, click **Check Results** to see which required components are not yet completed.

Task 5: Assign VLANs to Ports

Step 1.   Assign VLANs to access ports on S2.

Assign the PC access ports to VLANs:

- VLAN 10: PC1 connected to Fa0/11
- VLAN 20: PC2 connected to Fa0/18
- VLAN 30: PC3 connected to Fa0/6

Step 2.   Verify the VLAN implementation.

Use the appropriate commands to verify your VLAN implementation.

Step 3.   Check results.

Your completion percentage should be 75 percent. If not, click **Check Results** to see which required components are not yet completed.

Task 6: Configure STP

Step 1.   Ensure that S1 is the root bridge.

Set priorities to 4096.

Step 2.   Verify that S1 is the root bridge.

Step 3.   Check results.

Your completion percentage should be 82 percent. If not, click **Check Results** to see which required components are not yet completed.

Task 7: Configure Router-on-a-Stick Inter-VLAN Routing

Step 1.   Configure the subinterfaces.

Configure the Fa0/1 subinterfaces on R1 using the information from the addressing table.

Step 2.   Check results.

Your completion percentage should be 100 percent. If not, click **Check Results** to see which required components are not yet completed.

Task 8: Verify End-to-End Connectivity

Step 1.   Verify that PC1 and the web/TFTP server can ping each other.

Step 2.   Verify that PC1 and PC2 can ping each other.

Step 3.   Verify that PC3 and PC1 can ping each other.

Step 4.   Verify that PC2 and PC3 can ping each other.

Step 5.   Verify that the switches can ping R1.

CHAPTER 7

Basic Wireless Concepts and Configuration

Managing a wired infrastructure can be challenging. Consider what happens when a worker decides they prefer their computer system in a different location. For wired-only networks, you would then have to physically add another connection in the new location. Wireless networks not only make mobility more economical, they actually encourage it.

The Study Guide portion of this chapter uses a combination of matching, fill-in-the-blank, open-ended question, and Packet Tracer exercises to test your knowledge of wireless concepts and configurations.

The Labs and Activities portion of this chapter includes all the online curriculum labs to ensure that you have mastered the hands-on skills needed to understand wireless management and configuration.

As you work through this chapter, use Chapter 7 in *LAN Switching and Wireless, CCNA Exploration Companion Guide* or use the corresponding Chapter 7 in the Exploration LAN Switching and Wireless online curriculum for assistance.

Study Guide

The Wireless LAN

Business networks today are evolving to support people who are on the move. Employees and employers, students and faculty, government agents and those they serve, sports fans and shoppers, all are mobile and many of them are "connected." The exercises in this section cover the concepts behind wireless LANs (WLANs), including the standards, components, operation, and planning of the WLAN implementation.

Vocabulary Exercise: Matching

Match the definition on the left with a term on the right. All definitions and terms are used exactly one time.

Definitions

a. Organization that specifies how RF is modulated to carry information.

b. Frame used by WLAN clients to find their networks.

c. Modulation technique used by the 802.11a and 802.11g standards.

d. Modulation technique used by the 802.11b and 802.11g standards.

e. Organization that regulates allocation of RF bands.

f. Process that is an artifact from the original 802.11 standard, but is still required.

g. Unique identifier that client devices use to distinguish between multiple wireless networks.

h. Wireless topology in which two or more basic service sets are combined to allow roaming between access points without requiring client reconfiguration.

i. Used at the physical layer as the medium for WLANs.

j. Modulation technique used by the 802.11n standard.

k. Organization that ensures that vendors make devices that are interoperable.

l. Process for establishing the data link between an access point and a WLAN client.

m. Frame used by the WLAN network to advertise its presence.

n. Technique used by access points to resolve possible collisions.

o. Wireless topology in which mobile clients use a single access point for connectivity to each other or to the wired network.

Terms

____ association

____ authentication

____ beacon

____ BSS

____ CSMA/CA

____ DSSS

____ ESS

____ IEEE

____ ITU-R

____ MIMO

____ OFDM

____ probe

____ radio frequency

____ SSID

____ Wi-Fi Alliance

Wireless Concepts Exercise

Why Use Wireless?

Why is wireless access now considered a required component for business communications?

_____

_____

_____

_____

Wireless LANs share a similar origin with Ethernet LANs. The IEEE has adopted the 802 LAN/MAN portfolio of computer network architecture standards. The two dominant 802 working groups are _____ Ethernet and _____ wireless LAN.

WLANs use _____ (RF) instead of cables at the physical layer and MAC sublayer of the data link layer. Complete Table 7-1, which compares the characteristics of WLANs and Ethernet LANs.

Table 7-1   Comparing a WLAN to a LAN

Characteristic	Wireless LANs	Ethernet LANs
Physical layer		
Media access method		
Availability		
Signal interference		
Regulation		

Wireless LAN Standards

802.11 wireless LAN is an IEEE standard that defines how radio frequency (RF) in the unlicensed _____, _____, and _____ frequency bands is used for the physical layer and the MAC sublayer of wireless links.

When 802.11 was first released, it prescribed _____ data rates in the ____-GHz band. At that time, WLANs were operating at 10 Mbps, so the new wireless technology was not enthusiastically adopted. Since then, WLAN standards have continuously improved with the release of IEEE 802.11a, IEEE 802.11b, IEEE 802.11g, and draft 802.11n.

Complete Table 7-2, which compares WLAN standards.

Table 7-2   Wireless LAN Standards

Standard	Year Ratified	RF Band	Modulation	Data Rate	Range
802.11b					
802.11a					
802.11g					
802.11n					

The data rates of different wireless LAN standards are affected by something called a modulation technique. The two modulation techniques in this course are _____ (DSSS) and _____ (OFDM). You should be aware that when a standard uses _____, it will have faster data rates. Also, _____ is simpler than _____, so it is less expensive to implement.

Notice in Table 7-2 that only the 802.11a standard uses the 5-GHz RF band. List three reasons why:

■ _____

■ _____

■ _____
_____

What is a major disadvantage to using the 2.4-GHz RF band?

_____
_____

What is MIMO and how does it work?

_____
_____
_____
_____

Standards ensure interoperability between devices made by different manufacturers. Internationally, the three key organizations influencing WLAN standards are:

■ _____

■ _____

■ _____

The _____ regulates the allocation of the RF spectrum and satellite orbits.

The _____ develops and maintains the standards for local- and metropolitan-area networks with the IEEE 802 LAN/MAN family of standards.

The _____ is an association of vendors whose objective is to improve the interoperability of products that are based on the 802.11 standard by certifying vendors for conformance to industry norms and adherence to standards.

Wireless Infrastructure Components

The device that makes a client station capable of sending and receiving RF signals is the _____.
A _____ connects wireless clients to the wired LAN. Its job is to convert the TCP/IP
data packets from their _____ frame encapsulation format in the air to the _____
Ethernet frame format on the wired Ethernet network. Wireless clients must _____ with an access
point to join the 802.11 network and obtain network services. It is similar to plugging into a wired
LAN.

Access points oversee a distributed coordination function (DCF) called _____
with _____ (_____/____). This simply means that devices on a WLAN
must wait until the medium is free before sending.

Explain how access points and wireless clients resolve possible collisions.

_____

_____

_____

Explain how the hidden node problem causes collisions and how this problem is resolved with
CSMA/CA.

_____

_____

_____

_____

_____

_____

_____

Wireless routers, like the Linksys WRT300N, are really three devices in one box. List these three
devices:

- _____

- _____

- _____

Wireless Operation

A shared _____ (SSID) is a unique identifier that client devices use to
distinguish between multiple wireless networks in the same vicinity. Each SSID can be any alphanu-
meric, case-sensitive entry from ____ to ____ characters long.

The IEEE 802.11 standard establishes the channelization scheme for the use of the unlicensed ISM RF
bands in WLANs. The 2.4-GHz band is broken down into ____ channels for North America and ____
channels for Europe. These channels have a center frequency separation of only ____ MHz and an overall
channel bandwidth (or frequency occupation) of ____ MHz. The 22-MHz channel bandwidth combined
with the
5-MHz separation between center frequencies means there is an overlap between successive channels.

In North America, what three channels do not overlap?

_____

When implementing multiple access points in a network, what do best practices dictate?

_____

_____

_____

Explain what BSS and ESS are and the difference between the two:

_____

_____

_____

_____

A key part of the 802.11 process is discovering a WLAN and subsequently connecting to it. The primary components of this process are as follows:

- _____: Frames used by the WLAN network to advertise its presence

- _____: Frames used by WLAN clients to find their networks

- _____: A process that is an artifact from the original 802.11 standard, but is still required by the standard

- _____: The process for establishing the data link between an access point and a WLAN client

Wireless LAN Security

Security should be a priority for anyone who uses or administers networks. The difficulties in keeping a wired network secure are amplified with a wireless network. A WLAN is open to anyone within range of an access point and the appropriate credentials to associate to it. The exercise in this section covers threats to wireless security, wireless security protocols, and securing the WLAN.

Wireless LAN Security Exercise

Threats to Wireless Security

_____ refers to driving around a neighborhood with a laptop and an 802.11b/g client card looking for an unsecured 802.11b/g system to exploit.

Why are off-the-shelf wireless devices insecure?

_____

_____

_____

_____

A _____ access point is an access point that is placed on a WLAN and used to interfere with normal network operation; an example is an access point installed by employees without authorization.

Briefly explain how the man-in-the-middle attack might work in a WLAN:

_____

_____

_____

_____

_____

_____

_____

What are three ways a denial-of-service (DoS) attack can be used on a WLAN?

_____

_____

_____

_____

_____

_____

_____

_____

_____

_____

_____

Wireless Security Protocols

What are the two major flaws with WEP shared key encryption?

- _____

- _____

    _____

Today, the standard that should be followed in most enterprise networks is the _____ standard. This is similar to the Wi-Fi Alliance _____ standard. In networks that have strict security requirements, an additional authentication or login is required to grant clients such access. This login process is managed by the _____ (EAP). EAP is a framework for authenticating network access. IEEE developed the 802.11i standard for WLAN authentication and authorization to use IEEE _____.

Figure 7-1 illustrates the EAP authentication process. Fill in the missing steps.

Figure 7-1   Authenticating with EAP

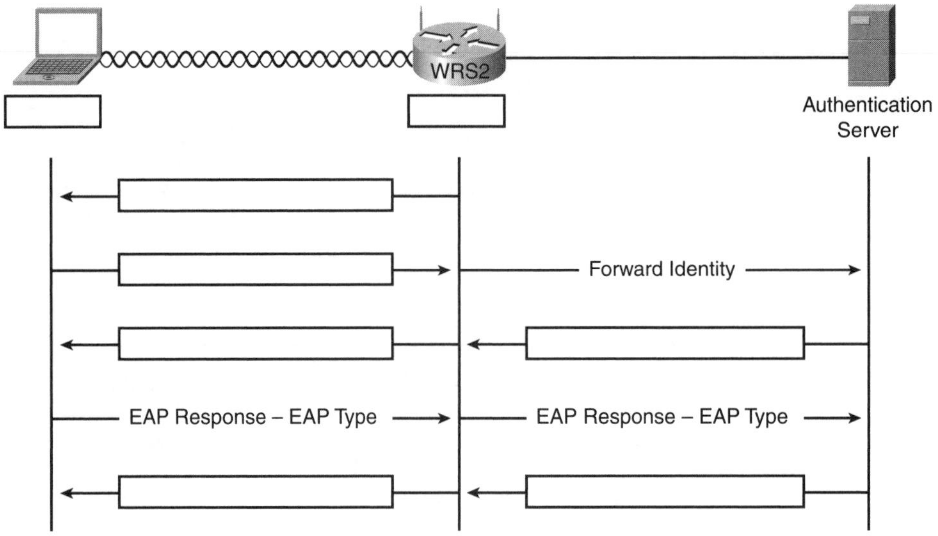

Two enterprise-level encryption mechanisms specified by 802.11i are certified as WPA and WPA2 by the Wi-Fi Alliance: _____ (TKIP) and _____ (AES).

List the two primary functions of TKIP:

■ _____

■ _____

_____

AES has the same functions as TKIP. What else does AES add to make it the preferred encryption method?

_____

_____

_____

Securing a Wireless LAN

Controlling access to the WLAN can be seen as implementing a three-step approach:

1. _____: Disable SSID broadcasts from access points.

2. _____: Manually construct tables on the access point to allow or disallow clients based on their physical hardware address.

3. _____: Implement WPA or WPA2.

Although steps 1 and 2 should be implemented, neither is considered a valid means of completely securing a WLAN. Why?

_____

_____

Configure Wireless LAN Access

The Packet Tracer exercise in this section covers how to configure a Linksys WRT300N wireless access point, including how to change the default IP addressing, change the SSID, enable security, and change the default administrative password. Packet Tracer supports only a limited set of Linksys WRT300N configuration skills. To practice all the skills required for this chapter, complete the labs in the Labs and Activities section.

Packet Tracer Exercise 7-1: Wireless LAN Configuration

Open file LSG03-0701.pka on the CD-ROM that accompanies this book to perform this exercise using Packet Tracer. The topology is shown in Figure 7-2 and the addressing scheme is shown in Table 7-3.

Figure 7-2   Wireless LAN Configuration Topology

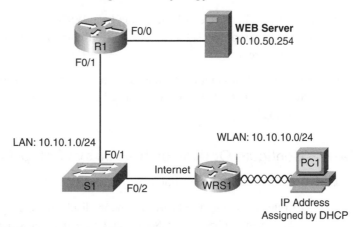

Table 7-3   Addressing Table for Wireless LAN Configuration Exercise

Device	Interface	IP Address	Subnet Mask	Default Gateway
R1	Fa0/0	10.10.50.1	255.255.255.0	N/A
	Fa0/1	10.10.1.1	255.255.255.0	
WRS1	WAN	10.10.1.2	255.255.255.0	10.10.1.1
	LAN/wireless	10.10.10.1	255.255.255.0	N/A
PC1	NIC	DHCP assigned	DHCP assigned	DHCP assigned
WEB Server	NIC	10.10.50.254	255.255.255.0	10.10.50.1

Note: The following instructions are also contained within the Packet Tracer Exercise.

Learning Objectives

Upon completion of this Packet Tracer Exercise, you will be able to

- Connect wirelessly to configure a Linksys router

- Configure options on the Linksys Setup tab

- Configure options on the Linksys Wireless tab

- Configure options on the Linksys Administration tab

- Verify connectivity

- Save the Packet Tracer file

Scenario

In this exercise, you will change the default Linksys configuration, including the IP addressing, SSID, authentication, and administrative password. The exercise is complete when your completion percentage is 100 percent and PC1 can ping the WEB Server.

Task 1: Connect Wirelessly to Configure a Linksys Router

You cannot directly access the Linksys router, WRS1, by clicking it. You must use the web browser on PC1:

- PC1 has already received IP addressing from WRS1. To check the IP addressing, click **PC1**, click the **Desktop** tab, and then click **IP Configuration**. Write down or memorize the default gateway address.

- Close the IP Configuration window and open your web browser. Type the default gateway address in the **URL** field. When prompted for a username and password, type **admin** for both and click **OK**.

Task 2: Configure Options on the Linksys Setup Tab

Step 1.   Set the Internet connection type to static IP.

At this point, the web browser window displaying the Linksys web page should show the Basic Setup subtab of the Setup tab. Under Internet Setup, for the Internet Connection Type option, click the drop-down menu and choose **Static IP**.

Step 2.   Configure the WAN IP address, subnet mask, and default gateway for WRS1:

- Set the Internet IP Address field to **10.10.1.2**.

- Set the Subnet Mask field to **255.255.255.0**.

- Set the Default Gateway field to **10.10.1.1**.

Step 3.   Configure the router IP parameters:

- Under Network Setup, in the Router IP options, set the IP Address field to **10.10.10.1** and the Subnet Mask field to **255.255.255.0**.

- In the DHCP Server Setting options, make sure that the DHCP server is enabled (the Enable radio button is chosen) and set the Start IP Address field to **10**.

Step 4.   Save settings and reconnect to WRS1.

Click the **Save Settings** button at the bottom of the Setup tab. The browser will refresh with the message "Savings are successful." But you will loose connectivity, because 192.168.1.1 is no longer a valid default gateway.

- Close the web browser window and click **Command Prompt**.

- Enter the commands **ipconfig /release** and then **ipconfig /renew**.

- PC1 should now have addressing from the 10.10.10.0/24 DHCP pool on WRS1.

- Close the Command Prompt window and click **Web Browser** again.

- Enter the new default gateway address, **10.10.10.1**, and reauthenticate with the **admin** username/password.

Step 5.   Check results.

Your completion percentage should be 62 percent. If not, click **Check Results** to see which required components are not yet completed.

Task 3: Configure Options on the Linksys Wireless Tab

Step 1.   Set the network name (SSID).

- In the web browser window displaying the Linksys web page, click the **Wireless** tab. The Basic Wireless Settings subtab is displayed by default.

- In the **Network Name (SSID)** field, rename the network from Default to **WRS1**.

Step 2.   Save settings and reconnect to WRS1.

Click the **Save Settings** button at the bottom of the Wireless tab. Again, you loose connectivity to WRS1.

- Close the web browser and click **PC Wireless**. The Linksys Wireless Network Monitor v1.0 opens. Click the **Connect** tab.

- If necessary, click **Refresh** to send a probe for wireless access points.

- The WRS1 network should be displayed under Wireless Network Name. Click this entry and then click **Connect**.

You should now be able to reconnect using the web browser.

Step 3.   Set the security mode.

- In the web browser window displaying the Linksys web page, click the **Wireless** tab. Then click the **Wireless Security** subtab.

- From the Security Mode drop-down list, choose **WEP**.

- Using the default Encryption setting of 40/64-Bit, set the Key 1 field to **1234567890**.

Step 4.   Save settings and reconnect to WRS1.

Click the **Save Settings** button at the bottom of the Wireless tab. Again, you loose connectivity to WRS1.

- Close the web browser and click **PC Wireless**. Click the **Connect** tab.

- If necessary, click **Refresh** to send a probe for wireless access points.

- The WRS1 network should display under Wireless Network Name. Click this entry and then click **Connect**.

- Enter the WEP Key 1 and click **Connect**.

You should now be able to reconnect using the web browser.

Step 5.   Check results.

Your completion percentage should be 88 percent. If not, click **Check Results** to see which required components are not yet completed.

Task 4: Configure Options on the Linksys Administration Tab

Step 1.   Set the router password.

- In the web browser window displaying the Linksys web page, click the **Administration** tab. The Management subtab is displayed by default.

- In the Router Access options, change the Router Password field to **cisco**. Re-enter the same password to confirm.

- Click **Save Settings** at the bottom of the tab. Then click the **Continue** hyperlink.

- When prompted, enter **admin** as the username and **cisco** as the password.

Close the web browser on the PC.

Step 2.   Check results.

Your completion percentage should be 100 percent. If not, click **Check Results** to see which required components are not yet completed.

Task 5: Test Connectivity

PC1 should now be able to ping the WEB Server at 10.10.50.254. Alternatively, you can click **Check Results** and then the **Connectivity Tests** tab. The status of both connectivity tests should be listed as Correct.

Task 6: Save the Packet Tracer File

Save your Packet Tracer file as LSG03-0701-end.pka.

Troubleshooting Simple WLAN Problems

The major troubleshooting considerations in simple WLAN implementations concern access point radio and firmware issues, channel settings, RF interference, access point placement, authentication, and encryption.

Troubleshooting Approach for WLANs

According to Chapter 7 of *LAN Switching and Wireless, CCNA Exploration Companion Guide*, a standard troubleshooting practice for WLANs involves three steps. List the steps and what to check for in each step:

Step 1.   _____

_____

_____

Step 2.   _____

_____

Step 3.   _____

_____

Labs and Activities

Lab 7-1: Basic Wireless Configuration (7.5.1)

Learning Objectives

Upon completion of this lab, you will be able to

- Configure options on the Linksys Setup tab

- Configure options on the Linksys Wireless tab

- Configure options on the Linksys Administration tab

- Configure options on the Linksys Security tab

- Add wireless connectivity to a PC

- Test connectivity

Figure 7-3 shows the topology diagram for this lab.

Figure 7-3   Topology Diagram for Lab 7-1

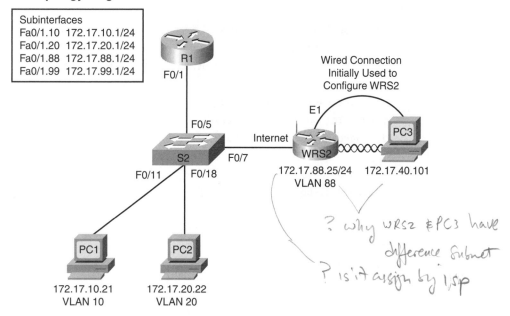

Introduction

In this lab, you will configure a Linksys wireless router, allowing for remote access from PCs and wireless connectivity with WEP security.

Task 1: Prepare the Network

Step 1.   Cable a network that is similar to the one shown in Figure 7-3.

Step 2.   Clear any existing configurations on the switch and router.

Step 3.   Apply the following configurations to R1 and S2. Alternatively, you can open the file LSG03-Lab751-Scripts.txt on the CD-ROM that accompanies this book and copy in the scripts for each device.

R1 Configuration

```
hostname R1
enable secret class
no ip domain-lookup
!
interface FastEthernet0/1
 no ip address
 no shutdown
!
interface FastEthernet0/1.10
 encapsulation dot1Q 10
 ip address 172.17.10.1 255.255.255.0
!
interface FastEthernet0/1.20
 encapsulation dot1Q 20
 ip address 172.17.20.1 255.255.255.0
!
interface FastEthernet0/1.88
 encapsulation dot1Q 88
 ip address 172.17.88.1 255.255.255.0
!
interface FastEthernet0/1.99
 encapsulation dot1Q 99 native
 ip address 172.17.99.1 255.255.255.0
!
line console 0
 password cisco
 login
!
line vty 0 4
 password cisco
 login
end
```

S2 Configuration

```
hostname S2
enable secret class
no ip domain-lookup
!
vlan 10
 name Students
vlan 20
 name Faculty/Staff
vlan 88
```

```
 name Wireless
vlan 99
 name Management
!
interface range FastEthernet0/1 - 24
 shutdown
interface range GigabitEthernet0/1 - 2
 shutdown
!
interface FastEthernet0/5
 switchport trunk native vlan 99
 switchport mode trunk
 no shutdown
!
interface FastEthernet0/7
 switchport access vlan 88
 switchport mode access
 no shutdown
!
interface FastEthernet0/11
 switchport access vlan 10
 switchport mode access
 no shutdown
!
interface FastEthernet0/18
 switchport access vlan 20
 switchport mode access
 no shutdown
!
interface vlan 99
 ip address 172.17.99.11 255.255.255.0
 no shutdown
!
line console 0
 password cisco
 login
!
line vty 0 15
 password cisco
 login
end
```

Task 2: Connect and Log into the Wireless Router

Note: Before beginning this task, check with your instructor to ensure that the wireless router is set to its factory default settings. If it is not, you must hard reset the router. To do so, find the reset button on the back of the router. Using a pen or other thin instrument, hold down the reset button for 5 seconds, after which the router should be restored to its factory default settings.

To configure the settings on the wireless router, you will use its web-based GUI utility. The GUI can be accessed by navigating to the router's LAN/wireless IP address with a web browser. The factory default address is 192.168.1.1.

Step 1.   Establish connectivity.

As shown in Figure 7-3, connect a straight-through cable from PC3 to the Ethernet 1 LAN port on WRS2. As long as PC3 is configured to obtain an IP address automatically, WRS2 will reply to DHCP requests from PC3. You can check the IP configuration on PC3 with the **ipconfig** command. By default, PC3 will obtain the following configuration:

IP address	192.168.1.100
Subnet mask	255.255.255.0
Default gateway	192.168.1.1

PC3 should be able to ping WRS2 at 192.168.1.1.

Step 2.   Open a web browser.

Step 3.   Navigate to the web-based GUI utility on WSR2:

- Open a browser window and enter the default gateway address for WRS2, **192.168.1.1**.

- The default login credentials are a blank username and the password, **admin**.

- Once you are successfully logged in, you should see the Basic Setup subtab of the Setup tab, as shown in Figure 7-4.

Note: The default login credentials for any networking device are very insecure, because these credentials can be easily found by searching the Internet. You will set a unique password in a later task.

Figure 7-4   Basic Setup: Default Web Page When First Logging In to the Linksys Router

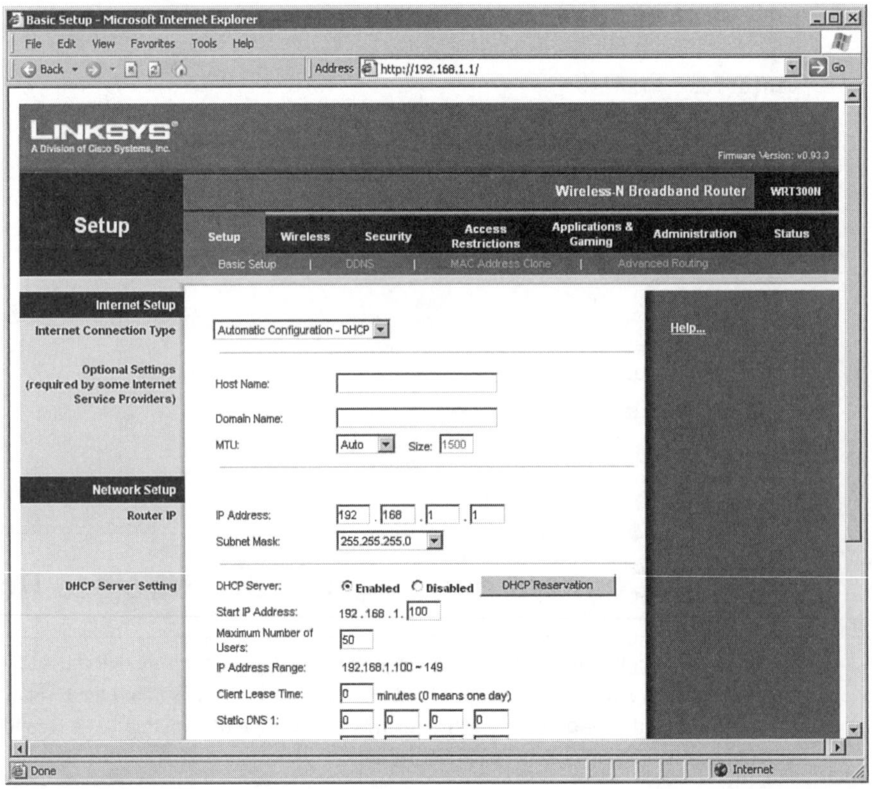

Task 3: Configure Options on the Linksys Setup Tab

Step 1.   Set the Internet connection type to static IP.

Under Internet Setup, for the Internet Connection Type option, click the drop-down menu and choose **Static IP**.

Step 2.   Configure the VLAN 88 IP address, subnet mask, and default gateway for WRS2:

- Set the Internet IP Address field to **172.17.88.25**.

- Set the Subnet Mask field to **255.255.255.0**.

- Set the Default Gateway field to **172.17.88.1**.

Step 3.   Configure the router IP parameters:

- Under Network Setup, in the Router IP options, set the IP Address field to **172.17.40.1** and the Subnet Mask field to **255.255.255.0**.

- In the DHCP Server Setting options, ensure that the DHCP server is enabled.

Note: The IP address range for the DHCP pool adjusts to a range of addresses to match the router IP parameters. These addresses are used for wireless clients and clients that connect to the wireless router's internal switch. Clients receive an IP address and mask and are given the router IP to use as a gateway.

Step 4.   Save settings.

Scroll to the bottom of the Setup tab and click the **Save Settings** button. You will loose connectivity to WRS2, because the 192.168.1.1 address is no longer valid.

Step 5.   Reconnect to WRS2.

Because you changed the IP address and DHCP pool, you will have to reconnect to WRS2 using the new address:

- Verify PC3 has obtained a new IP address that belongs to the 172.17.40.0/24 network. If not, then enter the **ipconfig/renew** command to force a DHCP release and then a DHCP request.

- Reconnect to the web-based configuration utility using the new default gateway IP address of **172.17.40.1**.

Task 4: Configure Options on the Linksys Wireless Tab

Step 1.   Set the network name (SSID):

- Click the **Wireless** tab. The Basic Wireless Settings subtab is displayed by default.

- In **Network Name (SSID)** field, rename the network from linksys to **WRS_LAN**.

- Click **Save Settings**.

Step 2.   Set the security mode:

- Click the **Wireless Security** subtab, as shown in Figure 7-5.

- From the Security Mode drop-down list, choose **WEP**.

- Use the default Encryption setting of 40/64-Bit.

- Set the Key 1 field to **1234567890**.

- Click **Save Settings**.

Figure 7-5   Wireless Security Configuration Window

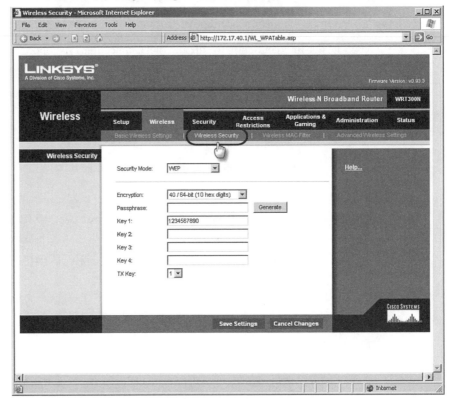

Task 5: Configure Options on the Linksys Administration Tab

Step 1.   Set the router password:

- Click the **Administration** tab, as shown in Figure 7-6. The Management subtab is displayed by default.

- In the Router Access options, change the Router Password field to **cisco123**. Re-enter the same password to confirm.

Step 2.   Enable remote management:

- In the Remote Access options, click the **Enabled** radio button to enable remote management.

- Click **Save Settings** at the bottom of the tab.

- You may be prompted to log in again using the new password, **cisco123**.

Figure 7-6   Management Administration Configuration Window

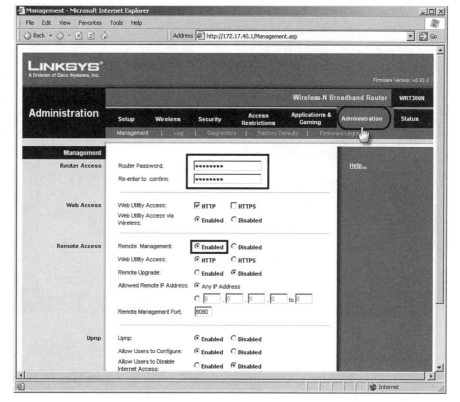

Task 6: Configure Options on the Linksys Security Tab

By default, inbound ping requests to the Internet interface on WRS2 are blocked for security reasons. For the purpose of verifying connectivity in this lab, you need to configure WRS2 to allow these inbound ping requests:

- Click the **Security** tab, as shown in Figure 7-7. The Firewall subtab is displayed by default.

- In the Internet Filter options, uncheck **Filter Anonymous Internet Requests** and then click **Save Settings**.

Figure 7-7   Security Firewall Configuration Window

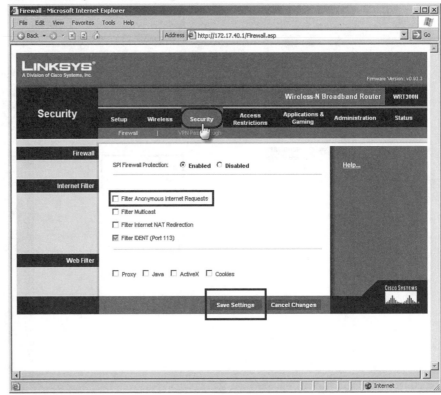

Task 7: Add Wireless Connectivity to a PC

Now that WRS2 is fully configured, you can test wireless connectivity from PC3 to WRS2:

Step 1.   Disconnect the Ethernet connection from PC3 to WRS2.

Step 2.   Use Windows XP to connect to the wireless router:

- Locate the Wireless Network Connection icon in your taskbar, or choose **Start > Control Panel > Network Connections**.

- Select **Wireless Network Connection**.

- From the File menu, choose **Status**.

- Click **View Wireless Networks**.

- Locate the WRS_LAN SSID in the list of available networks and connect to it.

- When prompted for the WEP key, enter it as in Task 3, **1234567890**, and click **Connect**.

Step 3.   Verify the connection:

- In the Wireless Network Connection Status dialog box, click the **Support** tab.

- Verify that PC3 has received an IP address from WRS2's DHCP address pool. Your IP address may be different from the one shown in Figure 7-8. However, it should belong to the 172.17.40.0/24 network.

Figure 7-8   Verifying the PC's Wireless Network Connection Status

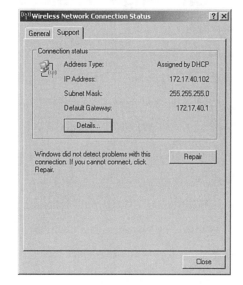

Task 8: Test Connectivity

If you have not done so yet, configure PC1 and PC2 with IP addressing according to what is shown in Figure 7-3, at the beginning of this lab. From PC3, test connectivity by pinging the following:

- Ping the LAN/wireless interface on WRS2 at 172.17.40.1.

- Ping the Internet interface on WRS2 at 172.17.88.25.

- Ping R1 at 172.17.88.1.

- Ping PC1 at 172.17.10.21.

- Ping PC2 at 172.17.20.22.

Note: If you try to ping PC3 from PC1 or PC2, you will receive a "destination host unreachable" error message. PC3 is protected by a NAT firewall. The 172.17.40.0/24 network is private and only known inside the LAN/wireless side of WRS2. The operation of NAT is covered in another course. However, you will learn how to disable NAT in the next lab.

Task 9: Clean Up

Unless directed otherwise by your instructor, erase the configurations and reload the router and switch. For the WRT300N routers, click the **Administration** tab and click the **Factory Defaults** sub-tab. Then, click the **Restore Factory Defaults** button. You can also hard reset the router. To do so, find the reset button on the back of the router. Using a pen or other thin instrument, hold down the reset button for 5 seconds, after which the router should be restored to its factory default settings. Disconnect and store the cabling. For PC hosts that are normally connected to other networks (such as the school LAN or to the Internet), reconnect the appropriate cabling and restore the TCP/IP settings.

Note difference from PT.

Lab 7-2: Challenge Wireless WRT300N (7.5.2)

Learning Objectives

Upon completion of this lab, you will be able to

- Cable a network according to the topology diagram
- Configure switches and routers for inter-VLAN routing
- Hard reset a Linksys WRT300N router
- Connect and verify connectivity to a wireless router
- Configure the IP settings for a Linksys WRT300N router
- Configure DHCP on a Linksys WRT300N router
- Configure basic wireless settings and wireless security on a Linksys WRT300N router
- Configure a wireless MAC filter
- Configure access restrictions on a Linksys WRT300N router
- Perform Linksys WRT300N router administration and management
- Establish full connectivity
- Configure static routes on both standard Cisco routers and on a Linksys WRT300N router

Figure 7-9 shows the topology diagram for this lab.

Figure 7-9   Topology Diagram for Lab 7-2

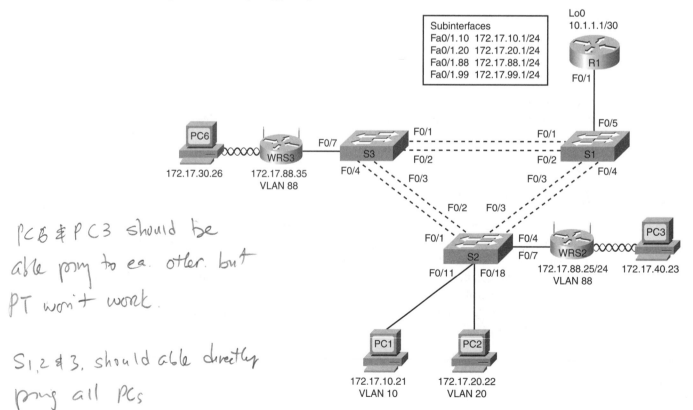

*PCB & PC3 should be
able pony to ea. other. but
PT won't work.*

*S1,2 &3. should able directly
pring all PCs*

Table 7-4 shows the addressing scheme used in this lab.

Table 7-4   Addressing Table for Lab 7-2

Device	Interface	IP Address	Subnet Mask	Default Gateway
R1	Fa0/1.10	172.17.10.1	255.255.255.0	N/A
	Fa0/1.20	172.17.20.1	255.255.255.0	N/A
	Fa0/1.88	172.17.88.1	255.255.255.0	N/A
	Fa0/1.99	172.17.99.1	255.255.255.0	N/A
	Lo0	10.1.1.1	255.255.255.252	N/A
S1	VLAN 99	172.17.99.11	255.255.255.0	172.17.99.1
S2	VLAN 99	172.17.99.12	255.255.255.0	172.17.99.1
S3	VLAN 99	172.17.99.13	255.255.255.0	172.17.99.1
WRS2	WAN	172.17.88.25	255.255.255.0	172.17.88.1
	LAN/wireless	172.17.40.1	255.255.255.0	N/A
WRS3	WAN (internet)	172.17.88.35	255.255.255.0	172.17.88.1
	LAN/wireless	172.17.30.1	255.255.255.0	N/A
PC1	NIC	172.17.10.21	255.255.255.0	172.17.10.1
PC2	NIC	172.17.20.22	255.255.255.0	172.17.20.1

(Handwritten margin notes: "Assign by ISP?", "Static assign for the Router. It will become ip gateway for the client PCs", "Same")

Table 7-5 shows the port assignments used in this lab.

Table 7-5   Port Assignments and VLANs

Port(s)	Assignment	Network
Fa0/1–0/5	802.1Q Trunks (Native VLAN 99)	172.17.99.0/24
Fa0/7	VLAN 88—Wireless	172.17.88.0/24
Fa0/11–0/17	VLAN 10—Faculty/Staff	172.17.10.0/24
Fa0/18–0/24	VLAN 20—Students	172.17.20.0/24

Scenario

In this lab, you will configure inter-VLAN routing with three switches and one router. In addition, you will add wireless access using two Linksys WRT300N routers. There are some tasks labeled as "Optional" in this lab. If your instructor does not require you to complete these tasks, simply review the descriptions and screenshots. Then move on to the next task.

Task 1: Prepare the Network

Step 1. Cable a network that is similar to the one shown in Figure 7-9.

Step 2. Clear any existing configurations on the switches, and initialize all ports in the shutdown state.

Task 2: Perform Basic Switch Configurations

Step 1. Configure the switches according to the following guidelines:

- Configure the switch hostname.

- Disable DNS lookup.

- Configure an EXEC mode password of **class**.

- Configure a password of **cisco** for console connections.

- Configure a password of **cisco** for vty connections.

Step 2. Reenable the user ports on S2 and S3.

Task 3: Configure Host PCs

Configure the PCs. You can complete this lab using only two PCs by simply changing the IP addressing for the two PCs specific to a test you want to conduct. Alternatively, you can use all four PCs. PC3 and PC6 will be automatically configured by the wireless router (WRS2 or WRS3, respectively). For now, connect PC1 and PC2 and manually configure their IP addressing.

Task 4: Configure VTP and VLANs

Step 1. Configure VTP.

Configure VTP on the three switches using the following guidelines:

- S1 is the VTP server; S2 and S3 are VTP clients.

- The VTP domain name is **Lab7**.

- The VTP password is **cisco**.

Remember that VTP domain names and passwords are case sensitive. The default operating mode is server.

Step 2. Configure trunk links and the native VLAN.

For each switch, configure ports Fa0/1 through Fa0/4 as trunking ports. The Fa0/5 on S1 also needs to be configured as a trunking port because it will trunk to the router, R1. Designate VLAN 99 as the native VLAN for these trunks. Remember to activate the ports.

Step 3. Configure the VTP server with VLANs.

Configure the following VLANS on the VTP server only:

- VLAN 10: Faculty/Staff

- VLAN 20: Students

- VLAN 88: Wireless

- VLAN 99: Management

Step 4.   Verify the VLANs.

Verify that all four VLANs have been distributed to the client switches. You should have output similar to the following:

S2#**show vlan brief**

```
LAN  Name              Status    Ports
––   ––––––––––––––––  ––––.     ––––––––––––––––––.
1    default           active    Fa0/5, Fa0/6, Fa0/7, Fa0/8
                                 Fa0/9, Fa0/10, Fa0/11, Fa0/12
                                 Fa0/13, Fa0/14, Fa0/15, Fa0/16
                                 Fa0/17, Fa0/18, Fa0/19, Fa0/20
                                 Fa0/21, Fa0/22, Fa0/23, Fa0/24
                                 Gi0/1, Gi0/2
10   Faculty/Staff     active
20   Students          active
88   Wireless          active
99   Management        active

<output omitted>


S3#show vlan brief

––   ––––––––––––––––  ––––.     ––––––––––––––––––.
1    default           active    Fa0/5, Fa0/6, Fa0/7, Fa0/8
                                 Fa0/9, Fa0/10, Fa0/11, Fa0/12
                                 Fa0/13, Fa0/14, Fa0/15, Fa0/16
                                 Fa0/17, Fa0/18, Fa0/19, Fa0/20
                                 Fa0/21, Fa0/22, Fa0/23, Fa0/24
                                 Gi0/1, Gi0/2
10   Faculty/Staff     active
20   Students          active
88   Wireless          active
99   Management        active
<output omitted>
```

Step 5.   Configure the management interface address on all three switches.

Verify that the switches are correctly configured by pinging between them. From S1, ping the management interface on S2 and S3. From S2, ping the management interface on S3.

Were the pings successful? _____

If not, troubleshoot the switch configurations and try again.

Step 6.   Assign switch ports to the VLANs.

Assign ports to VLANs on S2 and S3 according to Table 7-5 at the beginning of the lab. Activate the ports connected to the PCs.

Task 5: Configure the Router

Step 1.   Clear the configuration on the router and reload.

Step 2.   Create a basic configuration on the router.

Configure R1 according to the following guidelines and the information in Table 7-4:

- Configure the router with hostname **R1**.
- Disable DNS lookup.
- Configure an EXEC mode password of **class**.
- Configure a password of **cisco** for console connections.
- Configure a password of **cisco** for vty connections.
- Fa0/1 and its subinterfaces
- Configure Loopback 0.

Step 3.   Test connectivity between PC1 and PC2.

To verify that the VLANs and inter-VLAN routing are configured correctly, ping between PC1 and PC2. If unsuccessful, troubleshoot your router and switch configurations and test again.

Task 6: Connect to WRS3

Step 1.   Hard reset the Linksys WRT300N.

To hard reset the router to its factory defaults, find the reset button on the back of the router. Using a pen or other thin instrument, hold down the reset button for 5 seconds, after which the router should be restored to its factory default settings.

Step 2.   Establish connectivity.

Choose **Start > Control Panel > Network Connections**. Then, right-click the **Wireless Network Connection** icon and choose **View Available Wireless Networks**, as shown in Figure 7-10.

Figure 7-10   Viewing a PC's Available Wireless Network Connections

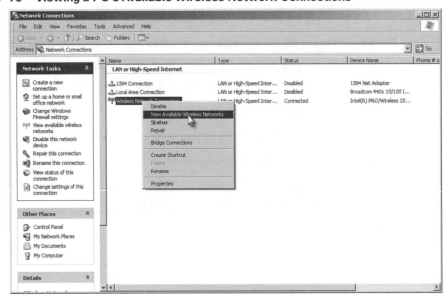

In the Wireless Network Connection window, in the Choose a Wireless Network list, click the **linksys** option and then click **Connect**, as shown in Figure 7-11. (Whereas Figure 7-11 shows only one wireless network, your PC will likely show many options.) After WRS3 and PC6 successfully negotiate DHCP parameters, you will be connected.

Figure 7-11   Choosing a Wireless Network Connection

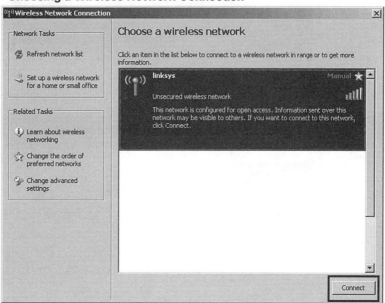

Step 3.   Verify that PC6 received IP addressing parameters from WRS3.

By default, PC6 will obtain the following configuration:

IP address   192.168.1.100

Subnet mask   255.255.255.0

Default gateway   192.168.1.1

PC6 should be able to ping WRS3 at 192.168.1.1.

Step 4.   Open a web browser and navigate to the web-based GUI utility on WSR3.

The default login credentials are a blank username and the password, **admin**. You should now be viewing the default page of the Linksys WRT300N web utility, which is the Basic Setup subtab of the Setup tab, as shown in Figure 7-12.

Figure 7-12   Accessing the Default Linksys Router Web Page

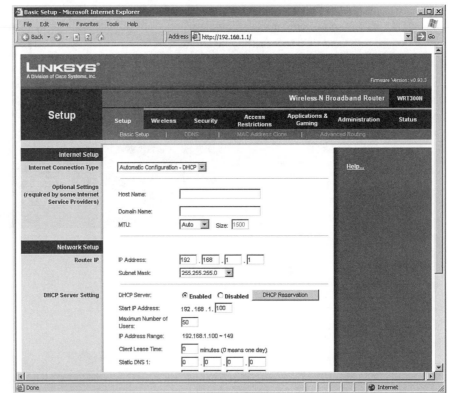

Task 7: Configure Options on the Linksys Setup Tab

Step 1.   Set the Internet Connection Type drop-down list box to **Static IP**.

Step 2.   Configure the WAN (Internet) IP address, subnet mask, and default gateway for WRS3 according to Table 7-4.

Step 3.   Under Network Setup, configure the Router IP parameters for the LAN/wireless side of WRS3.

Step 4.   Verify that the DHCP server is enabled.

Step 5.   Save the settings.

Step 6.   Reconnect to WRS3 at its new LAN/wireless IP address:

-   Verify that PC6 has obtained a new IP address that belongs to the 172.17.30.0/24 network.

-   Reconnect to the web-based configuration utility using the new default gateway IP address of **172.17.30.1**.

Task 8: Configure DHCP Settings and Router Time Zone Settings

Step 1.   Configure a static DHCP binding for PC6.

From the Basic Setup subtab under Setup on the Linksys web page, click **DHCP Reservations** button and find PC6 in the list of current DHCP clients.

Step 2.   Assign PC6 the 172.17.30.26 address.

By entering the PC6 address in the Manually Adding Client fields, whenever PC6 connects to the wireless router, it receives the IP address 172.17.30.26 via DHCP. As shown in Figure 7-13, type in the MAC address for PC6, click **Add**, and then click **Save Settings**.

Figure 7-13   Manually Reserving an IP Address

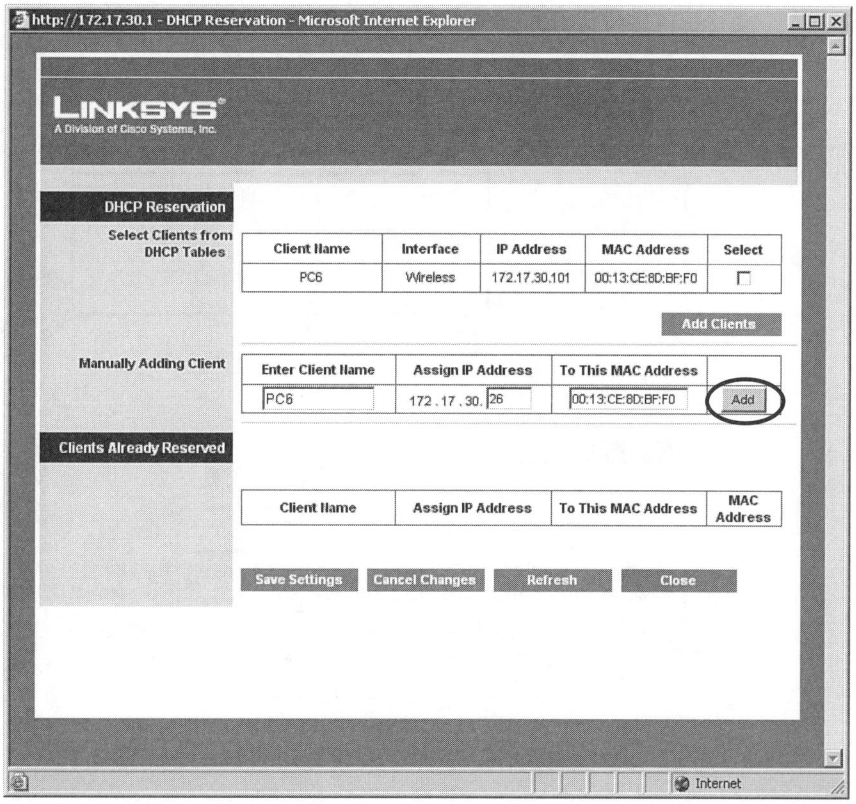

Step 3.   Verify that PC6 will now receive the DHCP address.

Use the **ipconfig /release** command to force PC6 to release its current IP address parameters. Then use the **ipconfig /renew** command to request new IP address parameters. PC6 should receive the 172.17.30.26 address. If not, try the **release** and **renew** commands again.

Step 4.   Configure the DHCP server settings.

Close the DHCP Reservation window if you have not done so already. In the DHCP Server Setting options, set the Start IP Address field to **50**, set the Maximum Number of Users field to **25**, and set the Client Lease Time field to **120** minutes (2 hours) as shown in Figure 7-14.

PCs that connect wirelessly or through a LAN port and send DHCP requests will receive an address between 172.17.30.50 and 172.17.30.74. Only 25 clients at a time are able to get an IP address. In addition, each client can have the IP address for only two hours, after which time they must request a new one.

Step 5.   Configure the router for the appropriate time zone.

At the bottom of the Basic Setup subtab, change the time zone of the router to reflect your location, as shown in Figure 7-14. Then click **Save Settings**.

Figure 7-14   Configuring the DHCP Server Setting

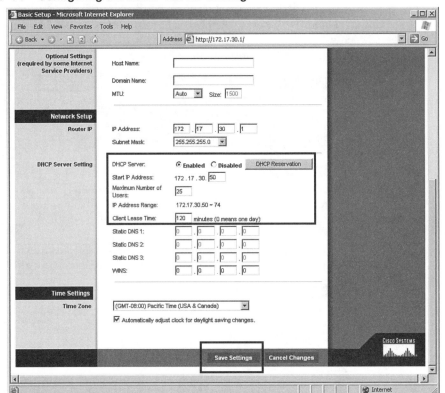

Task 9: Configure Basic Wireless Settings

Step 1.   Set the network mode.

The Linksys WRT300N router allows you to choose in which network mode to operate. Currently, the most used network mode for clients is Wireless-G and for routers is BG-Mixed. When a router is operating in BG-Mixed mode, it can accept both 802.11b and 11g clients. However, if a 802.11b client connects, the router must scale down to the slower level of 802.11b. For this lab, we are assuming all clients are running 802.11b only. Click the **Wireless** tab and then choose **Wireless-B Only**, as shown in Figure 7-15.

Step 2.   Configure other settings, as shown in Figure 7-15:

- From the Network Name (SSID) drop-down list, choose **WRS3**.

- From the Standard Channel drop-down list, choose **6 – 2.437GHZ.**

- For the **SSID Broadcast** option, choose the **Disabled** radio button.

Why is it good to change the wireless channel to be different from the default channel?

_____

Why is disabling SSID broadcast recommended?

_____

_____

Figure 7-15   Configuring the Basic Wireless Settings

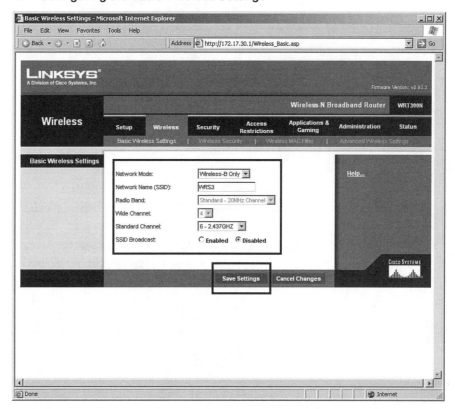

Step 3.   Click **Save Settings**.

You should now no longer be able to access the router's web page, and pinging the default gateway at 172.17.30.1 should fail. Why?

_____

Step 4.   Reconnect to the wireless network.

Choose **Start > Control Panel > Network Connections**. Then, right-click the **Wireless Network Connection** icon and choose **Properties**, as shown in Figure 7-16.

Click the **Wireless Networks** tab and click **Add**. The Wireless Network Properties dialog box opens with the Association tab displayed by default.

As shown in Figure 7-17, enter **WRS3** as the SSID and choose **Disabled** in the Data Encryption drop-down list. Click **OK** and then **OK** again. Windows should now try to reconnect to the wireless router.

Figure 7-16   Selecting the Wireless Network Connection Properties

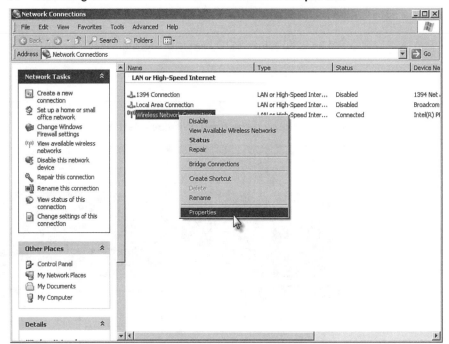

Figure 7-17   Configuring a PC's Wireless Network Properties

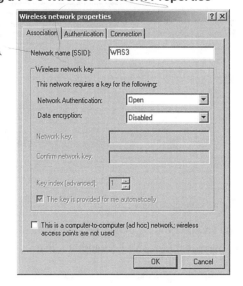

Step 5.   Verify the settings.

Now that you have reconnected to the network, you have the new DHCP settings that you configured previously in Task 8. Verify this at the command prompt with the **ipconfig** command and successfully ping the default gateway at 172.17.30.1.

Task 10: Enable Wireless Security

Step 1.   Reconnect to the Setup tab.

Step 2.   Click the **Wireless** tab and then click the **Wireless Security** subtab. Configure the following:

- From the Security Mode drop-down list, choose **WEP**.

- In the Key 1 field, enter the WEP key, **1234567890**.

- Click **Save Settings** to save your settings.

You will become disconnected from the network.

Step 3.   Configure Windows to use WEP authentication.

Choose **Start > Control Panel > Network Connections**. Then, right-click the **Wireless Network Connection** icon and choose **Properties**, as shown previously in Figure 7-16.

Click the **Wireless Networks** tab, select **WRS3 (Automatic)** in the Preferred Networks list, and then click **Properties**, as shown in Figure 7-18.

Figure 7-18   Selecting the Preferred Wireless Network and Accessing the Wireless Network Connection Properties

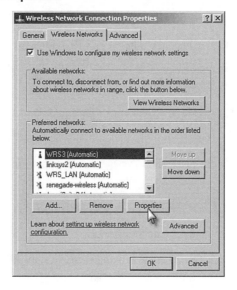

In the WRS3 Properties dialog box, shown in Figure 7-19, configure the following:

Figure 7-19   Configuring the Wireless Network Key Parameters Under WRS3 Properties

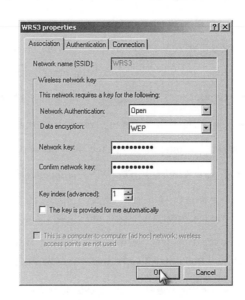

- From the Data Encryption drop-down list, choose **WEP**.

- Uncheck the **The Key Is Provided for Me Automatically** check box next.

- In the Network Key and Confirm Network Key fields, enter the network key of **1234567890**.

    Click **OK**, and then click **OK** again. Windows should now reconnect to the network.

Step 4.   Test connectivity to the default gateway.

    Before proceeding, verify that PC6 can ping WRS3 at 172.17.30.1.

Task 11: Configure a Wireless MAC Filter (Optional)

Step 1.   Reconnect to the Setup tab.

Step 2.   Click the **Wireless** tab and then click the **Wireless MAC Filter** subtab, shown in Figure 7-20. Configure the following:

- Click the **Enabled** radio button to enable wireless MAC filtering.

- Click the **Permit PCs Listed Below to Access the Wireless Network** radio button.

- Click the **Wireless Client List** button.

Figure 7-20   Setting Up a Wireless MAC Filter

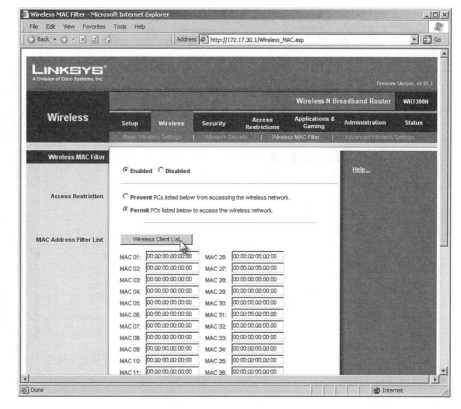

The Wireless Client List (see Figure 7-21) shows any clients currently connected to the router via a wireless connection. Check the **Save to MAC Address Filter List** check box and then click the **Add** button to automatically add the MAC address of PC6 to the wireless client list.

Figure 7-21   Adding a Client to Wireless Client List

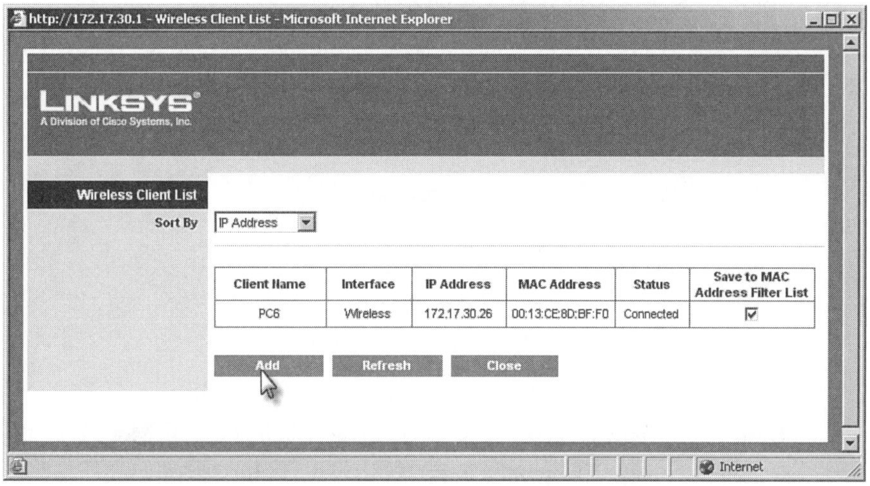

The MAC address for PC6 is automatically added to the MAC Address Filter List, as shown in Figure 7-22.

Figure 7-22   Verifying Client Is Now Listed in the Wireless MAC Filter

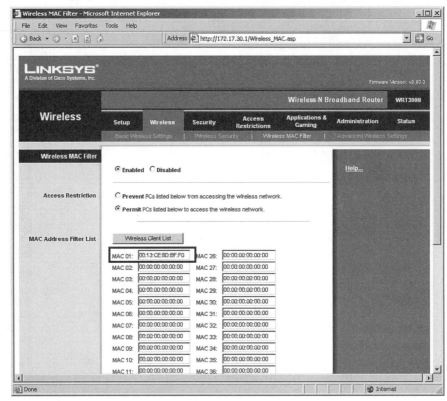

Task 12: Set Access Restrictions (Optional)

The WRT300N router is capable of filtering traffic based on your configured access restrictions. In this task, you will configure an access restriction that prevents Telnet access Monday through Friday to users in the 172.17.30.0/24 network.

Step 1.   Test Telnet access from PC6.

Currently, PC6 should be able to telnet freely to R1 at any IP address configured and active on R1. Verify connectivity to R1 by pinging 172.17.30.1. Then telnet as shown here:

```
C:\>telnet 172.17.88.1

User Access Verification
Password:cisco
R1>exit

Connection to host lost.
C:\>
```

Step 2.   Apply an access restriction to deny Telnet access Monday through Friday to any IP address belonging to the 172.17.30.0/24 network.

As shown in Figure 7-23, click the **Access Restrictions** tab and set the following:

- Enter Policy Name: **No_Telnet**

- Status: **Enabled**

- Access Restriction: **Allow**

- Days: check **Mon** through **Fri**

- Blocked List: add **Telnet**

Figure 7-23   Configuring an Internet Access Policy

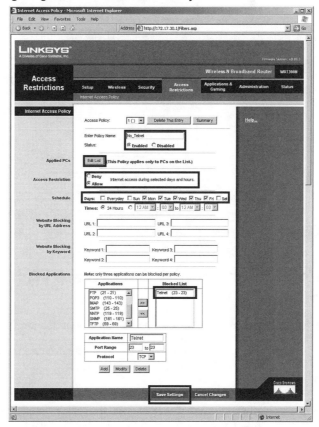

Step 3.   Set the IP address range.

The last step is to apply the policy to PCs. Click the **Edit List** button and then enter the IP address range for 172.17.30.0/24, as shown in Figure 7-24.

Click **Save Settings** on the List of PCs page, and then click **Save Settings** again on the Access Restrictions tab.

Step 4.   Test the access restriction by attempting to telnet to R1.

First, verify PC6 can ping R1 at 172.17.88.1. This should be successful. However, attempting to telnet will fail:

```
C:\>telnet 172.17.88.1
Connecting to 172.17.88.1...Could not open connection to the host, on port
23: Connection failed.

C:\>
```

Figure 7-24   Applying an Internet Access Policy

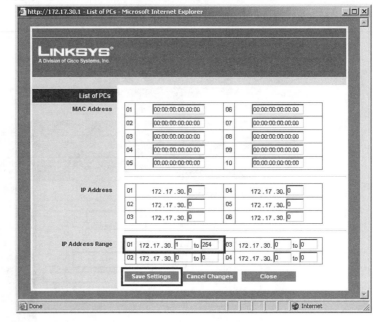

Task 13: Manage and Secure the Web Utility of the Router (Optional)

Step 1.   Configure router access and administration management:

- Click the **Administration** tab. On the Management subtab, change the Router Password field to **cisco** and confirm it.

- For Web Utility Access, check both **HTTP** and **HTTPS**. Checking HTTPS allows a network administrator to manage the router via https://172.17.30.1 with SSL, a more secure form of HTTP. If you choose to do this in the lab, you may have to accept certificates.

- For Web Utility Access via Wireless, click **Enabled**. If you disable this option, managing WRS3 from wireless clients is not available.

- In the Remote Access options, enabling Remote Management allows access to the WRS3 web utility through its Internet interface. Doing so now would allow PC1 or PC2 to remotely manage WRS3. As a security precaution, keep this feature disabled (click **Disabled**).

- Click **Save Settings**. You will be prompted for a password again. Enter the password **cisco** and return to the Management subtab.

Step 2.   Back up and restore the current configuration.

To back up the configuration, click the **Backup Configurations** button. When prompted, save the file to your desktop.

If your settings are accidentally or intentionally changed or erased, you can restore them from a working configuration using the Restore Configurations button. Click the **Restore Configurations** button now. In the Restore Configurations window, shown in Figure 7-25, browse to the previously saved configuration file. Click the **Start to Restore** button. Your previous settings should be successfully restored. You may have to refresh your connection to 172.17.30.1.

Figure 7-25   Restoring a Saved Configuration

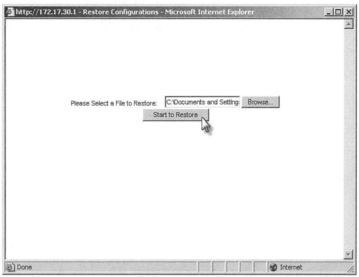

Step 3.   Enable logging.

On the Administration tab, click the **Log** subtab and enable logging. Click **Save Settings**. You are now able to view the log of the router, which will update every time you make a change to the configuration.

Task 14: Create and Verify Full Connectivity

Step 1.   Filter anonymous Internet requests.

Click the **Security** tab and uncheck **Filter Anonymous Internet Requests**, as shown in Figure 7-26. Then click **Save Settings**.

Figure 7-26   Filtering Anonymous Internet Requests

Disabling this option allows you to ping the WRS3 WAN IP address, 172.17.88.35, from places connected to its WAN port. However, pings to inside addresses belonging to the 172.17.30.0/24 network are still blocked because of the NAT firewall.

Step 2.   Disable NAT to allow pings to inside hosts on the 172.17.30.0/24 network.

Click the **Setup** tab and then click the **Advanced Routing** subtab. Disable NAT, as shown in Figure 7-27. Then click **Save Settings**.

Note: R1 will not be able to route traffic to the inside networks at 172.17.30.0/24 and 172.17.40.0/24 until later in the lab when static routing is configured.

Step 3.   Configure WRS2.

Connect to WRS2 either wirelessly or through a LAN interface. Access the web utility for WRS2 as previously done in this lab for WRS3.

Use the addressing in Table 7-4 and previous skills you have learned to configure the following:

- Configure the static IP address, subnet mask, and default gateway.

- Configure the router IP address and subnet mask.

- Statically bind the MAC address of PC3 to the DHCP address 172.17.40.23.

- Change the wireless SSID to **WRS2**.

- Uncheck the **Filter Anonymous Internet Requests** check box.

- Disable NAT.

Figure 7-27   Disabling NAT

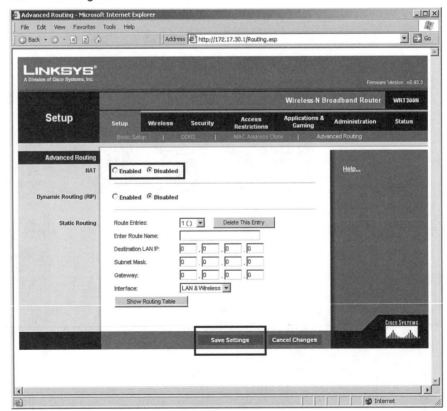

Step 4. Configure R1 with the following static routes:

```
R1(config)#ip route 172.17.30.0 255.255.255.0 172.17.88.35
R1(config)#ip route 172.17.40.0 255.255.255.0 172.17.88.25
```

Note: The configuration and administration of static routes is covered in the CCNA Exploration: Routing and Routing Protocols course.

Step 5. Verify full connectivity.

Verify that R1 has routes to PC3 and PC6 and that it can successfully ping them:

```
R1#show ip route
<output deleted>

Gateway of last resort is not set

     172.17.0.0/24 is subnetted, 5 subnets
S        172.17.40.0 [1/0] via 172.17.88.25
S        172.17.30.0 [1/0] via 172.17.88.35
C        172.17.20.0 is directly connected, FastEthernet0/1.20
C        172.17.10.0 is directly connected, FastEthernet0/1.10
C        172.17.88.0 is directly connected, FastEthernet0/1.88
     10.0.0.0/24 is subnetted, 1 subnets
C        10.1.1.0 is directly connected, Loopback0
R1#ping 172.17.30.26

Type escape sequence to abort.
Sending 5, 100-byte ICMP Echos to 172.17.30.26, timeout is 2 seconds:
!!!!!
Success rate is 100 percent (5/5), round-trip min/avg/max = 1/1/4 ms
R1#ping 172.17.40.23

Type escape sequence to abort.
Sending 5, 100-byte ICMP Echos to 172.17.40.23, timeout is 2 seconds:
!!!!!
Success rate is 100 percent (5/5), round-trip min/avg/max = 1/2/4 ms
```

Verify that PC3 and PC6 can ping the loopback interface on R1:

```
C:\>ping 10.1.1.1

Pinging 10.1.1.1 with 32 bytes of data:

Reply from 10.1.1.1: bytes=32 time=1ms TTL=254
Reply from 10.1.1.1: bytes=32 time=1ms TTL=254
Reply from 10.1.1.1: bytes=32 time=1ms TTL=254
Reply from 10.1.1.1: bytes=32 time=2ms TTL=254

Ping statistics for 10.1.1.1:
    Packets: Sent = 4, Received = 4, Lost = 0 (0% loss),
Approximate round trip times in milli-seconds:
    Minimum = 1ms, Maximum = 2ms, Average = 1ms
```

Verify that PC3 and PC6 can ping each other.

From PC6 to PC3:

```
C:\>ping 172.17.40.23

Pinging 172.17.40.23 with 32 bytes of data:

Reply from 172.17.40.23: bytes=32 time=2ms TTL=253
Reply from 172.17.40.23: bytes=32 time=2ms TTL=253
Reply from 172.17.40.23: bytes=32 time=2ms TTL=253
Reply from 172.17.40.23: bytes=32 time=2ms TTL=253

Ping statistics for 172.17.40.23:
    Packets: Sent = 4, Received = 4, Lost = 0 (0% loss),
Approximate round trip times in milli-seconds:
    Minimum = 2ms, Maximum = 2ms, Average = 2ms
```

Verify that PC3 and PC6 can ping PC1 and PC2.

From PC6 to PC1:

```
C:\>ping 172.17.10.21

Pinging 172.17.10.21 with 32 bytes of data:

Reply from 172.17.10.21: bytes=32 time=2ms TTL=253
Reply from 172.17.10.21: bytes=32 time=2ms TTL=253
Reply from 172.17.10.21: bytes=32 time=2ms TTL=253
Reply from 172.17.10.21: bytes=32 time=2ms TTL=253

Ping statistics for 172.17.10.21:
    Packets: Sent = 4, Received = 4, Lost = 0 (0% loss),
Approximate round trip times in milli-seconds:
    Minimum = 2ms, Maximum = 2ms, Average = 2ms
```

Task 15: Configure Routing Efficiency (Optional)

Step 1.   Use Traceroute to view the network connection.

From WRS3, trace the route to PC3 at 172.17.40.23. Click the **Administration** tab and then click the **Diagnostics** subtab. For the Traceroute Test, type the IP address **172.17.40.23** and then click the **Start to Traceroute** button. The Traceroute window will open, as shown in Figure 7-28.

Because R1 is the default gateway, WRS3 will route traffic to R1 to get to a network it does not know how to get to, including the clients of WRS2.

A packet from PC6 to PC3 first reaches its default gateway at 172.17.30.1. Then it is sent out the WRS3 WAN interface toward the WRS3 default gateway at 172.17.88.1. From there, R1 sends the packet to the WRS2 WAN interface, 172.17.88.25. WRS2 then routes the packet to PC3.

Figure 7-28   Completing a Traceroute

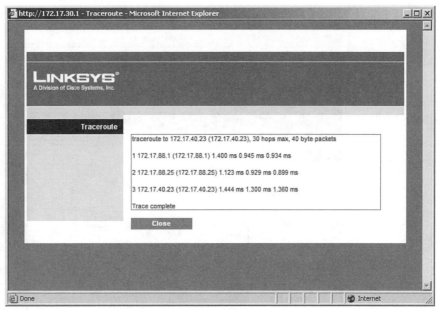

Step 2.   Configure a static route on WRS3.

You can configure WRS3 to send traffic destined for the 172.17.40.0/24 network directly to WRS2 at 172.17.88.25.

Click the **Setup** tab, and then click the **Advanced Routing** subtab. For the Static Routing options, enter the following settings, as shown in Figure 7-29:

- Enter Route Name: **To WRS3 Clients**

- Destination LAN IP: **172.17.30.0**

- Subnet Mask: **255.255.255.0**

- Gateway: **172.17.88.25**

- Interface: **Internet (WAN)**

Click **Save Settings**.

Figure 7-29   Configuring a Static Route

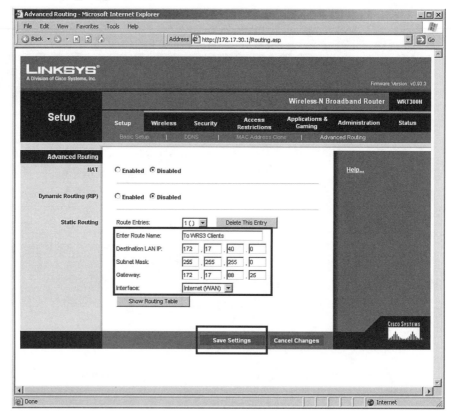

Step 3.   Verify the new route.

Click the **Administration** tab and then click the **Diagnostics** subtab. For the Traceroute Test, type the IP address **172.17.40.23** and click the **Start to Traceroute** button. This time, Traceroute should show WRS3 sending traffic directly to WRS2 as shown in Figure 7-30.

Step 4.   Configure a static route on WRS2.

Traffic from the WRS3 LAN to the WRS2 LAN is now routed directly to WRS2. However, return traffic from WRS2 back to WRS3 will still be routed through R1.

To optimize both sides of the link, configure WRS2 with a static route pointing to WRS3 for traffic destined to the 172.17.30.0/24 network.

Test the new static route by tracing from WRS2 to PC6 at 172.17.30.26.

Figure 7-30   Verifying a Static Route with Traceroute

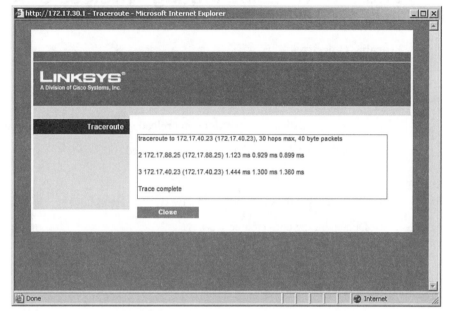

Task 16: Clean Up

Unless directed otherwise by your instructor, erase the configurations and reload the router and switches. For the WRT300N routers, click the **Administration** tab and then click the **Factory Defaults** subtab. Then, click the **Restore Factory Defaults** button. You can also hard reset the router as you did at the beginning of this lab. Disconnect and store the cabling. For PC hosts that are normally connected to other networks (such as the school LAN or to the Internet), reconnect the appropriate cabling and restore the TCP/IP settings.

Packet Tracer Companion: Challenge Wireless WRT300N (7.5.2)

You can now open the file LSG03-Lab752.pka on the CD-ROM that accompanies this book to repeat this hands-on lab using Packet Tracer. Remember, however, that Packet Tracer is not a substitute for a hands-on lab experience with real equipment.

Lab 7-3: Troubleshooting Wireless Configuration (7.5.3)

Learning Objectives

Upon completion of this lab, you will be able to

- Cable a network according to the topology diagram

- Erase any existing configurations and reload switches and the router to the default state

- Load the switches and the router with supplied scripts

- Find and correct all configuration errors

- Configure wireless network connectivity

- Document the corrected network

Figure 7-31 shows the topology diagram for this lab.

Figure 7-31   Topology Diagram for Lab 7-3

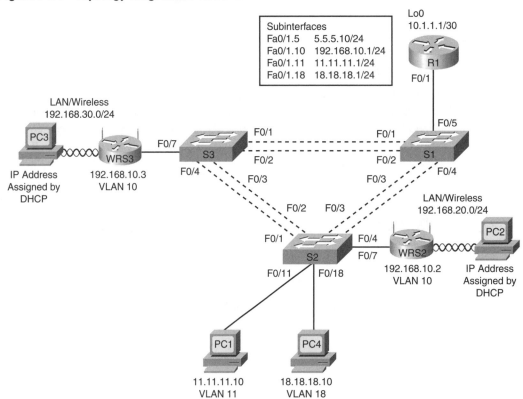

Table 7-6 shows the addressing scheme used in this lab.

Table 7-6   Addressing Table for Lab 7-3

Device	Interface	IP Address	Subnet Mask	Default Gateway
R1	Fa0/1.5	5.5.5.10	255.255.255.0	N/A
	Fa0/1.10	192.168.10.1	255.255.255.0	N/A
	Fa0/1.11	11.11.11.1	255.255.255.0	N/A
	Fa0/1.18	18.18.18.1	255.255.255.0	N/A
	Lo0	10.1.1.1	255.255.255.252	N/A
S1	VLAN 5	5.5.5.1	255.255.255.0	N/A
S2	VLAN 5	5.5.5.2	255.255.255.0	N/A
S3	VLAN 5	5.5.5.3	255.255.255.0	N/A
WRS2	WAN	192.168.10.2	255.255.255.0	192.168.10.1
	LAN/wireless	192.168.20.1	255.255.255.0	N/A
WRS3	WAN	192.168.10.3	255.255.255.0	192.168.10.1
	LAN/wireless	192.168.30.1	255.255.255.0	N/A
PC1	NIC	11.11.11.10	255.255.255.0	11.11.11.1
PC4	NIC	18.18.18.10	255.255.255.0	18.18.18.1

Scenario

The network is designed and configured to support four VLANs and two wireless networks. Inter-VLAN routing is provided by an external router in a router-on-a-stick configuration. However, the network is not working as designed and complaints from your users do not provide much insight into the source of the problems. Before configuring wireless access, you must first define what is not working as expected in the wired portion of the network. Analyze the existing configurations to determine and correct the source of the problems.

This lab is complete when you can demonstrate IP connectivity between each of the wired and wireless user VLANs and between the switch management VLAN interfaces.

Task 1: Prepare the Network

Step 1.   Cable a network that is similar to the one shown in Figure 7-31.

Step 2.   Clear any existing configurations on the router and switches.

Step 3.   Configure the Ethernet interfaces on the host PCs and the server.

Step 4.   Apply the following configurations to the router and switches. Alternatively, you can open the file LSG03-Lab753-Scripts.txt on the CD-ROM that accompanies this book and copy in the scripts for each of the switches.

R1 Configuration

```
hostname R1
!
no ip domain-lookup
enable secret class
!
interface Loopback0
 ip address 10.1.1.1 255.255.255.0
!
interface FastEthernet0/1
 no ip address
 duplex auto
 speed auto
 no shutdown
!
interface FastEthernet0/1.5
 encapsulation dot1Q 5 native
 ip address 5.5.5.10 255.255.255.0
!
interface FastEthernet0/1.10
 encapsulation dot1Q 10
 ip address 192.168.10.1 255.255.255.0
!
interface FastEthernet0/1.18
 encapsulation dot1Q 18
 ip address 18.18.18.1 255.255.255.0
!
ip route 192.168.20.0 255.255.255.0 192.168.10.2
ip route 192.168.30.0 255.255.255.0 192.168.10.3
!
line con 0
 password cisco
 login
!
line vty 0 4
password cisco
login
end
```

S1 Configuration

```
hostname S1
!
no ip domain-lookup
enable secret class
!
vtp mode server
```

```
vtp domain Lab7
vtp password cisco
!
vlan 5,10-11
!
interface range FastEthernet0/1 - 5
 switchport trunk native vlan 5
 switchport mode trunk
!
interface Vlan5
 ip address 5.5.5.1 255.255.255.0
 no shutdown
!
!
line con 0
 password cisco
 login
!
line vty 0 15
password cisco
login
end
```

S2 Configuration

```
hostname S2
!
no ip domain-lookup
enable secret class
!
vtp mode client
vtp domain Lab7
vtp password cisco
!
interface range FastEthernet0/1 - 4
 switchport trunk native vlan 5
 switchport mode access
!
interface FastEthernet0/7
 switchport access vlan 10
 switchport mode access
!
interface FastEthernet0/11
 switchport access vlan 11
 switchport mode access
!
interface FastEthernet0/18
 switchport access vlan 18
 switchport mode access
```

```
!
interface Vlan1
 no ip address
 shutdown
!
interface Vlan5
 ip address 5.5.5.2 255.255.255.0
 no shutdown
!
line con 0
 password cisco
 login
!
line vty 0 15
password cisco
login
end
```

S3 Configuration

```
hostname S3
!
no ip domain-lookup
enable secret class
!
vtp mode client
vtp domain Lab7
vtp password cisco
!
interface range FastEthernet0/1 - 4
 switchport trunk native vlan 5
 switchport mode trunk
!
interface FastEthernet0/7
 switchport access vlan 10
 switchport mode access
!
interface Vlan5
 ip address 5.5.5.3 255.255.255.0
 no shutdown
!
line con 0
 password cisco
 login
!
line vty 0 15
password cisco
login
end
```

Task 2: Troubleshoot and Correct the Inter-VLAN Configuration

The following is a suggested method for approaching the connectivity problems in the network:

Step 1.   Test and establish connectivity between devices.

When all errors are corrected, you should be able to freely ping and telnet between R1, S1, S2, and S3. PC1 and PC4 should be able to ping each other and the loopback interface on R1.

Do you have connectivity between any of the devices?

_____

If yes, which ones?

_____

_____

Step 2.   Investigate connectivity issues between the devices and implement solutions. Document the results of your investigation and the solutions you implemented.

_____
_____
_____
_____
_____
_____
_____
_____
_____
_____
_____
_____
_____
_____
_____
_____
_____
_____
_____
_____

_____

_____

_____

_____

_____

_____

_____

_____

_____

_____

_____

_____

_____

_____

Task 3: Configure Wireless Network Access

Instead of uploading corrupted configuration files to the Linksys WRT300N routers, you will configure wireless access for the 192.168.20.0/24 and 192.168.30.0/24 network with minimal guidance.
Make sure both routers are reset to the factory defaults. Use Figure 7-31, Table 7-6, and the following
requirements to configure the wireless portion of this lab.

1. Connect the Linksys WRT300N routers and configure the IP addressing on each according to
   Figure 7-31 and Table 7-6.

2. Starting with the .26 address, configure DHCP to allow 25 clients to obtain an IP address
   dynamically. The lease should expire after 2 hours.

3. Clients using both 802.11b and 802.11g wireless network modes can connect, but 802.11n
   clients cannot. SSIDs should match the router name (WRS2 and WRS3).

4. Wireless clients must be authenticated using WEP with a key of **5655545251**.

5. Use static routes to ensure traffic between PC2 and PC3 takes the most efficient route.

6. Ping requests inbound through the WAN ports of the Linksys routers to the inside LAN/wire-
   less IP addresses (192.168.20.1 and 192.168.30.1) must be successful.

7. Challenge: The two wireless networks must not interfere with each other. You can achieve non-
   interference by setting each router to a different channel.

Document the steps you took to meet the requirements in the space provided here:

_____

_____

_____

_____

_____

Task 4: Document the Configurations

On the router, R1, and each switch, capture the running configuration to a text file and save it for future reference. These scripts can be edited to expedite configuring switches in future labs.

Task 5: Clean Up

Unless directed otherwise by your instructor, erase the configurations and reload the router and switches. For the WRT300N routers, click the **Administration** tab and then click the **Factory Defaults** subtab. Then, click the **Restore Factory Defaults** button. You can also hard reset the router as you did at the beginning of this lab. Disconnect and store the cabling. For PC hosts that are normally connected to other networks (such as the school LAN or to the Internet), reconnect the appropriate cabling and restore the TCP/IP settings.

Packet Tracer Companion: Troubleshooting Wireless WRT300N (7.5.3)

You can now open the file LSG03-Lab753.pka on the CD-ROM that accompanies this book to repeat this hands-on lab using Packet Tracer. Remember, however, that Packet Tracer is not a substitute for a hands-on lab experience with real equipment.

Packet Tracer Skills Integration Challenge

Open the file LSG03-PTSkills7.pka on the CD-ROM that accompanies this book. You will use the topology in Figure 7-32 and the addressing table in Table 7-7 to document your design.

Figure 7-32   Packet Tracer Skills Integration Challenge Topology

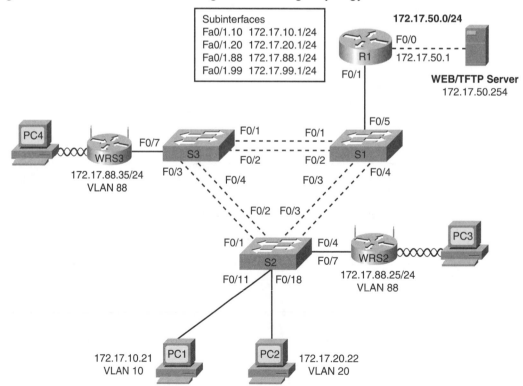

Table 7-7   Addressing Table for the Packet Tracer Skills Integration Challenge Activity

Device	Interface	IP Address	Subnet Mask	Default Gateway
R1	Fa0/0	172.17.50.1	255.255.255.0	N/A
	Fa0/1.10	172.17.10.1	255.255.255.0	N/A
	Fa0/1.20	172.17.20.1	255.255.255.0	N/A
	Fa0/1.88	172.17.88.1	255.255.255.0	N/A
	Fa0/1.99	172.17.99.1	255.255.255.0	N/A
WRS2	Internet	172.17.88.25	255.255.255.0	172.17.88.1
	LAN	172.17.40.1	255.255.255.0	N/A
WRS3	Internet	172.17.88.35	255.255.255.0	172.17.88.1
	LAN	172.17.30.1	255.255.255.0	N/A
S1	VLAN 99	172.17.99.31	255.255.255.0	172.17.99.1
S2	VLAN 99	172.17.99.32	255.255.255.0	172.17.99.1
S3	VLAN 99	172.17.99.33	255.255.255.0	172.17.99.1
PC1	NIC	172.17.10.21	255.255.255.0	172.17.10.1
PC2	NIC	172.17.20.22	255.255.255.0	172.17.20.1

Learning Objectives

Upon completion of this lab, you will be able to

- Configure and verify basic device configurations
- Configure VTP
- Configure trunking
- Configure VLANs
- Assign VLAN to ports
- Configure STP
- Configure router-on-a-stick inter-VLAN routing
- Configure wireless connectivity
- Verify end-to-end connectivity

Introduction

In this final Packet Tracer Skills Integration Challenge activity for the Exploration: LAN Switching and Wireless course, you will apply all the skills you have learned, including configuring VLANs and VTP, optimizing STP, enabling inter-VLAN routing, and integrating wireless connectivity.

Task 1: Configure and Verify Basic Device Configurations

Step 1.   Configure basic commands.

Configure each switch with the basic commands to apply the following. Packet Tracer only grades the hostnames and default gateways.

- Hostnames
- Banner
- Enable secret password
- Line configurations
- Service encryption
- Switch default gateways

Step 2.   Configure the management VLAN interface on S1, S2, and S3.

Create and enable interface VLAN 99 on each switch. Use the addressing table (Table 7-7) for address configuration.

Step 3.   Check results.

Your completion percentage should be 13 percent. If not, click **Check Results** to see which required components are not yet completed.

Task 2: Configure VTP

Step 1.   Configure the VTP mode on all three switches.

Configure S1 as the server. Configure S2 and S3 as clients.

Step 2.   Configure the VTP domain name on all three switches.

Use **CCNA** as the VTP domain name.

Step 3.   Configure the VTP domain password on all three switches.

Use **cisco** as the VTP domain password.

Step 4.   Check results.

Your completion percentage should be 21 percent. If not, click **Check Results** to see which required components are not yet completed.

Task 3: Configure Trunking

Step 1.   Configure trunking on S1, S2, and S3.

Configure the appropriate interfaces in trunking mode and assign VLAN 99 as the native VLAN.

Step 2.   Check results.

Your completion percentage should be 44 percent. If not, click **Check Results** to see which required components are not yet completed.

Task 4: Configure VLANs

Step 1.   Create the VLANs on S1.

Create and name the following VLANs on S1 only. VTP advertises the new VLANs to S2 and S3.

- VLAN 10: Faculty/Staff
- VLAN 20: Students
- VLAN 88: Wireless (Guest)
- VLAN 99: Management&Default

Step 2.   Verify that VLANs have been sent to S2 and S3.

Use the appropriate commands to verify that S2 and S3 now have the VLANs you created on S1. It may take a few minutes for Packet Tracer to simulate the VTP advertisements.

Step 3.   Check results.

Your completion percentage should be 54 percent. If not, click **Check Results** to see which required components are not yet completed.

Task 5: Assign VLANs to Ports

Step 1.   Assign VLANs to access ports on S2 and S3.

Assign the PC access ports to VLANs:

- VLAN 10: PC1
- VLAN 20: PC2

Assign the wireless router access ports to VLAN 88.

Step 2.   Verify VLAN implementation.

Use the appropriate commands to verify your VLAN implementation.

Step 3.   Check results.

Your completion percentage should be 61 percent. If not, click **Check Results** to see which required components are not yet completed.

Task 6: Configure STP

Step 1.   Ensure that S1 is the root bridge for all spanning tree instances.

Use 4096 priority.

Step 2.   Verify that S1 is the root bridge.

Step 3.   Check results.

Your completion percentage should be 66 percent. If not, click **Check Results** to see which required components are not yet completed.

Task 7: Configure Router-on-a-Stick Inter-VLAN Routing

Step 1.   Configure subinterfaces.

Configure the Fa0/1 subinterfaces on R1 using the information from the addressing table, Table 7-7.

Step 2.   Check results.

Your completion percentage should be 79 percent. If not, click **Check Results** to see which required components are not yet completed.

Task 8: Configure Wireless Connectivity

Step 1.   Configure IP addressing for WRS2 and WRS3.

Configure LAN settings and then static addressing on the Internet interfaces for both WRS2 and WRS3 using the addresses from the topology (see Figure 7-32).

Note: A bug in Packet Tracer may prevent you from assigning the static IP address first. A workaround for this issue is to configure the LAN settings first under Network Setup. Save the settings. Then, configure the static IP information under Internet Connection Type and save the settings again.

Step 2.   Configure wireless network settings:

- The SSIDs for the routers are **WRS2_LAN** and **WRS3_LAN**, respectively. The SSID names are case sensitive.

- The WEP for both is **12345ABCDE**. This key is case sensitive.

Step 3.   Configure the wireless routers for remote access.

Configure the administration password as **cisco123**.

Step 4.   Configure PC3 and PC4 to access the network using DHCP.

PC3 connects to WRS2_LAN, and PC4 connects to WRS3_LAN.

Step 5.   Verify remote access capability.

Step 6.   Check results.

Your completion percentage should be 100 percent. If not, click **Check Results** to see which required components are not yet completed.

Task 9: Verify End-to-End Connectivity

Step 1.   Verify that PC1 and WEB/TFTP Server can ping each other.

Step 2.   Verify that PC1 and PC2 can ping each other.

Step 3.   Verify that PC3 and PC1 can ping each other.

Step 4.   Verify that PC3 and PC2 can ping each other.

Step 5.   Verify that PC4 and PC1 can ping each other.

Step 6.   Verify that PC4 and PC2 can ping each other.